THE
INTELLECTUAL
FOLLIES

THE INTELLECTUAL FOLLIES

A Memoir of the Literary Venture
in New York and Paris

LIONEL ABEL

W · W · NORTON & COMPANY · NEW YORK · LONDON

The text of this book is composed in Janson, with display type set in Weiss.
Composition and manufacturing by The Haddon Craftsmen, Inc.
Book design by Nancy Dale Muldoon

Portions of this book have appeared, in another form, in the following publications:
Commentary, Dissent, This World, Salmagundi, and *The American Scholar*

First Edition

Library of Congress Cataloging in Publication Data
Abel, Lionel.
  The intellectual follies.
  Includes index.
  1. Abel, Lionel. 2. Critics—New York (N.Y.)—
Biography. 3. New York (N.Y.)—Biography. I. Title.
PN75.A24A34 1984   801′.95′0924 [B] 84-16688

ISBN 0-393-01841-5

W.W. Norton & Company, Inc., 500 Fifth Avenue, New York, N.Y. 10110
W.W. Norton & Company Ltd., 37 Great Russell Street, London WC1B 3NU

1 2 3 4 5 6 7 8 9 0

For Gloria

CONTENTS

One
THE MODERN MOON—A YOUNG MAN BEGINNING, 11

Two
THE THIRTIES, 29

Three
AS THROUGH A GLASS DARKLY, 61

Four
THE SURREALISTS IN NEW YORK, 88

Five
SARTRE REMEMBERED, 116

Six
READING CATASTROPHE, 145

Seven
AS PARIS WAS (1948–1951), 159

Eight
LOST BLOOM IN GENEVA, THE MAD GRASS IN NEW YORK, 193

Nine
OFF-BROADWAY, 217

Ten
BREAKUP, 242

CONTENTS

Eleven
JEWS WITHOUT "THE JEWS," 258

Twelve
A LETTER FROM—AND FOR—NEW YORK, 280

INDEX, 291

THE
INTELLECTUAL
FOLLIES

≺ One ≻

THE MODERN MOON—
A YOUNG MAN BEGINNING

On a warm afternoon in late November of 1929—the whole fall season that year had been quite summery—I might have been seen, if anyone had wanted to take note of me, sauntering across Greenwich Avenue and then turning down Sixth Avenue under the El; I even remember that I followed as it swung around Third Street carrying its iron clatter to points east. I was in no hurry at all; in fact I was much too early for the appointment I had scheduled after dark, with someone I had never before met, at a place I had not yet been in, and which I do not clearly remember, even now. The person I was going to meet was the actor, Lionel Stander, to whom I had a letter of introduction from a classmate at the University of North Carolina, from which Stander had graduated two years before.

I knew that Stander, whom I had spoken to just once over the telephone, might be late or not come at all. Yet I felt that he would come, and on time. And I was in Greenwich Village, which was interesting. I was curious about it as I turned up MacDougal Street from Third Street to the Park, which was then quite empty, without professional park sitters, stragglers, or mendicants. And it was beautiful then, too, its trees graceful and lithe, if almost leafless, in the fall wind. Washington Square Park is too crowded nowadays for one to feel quite sad in it; sadness requires a certain amount of space and time, the time to recognize that you are sad, and the space to feel yourself sufficiently distanced from anyone who is not. Now both these options are taken from you when there are too many people around. But there were not many persons there that afternoon, and I was able to stroll with enjoyable loneliness around the park. I soon found an empty bench for myself and could savor for awhile the steady and continuing silence, and feel in touch with the bare, stripped trees around me.

I would be nineteen at the end of November. I had some prospects but little money; however, I was not thinking about money. I did not even know that there had been a crash on Wall Street during the previous month. When I say I did not know about the crash, I do not mean that I had not read of it. I mean merely that it had no special significance to me. I had not yet been involved with anyone ruined or hurt in the foundering of the many financial empires which had gone down. And the crash, too, had not yet visibly affected the rest of the country, which it would do within a few months' time. No doubt there were many positions in the city in which I would have liked to be placed; some were being eliminated from New York's life-possibilities even as I sat and enjoyed my feeling of sadness in Washington Square Park. No doubt with each breath I took in, some favorable situation was being lost. But I was wholly unaware that this was happening, looking forward as I did to the adventure before me, my scheduled meeting after dark with Lionel Stander.

In the park I thought, "This is the place for a tryst." But the fact was I knew nobody in New York City with whom a tryst was possible. A tryst with the park itself? Why not? I write down here the very words I used about fifty years back: "Tomorrow at the same time of day I shall sit here on this same bench, with the same tender feelings for this place." So I sat there until the evening came on, and then went to the place of rendezvous, which might very well have been Louis', a bar and restaurant on the corner of Fourth Street and Sixth Avenue, favored at the time by the Fourth Street gangsters. Lionel Stander was already there and I recognized him at once. After all, I had seen the actor at the Provincetown Players' theater on

Twenty-third Street at a matinee during the winter in O'Neill's *SS Glencairn*. In 1929, Stander looked very much as he would in 1936 in *Mr. Deeds Goes to Town*. He was well set up, quite tall, with a boxer's long arms and wide shoulders, and the broad, smiling face of someone who likes to laugh and often finds sufficient reason to. And his voice was of a wonderfully sarcastic bass that seemed to come up from the depth of his belly, so that everything he said was in a way a gut statement, and you tended to believe him even if you had some evidence that he was lying. He was extremely friendly to me even before he had perused my letter of introduction, and after that he announced that he would show me the Village and make me acquainted with this most wonderful of all places. Shortly afterwards, Stander was joined by his girlfriend, Lucy Deats, a very handsome long-legged girl from Norwalk, Connecticut, and the two of them took me on a sight-seeing tour of Greenwich Village. The "sights" though, were not picturesque places, but people—those who were outstanding in the Village life of that period.

Thus it was that I was introduced to Maxwell Bodenheim, who had made something of a stir with his poems and novels and was soon to be savagely attacked in *The Dial* by Malcolm Cowley (then a young poet about to take over the literary editorship of *The New Republic*). Bodenheim, when he spoke to you, closed his eyes to shut you from his field of vision so that he could see only the words that came into his mind. Not looking at me he said, after we were introduced, "The Village is no place for you." "What place is?" I asked, though it had not yet occurred to me that there was any place that was *for* or *not for* me. "Capri," said Bodenheim, with his eyes still closed. "At this very moment I can see the intense blue of the sea around it, and I wish I was back there myself right now." "When you're in Capri," Stander put in, "do you look at that intense blue sea with your eyes *closed*, as you're looking at us?" Bodenheim was offended. "I don't have to tell you what I do in Italy. But I can tell you this, young man, it's very beautiful." And he stalked off.

"I assure you," Stander said to me, "this *is* the place for you. Let's make the rounds." And he and Lucy Deats each took me by an arm and walked me about the Village. On Third Street

we passed Charles Wagner, a poet who was then the book reviewer of the *New York Daily News*, and later we came upon the
poet, Eli Siegel, who had a saturnine expression and the bent
bearing of a *yeshivah bocher*. A few years before, he had won *The
Nation* prize for his poem "Hot Afternoons Have Been in Montana." "There've been some hot afternoons in New York City,"
Stander said to him. "Why don't you write a poem about that?"
"I like to think of hot afternoons in Montana, and not in New
York City," responded Siegel, "but I'll give you right on the spot
a one-line poem about poetry, and maybe it'll explain to you
why I like to think of hot afternoons in Montana." The one-liner
was this: "What is a poem? A whirlwind with details." "Think
it over," said Eli Siegel, and he went off.

As we walked through the Village, at some point Lucy
Deats called out, "There he is! Let's catch him." Who could it
be? "Not a doubt of it," I thought, "it's someone who's important." And Lionel Stander and Lucy Deats both insisted that the
one they had to catch up with and introduce me to was *very*
important. He was the oral historian of American action,
praised and published by Pound, and to whom the poet e. e.
cummings gave the sum of one dollar every Wednesday when
he appeared to collect his weekly wage for being the person he
was. They hurried down Third Street and called to a miniscule
man wrapped in rags, and with a grandiose beard. This was Joe
Gould. I noticed the twinkle in his eye. "What's your hurry?"
Joe Gould asked them. "We wanted to say hello to you," said
Stander. "That's not why," said Joe Gould. "After all, why do
you want to say hello to me? What good will it do you? You were
running after me, and I don't mean that just literally. You want
me to think well of you! And I don't. Let me tell you something.
I have some good advice for you. Don't run after Joe Gould.
Find out what Joe Gould runs after, and then run after *that*. But
I'm not gonna tell you what it is."

As Joe Gould left us, Stander was not discountenanced.
"There are all sorts of people here," he said. "Some are friendly,
some are unfriendly; most of them are interesting."

We kept walking. The next person they introduced me to
was Kenneth Fearing. He was slender, very youthful, with

straight black hair and intense dark eyes behind heavy horn-rimmed glasses. "Hello, Kenneth," said Stander. Pointing to me, "He's just come to the Village from college." And then, "This is the Village Bobby Burns, Kenneth Fearing." "Are you playing Virgil to this young Alighieri?" Fearing asked, "showing him the Village, pointing everybody out? Where do you think you are, in Hell?" "I think I'm in Heaven," I said. "Spoken like a neophyte," said Fearing, "but I'm glad to meet you. Let's all go have a drink." And he took us to his favorite gin mill. As we went, he recited one of his poems, one he evidently liked, which ended with these lines:

> *Here is the statue of Bobbie Burns . . .*
> *And there is the modern moon. . . .*

In the gin mills of the period, as I discovered that night, a glass of beer was twenty-five cents, and most people thought this quite expensive, although even when they protested the cost of beer, they would make a point of praising its quality and also of praising the gangster chieftain, Al Capone, who provided it. On this particular night I heard Kenneth Fearing say of Capone: "He makes good beer, and also, what I'd like myself, thirty-three million dollars a week."

"How do you know it isn't thirty-four million dollars a week he makes, or thirty-six and three quarters of a million?" Stander asked him. "You're cynical," Fearing told him. "And aren't *you* cynical?" Stander asked, indicating that he wanted a clear reply, by which he meant an admission. "Yes, I'm cynical," said Fearing, "but with a difference." And then, as we all ordered beer, he explained this to me. "Lionel Stander is going to tell you that this part of New York is blessed with insouciance and spirit, that most of the people who live here are wonderful, seeking the beautiful things in life, which they are prevented from finding elsewhere. According to him, they . . . ," he pointed around the gin mill, "and we, and all the people in the other ginmills at this hour—at least in the ones bounded by Greenwich Street and Second Avenue, by Fourteenth and Houston Streets—and all those people now in their studios painting pictures or banging on typewriters, writing, singing, dancing, kibitzing, screwing, listening to records, are all the salt of the earth. Well, I don't think so. I'm not, I know that, and Stander isn't. I don't know about Lucy. I don't want to say anything about her. As for you, young man, stay here in this place you think is like Heaven, and you won't be either. I promise you that."

But this was not the kind of analysis to convince me. It only made me more enthusiastic and more prone to believe everything positive that Stander and Lucy Deats had had to say about the Village.

Essentially, this is what Stander told me: Except for the museums, theatres, Carnegie Hall, and the opera, all that was humanly essential to the city was in Greenwich Village. Those who lived outside the area were just pariahs—or did not even exist, humanly, that is. There was no really "good" person then who would want to meet the Mayor; Wall Street might just as well have been in Illinois, and Madison Avenue "really" belonged in some part of Ohio. New York City was Greenwich Village, which was really, but *really:* e.e. cummings, Sam Schwartz's restaurant, Eugene O'Neill, the Provincetown Theatre, Hubert's Cafeteria, the eating and drinking places favored by certain people. For that's what New York City was then, certain people, and that's what a human community is, after all, certain people.

When, more than a year later, I had become a part of the Village, I discovered that in addition to the persons of reputation, the Village—that is to say, New York City—was a certain number of people who had never done anything, but whom one was seriously urged to meet. There was the splendid fellow, in the rhetoric of that time (it has continued into ours), "a beautiful person," who had unhappily done nothing at all in his life. There was the woman who had done very little with her talent for dancing, the young man who had never stopped denying his great and evident gifts. And in each case the reason the particular individual was wasting himself or herself was far more interesting than anything he or she might have done.

There was M.J., who at twenty-three was much too beautiful to think of doing anything whatever. It was shameful to think of her having to do anything short of the most sacred work. Quite naturally, she refused to go to Hollywood, to which Greta Garbo had yielded. M.J. was really beautiful: hers was a beauty that made one shudder. She felt that just to exhibit her beauty was quite sufficient; by showing herself she was giving others far more than they deserved. Now what did others give her? There was R.F.—a poet—who gave her his money and lived in a furnished room on practically nothing; then, with one violent act, he gave and took back from her everything. R.F. hanged himself. There was the novelist whom she had married, and who, in return for this, was going to give her his novel when he had finished it. M.J. was always referring to it as *her* novel, and often went on at great length about the pain and struggle involved in the writing, which she may actually have imagined herself doing. . . . But if it takes a single moment of time to promise a beautiful woman a book, it takes many moments of unbeautiful time to write a book. The novelist published the work under his own name.

(Let me note here that the author of the novel M.J. referred to as "hers" was Henry Miller, and the novel, *Tropic of Cancer*.)

But the important point that Stander and his girlfriend made to me that night was that in all the Village at that time there was not a single person who had not once in his life looked exultant, exalted, or, at the very least, distinguished. There was not one person who had not, at least once in his life, said something that could be, and maybe was, repeated.

That night I was convinced that Greenwich Village was indeed the place for me. And I spent another year visiting it, searching it out, trying to find some way to live there.

I⊤ took more than a year of shuttling between Lynbrook, Long Island to which my parents had recently moved, and places in the Village where I would spend some nights and then go back home, before I found a way to pay rent regularly for a furnished room at 10 Charles Street. A publisher, Joseph Felshin, had given me a contract to make a translation of Rimbaud's poems, and on the advance for this I was able to live in the Village.

And whom should I meet, once happily installed, but Lionel Stander, back for a visit East after a stay in Hollywood, where he was on his way to stardom.

"I'm living here now," I told Stander.

"You sound as if you're proud of it," Stander replied.

"In a way, yes. I have a publisher's contract, and I can pay for my rent and for my meals. And live in the Village, which you told me, when I first came, was the only part of New York for me to live in."

"Did I say that?" Stander asked. I insisted that he had said that and more.

"Well," said Stander, "if I did say anything like that, I want to take it all back. I can't tell you how happy I am to be away from the Village."

"Where do you live now?" I asked him.

"In Hollywood," Stander told me, "where one can make a buck. That is what I want most of all, and that is what I think people living in the Village also want; but they have little chance of getting it around here." And then Stander proceeded to repeat many of the things said against the Village and Villagers by Kenneth Fearing on my first night with him and Stander.

"Now you sound like Kenneth Fearing," I told him.

"And do you know who you sound like?" Stander asked.

"No, who?"

"You sound like Joseph R.," Stander said.

"Joseph R. is my best friend," I replied, at which point Stander threw up his hands to indicate there was no use in further discussion.

Joseph R. was a poet of Italian origin, in his middle twenties, who had captivated me with his lucid, and often lyrical, rhetoric. If the great despisers are also the great adorers, as Nietzsche claimed, then Joseph R. was not great at despising, for he certainly did not adore anything or anyone. But if not great at despising, he was certainly very good at it, and in any conversation with him, one's good opinion of somebody was bound to suffer. His dark curly hair fell into sculptural folds, and under heavy eyebrows his greenish, gold-flecked eyes were full of light and laughter. Probably what he enjoyed most was to maneuver anyone with whom he was engaged in talking into praising him for something. Once that had happened, the other person was bound to be judged pejoratively. Once I asked him, "Would you kill somebody who was trying to save your life?" "I'd love to," said Joseph R., smiling even as he revealed one of the darkest aspects of his nature.

He also represented the darkest aspects of bohemian life. I had already heard much about him when introduced to Joseph R., but I was not prepared to be told on first acquaintance about his illness (probably pretended). As he let go of my hand after our handshake on being introduced, Joseph R. held his own hand up and scrutinized it with raised eyebrows. "It didn't come off," he said. "What didn't come off?" "My hand," said Joseph R. "You sound as if you expected it to," I said. "Naturally I'm not looking forward to leaving my hand in someone else's, but I realize that this could happen, in fact is bound to happen some day." He went on to say that he had contracted the dreaded disease of so many of the nineteenth century's great. "You're trying to make it seem attractive," I said. "I don't want it to seem anything it is not," replied Joseph R. "What is syphilis, after all? A hurt that results from having been attracted, and maybe some attractiveness still hovers over the hurt."

The surprising thing about Joseph R. was that he made no secret of his affliction. He confided to me that he would take his girlfriends with him when he went to his doctor's office (on Fourth Street near Fifth Avenue) for treatment. He would say, "Wait in the park. I'll only be a few minutes. I have to get my mercury." (In those days doctors' offices were not crowded with patients, and Joseph R.'s girlfriends didn't have to wait long.) Joseph R. explained his tactic thus: "If they wait for me, I know that they are metaphysically mine." I was never sure, though, that when Joseph R. came out of the doctor's office that there was any real mercury in his veins. I was soon fairly convinced that the whole thing was a posture, a bluff, a part of Joseph R.'s rhetoric—in short, a literary attitude. Talking about Remy de Gourmont one day, Joseph R. had said, "You know why I like him, why I admire him? Not just because Pound likes him, and not just because he liked Mallarmé, and not just for his style or for his intelligence. Of course I admire him for all that, but I like him *most* for the sickness he contracted. You know, he was a leper. And there's absolutely nothing mediocre about leprosy."

Among the other things I admired Joseph R. for was his relation to the gangsters, who often dropped into the coffee shop on Fourth and Cornelia Streets. These gangsters were associated with a joint known as the Whoopee Club. Early in the evening they could be seen walking up and down Fourth Street soliciting customers. If a well-dressed man passed by, they would call after him: "For what you want—whatever you want —the best place is the Whoopee Club. It's on MacDougal Street!" This line met with success. Many a well-dressed man seen walking down Fourth Street was soon seen afterwards walking down MacDougal Street, towards the Whoopee Club. There was only one scenario. Having had some drinks, the man would be told that he had treated the whole house to champagne, and owed anything from hundreds to thousands of dollars, depending on his appearance of respectability and also the quality of his clothes. Informed what he owed, the man would write a check. But the owners of the Whoopee were, of course, not born yesterday. They knew perfectly well that checks can bounce. To defeat any such unpleasantness, Whoopee had its gangsters, whose role was to kidnap the one who had signed a check and detain him somewhere set up for this purpose until ten o'clock of the following morning, by which time the check would have been cashed. If it were a Saturday night, the signee would be detained until Monday, and if the night began a holiday weekend, he might be kept under surveillance for two, or even three, days. When not involved in detaining someone, and when not looking for Whoopee customers, the gangsters practiced being hard. One example: Paddy R., the leader, a chap with tremendous shoulders, would amuse himself and the other gangsters by slapping a new recruit around. The whole gang would walk down the block in a kind of phalanx, and suddenly Paddy R. would swing around and smack the cheek of the newest recruit with a sound like a whiplash, and all the gangsters, except the one smacked, would laugh. These were the chaps I admired Joseph R. for being acquainted with.

One of the gangsters did not admire me and on several occasions expressed himself to this effect. I wondered what I should do about it, and then, on one occasion, without having come to a decision, swung at the gangster and caught him flush on the jaw. Surprised by the unexpectedness of the act, and also confused by it, he hurled a sugar bowl at me which, happily, went off target. I, more confident now, launched another right, and again caught my opponent on the jaw. I knew then that I could beat him if he fought fairly. The gangster realized this too, and promptly kicked me in the balls. I passed out.

All this has interest now for what followed. When I came to, the gangsters from the Whoopee Club were split into two factions, arguing out the ethics of what had been done to me. One faction, supporting me, maintained, pointing to Ricky, the gangster who had laid me out, "Ricky shouldn't have kicked him in the balls." The other faction held to this doctrine: "Hands don't count." Finally, both factions turned to Joseph R., who was sitting at the counter, sipping his coffee, and surveying the whole scene sarcastically. They asked him: "Joe, which of us is right?" I, like the gangsters, waited for Joseph R.'s answer. After some thought he said, pointing to the gangster who had kicked me in the balls, "I think Ricky is wrong for not understanding him and not trying to." Then Joseph R. said: "But I think Ricky is quite right in wanting to kill him," at which the gangsters said with one voice, "See that, hands don't count." And the moral issue, assuming it was a problem to them, was solved. As for me, I had to consider: In what sense was Joseph R. my friend?

When I first met him, Joseph R. was sharing an apartment with a chap who worked as a soda jerk, got up every morning at eight o'clock to serve at his fountain, and regularly left Joe enough change to go to a soda fountain too—not to work there, but to be served breakfast. Naturally, Joseph R. had other needs besides those his roommate enabled him to satisfy, and for these needs he had to be funded in other ways. Well, he had many resources, and for a period I was one of them. But one night when we were both quite broke and rather hungry, Joe decided that he would reverse past roles and be the provider for the two of us. He suggested that we go up to Harlem, where he was well

21

acquainted—he had grown up there—and he would pay a call on Vito Marcantonio, then at the outset of his political career, make a loan, and we could both have dinner. I had just about enough subway fare (the fare in those days was five cents), to take us up to Harlem and back, and a quarter besides. The question in my mind was: Wouldn't the twenty cents, the fare for both of us up and back, be better spent on coffee? And as for the extra quarter I had, this seemed to me almost sacred, for as long as it was in my pocket, I knew that I would not feel quite destitute.

Well, we went up to Harlem and Joseph R. visited Marcantonio, was closeted with him for about twenty minutes, and emerged to announce that he had failed in his mission. I was quite sure he was lying, and had in fact made a touch, and the proof that he had came almost immediately, for on the way to the subway we passed a pool parlor in which there were some slot machines, and Joe announced that he was going to try his luck inside. "How will you do this? You didn't get any money from Marcantonio. Or are you going to change one of the bills he didn't give you?" Such were my questions. "I know the owner of the place," Joseph R. said, "and I'll borrow some quarters from him." The worst of it was that he didn't even care that I knew he was lying. So Joseph R. went inside, remained for a long time, and must have lost whatever it was that Marcantonio had given him. Finally he came out, disappointed, broke, still hungry; also, he had exposed himself to me. I said to him, "Joe, I'm going to try my luck with this remaining quarter." I went into the pool parlor, put in the quarter, hit the jackpot and took out of the machine some eighteen dollars in change. So it was quite a triumph. I then took Joe to Lindy's, where we feasted on hot roast beef sandwiches, after which he said, "You were the winner tonight, no doubt about that. But how did you win? What enabled you to?" And he answered his own question: "It was luck, sheer luck."

Yes, of course, it is only luck that enables one to hit the jackpot with one's last quarter, but to me Joe's remark did not seem calculated to deny me any merit. It was, rather, an expression of the coldness and hardness of New York life at that time

22

(of which some expression was to be found in Greenwich Village). And as Joseph R. said to me, "You have to admit you were lucky," I thought I saw the whole city of New York rising up before me in its elegance, hauteur, and hard, skeptical refusal to grant anything unprovable. It leaned over the table, patted me on the shoulders and I knew exactly where I was.

In what seemed a lifetime after this, I ran into Joseph R. one day —actually, I had not seen him for some forty years. I was coming down the steps of the New York Public Library and Joseph R. was going up the steps. He had already passed me when I realized I had recognized someone; I didn't yet know whom. I turned and watched the fellow. Yes, I did know him. Yes, it was Joe. His hair, which had been black, was now white, but it was still curly and close-cropped. I called to him. He stopped and I looked him over closely as I went up to him. His dark eyes were now inward looking and his expression meditative.

"Oh, it's you," he said, staring at me. "What do you see?" I asked him. "When I look at you," he replied, "I see something of what time has done to me."

"Maybe you'll tell me what it's done to you."

"Over coffee," he said. "Let's get some, like in the old days."

But there were very few places around Forty-second Street and Fifth Avenue where one could sit down to coffee as in the old days. Finally we went to a bar at Madison and Fortieth Street, and ordered some coffee, thus earning the frank enmity of the waiter. "I know you hate us," Joe said to the waiter as he brought us our coffee, "but I want you to know that we are both capable of hatred too." The waiter did not respond. "I talk and talk," said Joe, "and nobody listens to me."

What had happened to him?

For one thing, he was now fairly well-to-do. He had come into some money, invested it wisely, and was living on the income from it. His wife had died, and he had one son at Syracuse University, studying medicine as a matter of fact, and he claimed to be interested in the boy's future. "Are you really interested in things like that?" I asked him. "Of course I am.

23

Why should you doubt it?" Joe replied. "You used to be interested in sickness," I said, "and now you're interested in medicine." "Well," Joe replied, translating my question into his own
rhetoric, "You mean, when you say I was interested in sickness,
I was interested in myself. And now you can't imagine my being
interested in my own son. Well, that's your failure of imagination. The truth is that like so many others I've lost interest in
myself. That does happen to people, and it happened to me too."
And then he challenged me, "Are you going to tell me you're
just as interested in yourself as you used to be?" "Was I that
interested in myself?" I asked him. "You were infinitely interested in yourself," Joe replied, "if I can use the expression of
Sören Kierkegaard." "Even so," I answered, "this didn't make
me interested in being sick."

Then I asked him: "If one is infinitely interested in himself,
is one drawn to sickness?" "No question about it," Joe answered
dogmatically, "and if your interest in yourself is like mine in
myself now, quite finite, do you know what you're drawn to?
Medicine. I'm looking forward to a conversation with my son.
I'm going to call him at Syracuse tonight. We'll talk first about
diet and then about the new things in medicine that are not
sensational, that don't represent breakthroughs." "Why don't
you want to talk about them?" "Talking about them," he answered, "would remind me of the old times, and the interest I
once had in myself." I felt dismissed.

As I thought about my early experiences in the Village, I
could not but wonder why my recollections of Joseph R. figured
so prominently. Why was this? Was it because Joseph R. represented the darkest aspect of my bohemian days? Was the darkest
aspect the truest? Was that the essence of it? No, I thought, there
was something else. It was rather that in the world of the purely
possible, which bohemians strove to live in, anyone who called
attention to the dark side of the possible was bound to seem
more real, and Joseph R. had seemed very real to me, more real
than any other of those who in the Village had lived by what
Kierkegaard has called "the despair of the aesthetic."

This despair, Kierkegaard pointed out, results from sacrificing the real to the merely possible. To live aesthetically, he
noted, is more like dying than living, for it means to replace the

real with the imaginary. Now, could it be said that at any time a whole section of New York City was devoted to one single drastically staged experience, the despair of the aesthetic? Not exactly. People had come to Greenwich Village for many reasons: some, out of disgust for conventionally set relationships, some because they had made a cult of sexual promiscuity, and others simply to hide, if only from themselves. But what gave its tone to this part of the city in the late twenties and early thirties was the despair in the hearts of all those who came to the Village for another reason: to give up reality, to live by a standard which might make real life impossible.

Thinking thus, I recalled one evening—it might have been in 1931 or 1932—when I found myself in the Village, on Grove Street, in front of Hubert's Cafeteria. It was filled with a crowd of people who gesticulated uncontrollably and talked continually. I was very tired. It was quite late, and I wanted to go back to my room on Charles Street and get some sleep. But something drew me to that crowd in Hubert's, and when I went inside to have some coffee, and saw the crowd from closer quarters, I discovered what it was. Practically everybody in Hubert's was talking about art. Art in some form, if only the art of making cartoons—and indeed there were cartoonists there, making cartoons of those who were talking about drama, music, painting, and poetry. I hadn't known there were that many people in the City interested in art, and it seemed they all were in Hubert's. It was like a conference of the arts, like one of those festivals provincial cities try to get up regularly nowadays to show that some cultural explosion is going on. But the profuse strains of talk in Hubert's were certainly not the result of civic or commercial planning. Yes, the aesthetic was in Hubert's. And the despair of the aesthetic? That was everywhere in Hubert's, in the mood of everyone talking and gesticulating. It was even present in the fact that people remained in Hubert's to so late an hour (few left before 4 A.M.). If one talked about aesthetic questions at any time before midnight, if one did not sacrifice one's feeling of freshness on the morning after, just in order to talk about aesthetic matters very late at night, one could perhaps come in contact with the aesthetic and not feel the despair which Kierkegaard found latent in it. But it was this very despair which was in fact the most attractive part of the aesthetic. As interesting as art, and maybe even more interesting, was talking about it after midnight, close to four in the morning, just before Hubert's closed. And the faces of those who talked about it: emaciated, unwholesome, fevered, and mischievous, spoke, if one could hear what their looks said, much more of despair than of art. How wonderful that place was to any newcomer to the ways of bohemianism!

I focused on my first evening, or morning (it was past three A.M.), in Hubert's, when I had had a brush with a very particular expression of the despair which long afterwards, on reflection, I thought had hovered over my whole experience as a youth. At the table next to mine, there was just one person sitting, and there were two empty chairs, which was surprising because Hubert's was so crowded. The man sitting alone over his coffee was young, but quite unpleasant looking, with a large, ridiculously shapeless nose, very red cheeks, and a jaw that jutted beyond what should have been its natural limit. But I was not bothered by the man's appearance. I had never formed the idea that everyone in the world would have to be good-looking for me to be at ease with myself. As I was thinking about this, I noticed a very stylishly dressed, handsome young man approaching the table. The solitary one invited him to sit down. "No, I think I won't," said the young man. "You're much too ugly for me to sit down with you." And he turned his back and went off. The solitary man's red face became still more red. But the insult did not go without retaliation. Some weeks later, the solitary one the handsome young man would not sit with, put his fist through Hubert's plate glass window. He severed an artery in the process, and was taken to Bellevue, where he recovered. But Hubert's did not. After this incident, the depression, which was then mounting, closed it down for good.

POST SCRIPT

I have been asked this question by persons to whom I told what has gone before: "Didn't you have some ideas of your own before you ever met up with Lionel Stander?"

Now, I think I have chosen the right age, nineteen, to begin my account of what I did, saw, and heard insofar as my life has been serious, and I will cite here in my defense Rimbaud's line:

One is not serious at seventeen.

Nevertheless, I shall go back before 1929, and indicate how it was I reached the Village.

I came to Manhattan from Chapel Hill. Before that I had lived in Brooklyn with relatives, while attending St. John's University, and this is the reason I had been in Brooklyn: I had had to leave my parents' home. My father, rabbi at Niagara Falls, New York, would have been in great trouble with his community if I had been seen on the streets of that city in long pants. During my years at Niagara Falls High, my classmates, all of whom were older than I was, were used to spending Saturday nights playing pool for high stakes in the local pool parlors. The custom was for the winner to treat the others to whatever was offered in the Niagara Falls brothels, and I, whether a loser or winner, was entitled to go along too. Except for this: Though at fourteen I was captain of the debating team (I graduated from high school one year later), I still wore knickers, and I was told that the local brothels would not admit me. So my classmates at Niagara Falls High would not take me along with them on Saturday nights. As a result, my whole interest was centered on acquiring a pair of long pants. But the story got around about where I wanted to go in long pants, and it was even said I had been there, and been turned down. And then the thought struck me that I could never appear in the streets of Niagara Falls in adult trousers, for if I were so seen it would have immediately gone out that the rabbi's son had just come from a brothel. To grow up, I would have to leave the city. On graduating from high school I enrolled at St. John's University in Brooklyn, and, working over two summers as a waiter, I saved enough money to enter the University of North Carolina at Chapel Hill. If my father had been consulted about what happened to me, he would no doubt have said: "As a result of trying to get into a whore-

27

house" (he would purposely have used the strongest possible term), "my son arrived in Greenwich Village, which is where he belongs." I must add here that soon after I reached the Village my father lost his pulpit in Niagara Falls and had to take a less prestigious position in Lynbrook, Long Island. But this was not the result of anything I had done. His job in Niagara Falls was still another casualty of the depression.

‹ Two ›
THE THIRTIES

"I F only we had come of age during the thirties!" I have heard any number of young people voicing this complaint; they were faulting not themselves, and not even their parents, merely the time when they were born. I found, too, that I only excited their anger when I said their complaint was based on ignorance; in many ways the thirties was a depressing period. Could anyone who happened to be on Union Square as I was on May Day 1931, and saw Grover Whelan's police rout and then beat the May Day marchers, think it so wonderful to have come of age that year? And Whelan's May Day outing for the brutal was not just an isolated event. There were other happenings at the time, calling on the May Day violence to occur. There were the reactionary tirades of Father Coughlin over the radio, and the sinister addresses (also over the air) by Huey Long, telling us that what the nation needed most was the kind of mob-backed authoritarian government already fastened on the state of Louisiana.

Oh, there was so much that was painful in the time! The streets were full of the jobless, employment agencies overflowed, and the rudeness of secretaries, who were there presumably to help you find a job, gave you the disabling feeling that no one would ever pay you to do anything. The thought of apples became the thought of selling apples; in fact, apples were being hawked at all the street corners, and with this result: The fruit which Rilke tells us crams life and death into our mouths by being so delicious, was fast becoming a symbol not of the sweet, but of the bitter, of all we were denied. And counterpointing the more candid sounds of misery were the halfheard movements in officialdom, all leading up to World War II, which many of us knew might be delayed, but could nowise be prevented. Whatever one commenced doing would have to be dropped once the war began, and could anyone suppose the world would be the same after the war was over?

AND yet it is quite true that all was not privation and poverty during the thirties. There were some positive things, too, so that I can even understand—up to a point—the regret expressed by those who missed the period. I understand such regret but do not quite respect it, for I have generally found that those who are hard on the time in which they happen to live are rather soft on themselves for what they failed to achieve in it. About failure: some of the writers of the thirties told me they felt literary failure less keenly—was it somehow less shameful?—than they would have felt it had they come up in the twenties. And I can hardly think of a single person whom I heard say during the thirties: "I'm so glad I wasn't born earlier. I wouldn't have missed this time for anything." Whatever it was we who lived through the thirties enjoyed, we scarcely ever attributed to the thirties. So what is it you think you missed, you who had the luck (good or bad) to have come of age during the forties, the fifties, the sixties, the seventies?

You missed a New York City much less crowded than it is today. There was an abundance of gas then, and the cost was negligible. But there was no smell of gasoline in the air. Hardly ever did one see a plane cross the sky. But now I come to something which indeed *was* there, something people may rightly regret having missed. In all the depression of the period, which was not just economic, there was yet this exhilarating feeling: we were on the point of some real change, real change was possible. And this feeling is powerful, it is life-enhancing. You note that the institutions which have stood in the way of human realization are, after all, not that enduring. The strong were not as strong as the weak had thought they were, and the weak were not as weak as the strong had fancied them. Something new could occur. There were those, of course, who claimed to know what this new thing would be. Generally, they were the ones who had joined the Party, which in those days meant the Communist party; the Party told them what the country needed and what they were to expect.

I THINK it was in 1932, the year that Hitler became Reichschancellor and Franklin D. Roosevelt, President, that I was brought to a social-political gathering on the West Side of New York City. The place of meeting was a rather sumptuous apartment on Central Park West, a neighborhood which in those days was even more splendid than it is today. The meeting had been called by an ideologically orientated but fundamentally literary group of which Nathanael West was a member. I was told at the meeting about *Miss Lonelyhearts,* which had not yet appeared in print, but which many members of the group had already read in manuscript. They all spoke of West with great affection and they regretted his having gone off to California. Finally, they talked about their social ideas, which I had come there to be informed of, and by which, I was promised, I would be ennobled. One member explained that they were all committed to a new conception of human relations. What was this conception? It was a Christian view of true human contact, they said, and it had been revealed to them by Dostoevsky. I can still remember how I looked about me to see if there was even one non-Jew in that apartment. In fact, there was not one person there who was not, at the least, of Jewish origin. As I remember, I even brought the matter up. I said, "I think everyone here is Jewish." "What of it?" someone replied. "We're talking about our beliefs, not about what our parents believed. And as a matter of fact, my own parents never believed in anything." Another said this to me: "Jews need Dostoevsky's revelation more than Christians do." And then he quoted some remarks from *The Sleepwalkers,* a recently published novel by the Viennese writer, Hermann Broch: ". . . The Jews have carried to a still more

31

advanced stage [than the Protestants] . . . the neutralization of religious experience. . . . Perhaps they have already gotten as near to the coldness of the Absolute as ordinary men can bear. . . ." After this quotation, with its vaguely anti-Semitic flavor, they told me what was really on their minds, and what they said then made me think that I had indeed found my way into one of Dostoevsky's novels. The leader of the group, the very one who had convinced the other members to join with him in spreading the new Dostoevskian gospel, had, very recently, undergone a change of heart and joined the Communist party. Moreover, another of the group's members—he was not present at the meeting—had sent the group leader a telegram threatening to shoot him on sight unless he straightaway resigned from the Communist party. The group members were concerned to prevent this act of violence. But they were not prepared to go to the police. As they saw it, the problem facing them could be a test of the new truths which had been revealed to them. Their idea was to try, by utterly Dostoevskian, by Alyoshane methods, to persuade the terrorist member, whose name, by the way, was Ginsberg, to let their former leader waste some weeks in trying out the Communist party. They were convinced that he would soon resign from it of his own accord. I remember that as I left the meeting, they gave me some literature. That's what happened during the thirties after a meeting, often after a party: You were given something to read. The literature this time was made up of passages on the decay of values from Broch's *The Sleepwalkers*, which they had already cited to me. They had typed out passages on values for the newcomers to their ranks. And along with the pages from Broch, they also gave me what they no doubt considered sound advice. They said, "Don't just read this, memorize it."

I have recently reread *The Sleepwalkers*, in which there are some fine dramatic moments. But the essays on the degeneration of values included in the novel are of little interest. I couldn't help wondering how anybody of critical mind, even in 1932, could have thought them worth committing to memory. Broch's essays amount to little more than a collection of the pessimistic cultural platitudes fashionable in his period. But I do not want to suggest that the group which called my attention to this text of Broch's is to be judged by Broch's ideas. These ideas are, of course, quite dead today (I think they were dead in 1932), but the notion of a Dostoevskian approach to social problems is something else again. I have found references to contemporary groups in the USSR, groups with precisely this orientation, in Yanov's book *The New Russian Right,* so there might have been something prophetic after all about that little band of Dostoevskians on Central Park West.

Moreover, there *was* something in the period which did relate to Dostoevsky's insights, though for most people who thought about politics then, the time seemed inevitably related to those of Karl Marx. The interesting thing to recognize now, though, is that there really was some connection between the time, with its problems, and Dostoevsky's social and religious thought.

Until the economic catastrophe of 1929, there were not many Americans who gave serious consideration to what they should do in life besides trying to succeed (in some practical or intellectual enterprise). Thought tended to be focused on the *technical* problems which had to be met for a project to be successfully concluded. And, I think for many Americans, thought is just that—even today, even in philosophy, which has traditionally judged the meaning and value of *alternative* projects. But the main interest of our present-day philosophers still seems to be a technical one: To be clear about the basic elements in saying anything at all, to be clear about what might be called the structure of assertion as such. But during the thirties, because of the continuing difficulties people faced, they had to ask themselves what it was they really believed, what it was they really valued, which of their actions were worth the doing, and just what sacrifices they were ready to make. They began to ask themselves *Russian* questions, and this not because they had read Dostoevsky, Tolstoy, or Chekhov, but because questions of some depth were regularly raised for them by the problems of the day. So, come to think of it, that little group of Dostoevskians was not quite the anomaly I thought it was in 1932.

I discovered this in the thirties: Ordinary life remains quite as ordinary even when there is pain in it. As to ordinary life: Almost everyone went to the movies at least once a week, and admissions were generally no more than twenty-five cents— except after 5 P.M., when admissions went up to fifty cents. Now, as to the pain: Most people went to the movies not just to pass the time, but to win some money in the lotteries and bingo games that were regularly part of the show. As I remember, my mother, who went to the movies then exclusively for this purpose, never became absorbed in the films shown, and generally waited—tense, apprehensive, and hopeful—for the announcement of a winning number. But once, in despair at not having won on other occasions, and at having spent money uselessly, since she had not even watched the film, she left just before the announcement of a winner, and was not present to hear her own number called. Had she remained, she would have been awarded the sum of one hundred dollars. From this sad event she learned a lesson in patience, and from then on, no matter how boring the film—though, in fact, films were most often not boring in those days—she would stay to the very end, and was indeed repaid twice with one-hundred-dollar awards.

SOME restaurants or eating places—for cafeterias also counted in this way—are privileged in certain periods; they seem to absorb the qualities and values of those who frequent them. Before the depression, in the Village the privileged eating place was Romany Marie's. I don't think it was merely a restaurant, for it was other things too: a coffee house, a place for rendezvous, and a place to stay up until 3 A.M. When the depression came, Romany Marie's was frequented by Bertrand Russell when he was in New York (Will Durant brought him there), by John Cowper Powys, by two explorers who had been to the North Pole, by Glenway Wescott, and by Arshile Gorky and Mark Toby, who were then struggling to win reputations as painters. And Stuart Davis, already famous, came there often. Romany Marie's was notable not only for good food at low prices, its renowned clientele and warm atmosphere, but also for the machinations of the owner and hostess, Romany Marie, who tried her best to determine which boy took which girl seriously in her restaurant. She tried to have a hand as *entremetteuse* in every love affair that blossomed under the lights in her place, and she seemed to think that it would be unethical to leave serious sexual affairs to what might happen by chance. This might be all right in other restaurants, for which she had nothing but scorn, but not in her place. And, until the economic disaster of the early thirties, she held forth on the corner of Fourth Street and West Broadway, across from the Park, and those of us who cared for life in the Village went there either for dinner, or after dinner. I was almost always there. For a whole period there was nowhere else I wanted to go.

But with the depression one changed the places of pleasurable acquaintance. With the depression, people deserted Romany Marie's, and they began to go to the Jumble Shop, on MacDougal Street just below Eighth Street. Here the topics of conversation were also different, and so were the names bruited about. Here nobody talked about Glenway Wescott or Bertrand Russell, but one did hear the names of Hilquit and Browder and Marx. Although, as a matter of fact, when Marx's name was cited—perhaps because this was still the Village—it was invariably preceded by "Charlie" and not by "Karl." It was of Charlie Marx we spoke when we discussed the *Communist Manifesto* or *The Eighteenth Brumaire* in the Jumble Shop. But I had never heard any variant of his name mentioned at Romany Marie's.

The Sam Johnson, on West Third Street between MacDougal and Thompson Streets, was one night spot for eating, drinking, talking, and reciting poetry which, instituted before the depression, had its real life during that period. The Sam Johnson was a sort of proletarianized version of the Jumble Shop. Its leading figures were the poets: Maxwell Bodenheim, Eli Siegel, and John Rose Gildea, who was famous for, among other things, the denunciatory rhetoric with which he had assailed someone who had asked him to define the Holy Ghost. At the Sam Johnson, Gildea and Bodenheim would recite their latest poems and Eli Siegel would recite Vachel Lindsay's *The Congo*, a poem certainly intended for and suited for recitation. Eli made a theatrical production of it.

Villagers went to poetry recitals, but they went to the movies, too. Now one aspect of the films we saw is worth noting here. Some of the best films and the most popular were the ones known as gangster films. *Scarface* and *Little Caesar* immediately come to mind, and they brought to the fore actors like James Cagney, Paul Muni, and Edward G. Robinson. For my part, I have to say that of all the films I've seen, the gangster films of the thirties were the ones I most enjoyed. And I must note here that the next great input into exciting filmmaking came from the Nazis. Yes, the films in which Nazis figured during the forties and early fifties almost rivaled the thirties' films about American gangsters. The connection I am suggesting here between the gangsters and the Nazis has to do only with the dramatic forcefulness of film action, but a clever European friend, when I talked about this with him in Paris after the war, suggested quite a different connection which might be described as sociological. He suggested that the very *same* social forces which in European countries had led to the Communist, Fascist, and Nazi movements, had, in the United States, been expressed in the criminal gangs of the late twenties and early thirties. The American gangsters, he thought, were expressing in economic terms something very similar to what was expressed politically in Europe by the Communists, Nazis, and Fascists. I am inclined to think today that there is some depth in this notion, and that it explains to a very large degree what it was in the gangster films of the thirties that made them so fascinating: the gangsters were part of something like an ideological movement; they were not just criminals.

In line with this view, what I think should be emphasized today is that the gangster films raised, for the audiences of that period, questions about problems which were not truly seen when approached conventionally. These questions could be reduced to a few basic ones: To what length would one go to achieve some real goal? What would one do to escape from poverty? To get a good job after long periods of joblessness? There was another question, almost as basic: With what other persons, with what organized group, was one willing to be associated in the struggle to better one's condition? Here the Communists made their strongest pitch, and many persons, yielding to their propaganda, decided at that time to seek economic and also political salvation through the Party. And if, for whatever reason, one rejected the Party, it seemed in the thirties that there was no alternative but to find or to organize a better party than the Party. The goal of ethical action then might have been summed up in this alternative: to join, and work for, the Party, or to create some improvement of it in still another group. Here the Trotskyists made their appeal, claiming, "We have made precisely that improvement." But of course there were other groups who claimed to have improved on the Trotskyists, notably the Fieldites. Numbering somewhat less than ten members —among whom, though, there were individuals who are important today in the American academy: Professor Albert Wohlstetter, the military theorist, and the noted Harvard philosopher, Morton White—this group claimed to adhere more strictly to Leninist principles than the Trotskyists, whom they often described as "utterly compromised." When I first heard them talk about the Trotskyists, I thought the party they were discussing was the Republican party. I remember, too, that Harold Rosenberg was so struck by this political sect that he referred to them in a term suggesting both derogation and respect; "They are," he said, "our political cubists."

The thirties in New York City—but I am sure this was true in many other cities—were full of marchers shouting slogans. Up until the Works Progress Administration openings created by Franklin Roosevelt's government, the main slogan was "We want jobs." After the WPA jobs were set up, the slogans became more political; at first they were directed against "war and fascism," later on they were further particularized. Thus we had the anti-Japanese "Hands off China," and with the eruption of the Spanish counterrevolution in 1936, there were slogans in defense of the Spanish Republic. I was present at a political meeting during which Jay Lovestone (former secretary of the American Communist party, but after 1929 a heretic), introduced a member of the United Automobile Workers (then just being constituted) to a member of the Spanish POUM, sent here to collect money for that revolutionary group in its struggle with Franco. Lovestone introduced the two men, the Spaniard wearing the uniform of the Spanish Republican Army and the American auto worker in corduroys, and the two men publicly exchanged gifts. The man from the UAW gave the POUMist a tire chain which had been used in a struggle between strikers and auto plant detectives, and the soldier from the POUM gave the UAW representative a handful of bullets from his machine gun. To everyone in that room the ceremonial exchange signified the forging of an international unity against oppression.

So marching became a regular thing, a part of daily life. People got used to traveling to other cities in order to march there for some political purpose, and once one had begun marching, one was almost sure to become a member of a political organization, which was sure to promote still more marches. I recollect taking a train to Washington in the very early thirties just in order to march there. The slogan on this occasion had to do with jobs, but most of those on the train who had taken the trouble and the time to go to Washington had jobs; the real aim of some of them was not to obtain jobs for anyone, but to confront and expose the new government in Washington. On the train ride to Washington there was much talk of politics and no talk about jobs. People raised questions about the moral right to be violent, and Felix Morrow, who was in the group, announced for all to hear that he was not only not opposed to violence, but he in fact liked it very much. And Will Gruen, who was teaching philosophy downtown at New York University, speaking of Norman Thomas said, "I always thought well of him, but I never thought he was a revolutionary." And he said this as if "a revolutionary" was the thing to be.

Once the WPA jobs were opened to the unemployed, real change came over the city. The breadlines disappeared, and that was very important because of the psychological effect the lines had had. And then the WPA workers went into the parks and streets and cleaned and polished and decorated them so that this city of New York, with all its millions, among whom so many were certainly ill-housed and shabbily dressed, was suddenly spic-and-span, swept from one end to the other, its piles of trash removed. New York was, I think during this period, a model city with respect to the cleanliness of its streets and parks and the expeditious disposal of its waste—not all of the city to be sure, but yet at the height of the depression, for the most part, it looked better than it has ever looked since. Much has been written against the WPA projects, about the waste of government money on jobs poorly performed or simply not attended to, and no doubt some of the criticism has point. But in fact, the WPA workers did a great deal for the beauty and cleanliness of this city, whose features, so begrimed today, were well cared for at that time. Maybe the WPA workers were overpaid for what they did. Many of them worked only part of the time, and no doubt it was easier then to keep the city proper. But the WPA workers did more than keep the city clean; they also decorated it. Artists from the Artists Project, among whom were painters like Arshile Gorky, Willem de Kooning, Philip Evergood, and Philip Guston, painted murals in banks and government buildings. Malraux had said that no one wants to look at an art work in a sea of blood. The artists were helping the government by their work, saying, there can't possibly be a sea of blood here, for look, here are works of art!

As I have already noted, the time had come when people felt it was necessary to join a political party. Which party? Certainly not the Republican or the Democratic party, for these parties, in the rhetoric of that period, were politically "dead." Only in very much smaller organizations was there the possibility of political life. The Socialists? No, they were incompetent in the first place and right-wing in the second. So it was the Communist party that people joined. Those who remained Democrats or Republicans seldom told you of their party affiliations, but people who went Communist also went public with it, for one was proud to be a Communist. Gerard Manley Hopkins has written a poem, one of his poorest, yet somehow striking, in which the first line goes: "Why do I, seeing a soldier, feel ashamed?" An English poet of the period, C. Day Lewis, one day to be Poet Laureate, imitated Hopkins's poem, substituting for the word *soldier* the word *Communist.* So the first line of his poem ran, "Why do I, seeing a Communist, feel ashamed?" It's obvious that there's some difference between the two lines because, if you can clearly see that someone is a soldier from his uniform, how can you possibly see (from his expression?) that someone is a Communist? During the late thirties, Wyndham Lewis, in his novel *Revenge for Love,* parodied C. Day Lewis's transformation of Hopkins's line, describing the feelings of shame that come over a member of the British Communist party as he catches a glimpse of himself in the mirror. His face, a Communist's, made him ashamed of anything not strictly Communist in his thoughts and feelings.

In the great cities—but most of all in the city of New York —the choice of a party became one of the important spiritual decisions one could make.

In choosing a party one often chose whom one would marry, what friends one would have, and what one's children would be like. When I went to Chicago in 1940 (I was on the Writers Project there for one year), I found that the Trotskyists, all of them young, were married and already had had children. How had this happened? How had they altogether escaped a period of bohemianism? They told me, and by "they" I mean Saul Bellow, Isaac Rosenfeld, Harold J. Kaplan, that they had married in order to show their disapproval of the sexual promiscuity in the Communist party. They claimed that they married at an early age because of politics, and Saul expressed this in a literary way. He said: "My marriage broker was the Fourth International."

As I recall, I remained on speaking terms with one Stalinist up until the Moscow Trials—after that it was impossible to have friendly relations with anyone in the Party. (A person with Trotskyist views or affiliations was simply called a Fascist by Communist party members.) This particular supporter of things Stalinist, a very handsome widow, had one child, a son. When I knew his mother, he was about seven. I thought him the most delightful, the most intelligent and the manliest little boy I had ever met. His mother made sure that his education would be in accordance with strict Communist principles. She sent him to the Communist schools and in the summer to the Young Pioneer camps, and she said to me once, "When I joined the Communist party I introduced myself to my great-great-grand-children." She could not have been more wrong. Some three years after she said this to me, her son had run away from home, and to my knowledge she never saw him again.

The choice of a political party holding extreme views on society, the state, the economy, and on many other matters, required mature judgment and political experience, and very few of those of us who felt obliged to choose a party had the needed experience of politics. Necessarily one came to depend on the judgment of someone older than oneself, and it is in this way that the choice was most often made. But of course there are always exceptions. I remember a meeting of the Trotskyist faction in the Socialist party to which I belonged at one period in the thirties, in which there was another Trotskyist, older than I but with whom I found I had something in common. We both wore freshly laundered white shirts to Party meetings. He confided to me that he had become a Trotskyist when Trotsky was expelled from the Russian Communist party and exiled to Turkey, and not because he had been instructed in politics by someone older than he. What he said was this: He had so resented the unconcealed delight in the "capitalist" press at Trotsky's fate when exiled from the USSR that he could not help but equate, in his feelings at least, the support of Stalin with the support of capitalism.

I'LL return to the matter of parties, but I want to take some note here of my literary activities at that time, which of course could not but have some connection with the political judgments I was making. In 1933, I began to write for *The Nation*. I sent the review a couple of literary articles, one an essay on Malraux's *Man's Fate*, which had just appeared and which I believe I gave its first favorable review in this country. Praised by Trotsky, it had had unfavorable reviews in the Communist press. I published poems in *The Nation*, *Blues*, and *Poetry*. Joseph Wood Krutch, the editor of *The Nation*, having published two of my pieces which I sent in unsolicited, then asked me to review books for the magazine, and I reviewed, among other works, a novel by Josephine Herbst, *The Executioner Waits*, which I judged unfavorably for the deadness of its characters, which I laid up to the author's ideology. I met Miss Herbst at a party many years later and we talked about her book and my piece on it. She had long since forgiven me for the review; in fact she had come to think I was quite right in what I had written against her. Moreover, she was no longer the enthusiastic pro-Communist she had been in the thirties. We talked about her husband, John Hermann, who back in the thirties had won a *Scribner's Magazine* prize for a novel which I thought was rather imitative of her style. I had met him some years before, and Josephine Herbst wanted to talk about him. He was a big, gawky, handsome midwesterner, but quite enthusiastic about politics, literature, and sex. His aim, Josephine told me, had been to go to Iowa, sleep with the Iowa farm girls in the cornfields, and get them and their families to join the Communist party. Did he do this? "Yes, this is what he did," she said. And that is why she had broken off with him. But she told me something else which I find interesting. There had been many young persons in the Communist movement who believed in the goodness of the farm population and actually thought the industrial workers already corrupted by capitalism. This faith in the goodness of the people on the farms who were still in contact with nature and had not yet submitted to the discipline of the assembly line, was, according to Josephine Herbst, much more widespread than anyone realized. Thinking about it today, I am struck that it was this kind of faith in the unspoiled which was reasserted in the sixties in the youth cult of that period. The belief in the young and their goodness, propounded for a while by Paul Goodman (he did finally renounce it), was, I believe, a sixties version of an older faith, which, in the thirties, projected the figure of the farm boy—or farm girl—as uncorrupted. And the problem of where to find—or even look for—some social group in which human nature can be said to be still unspoiled, has been raised for us once again in two connections: first, as an explanation for the failure of the Left to revolutionize society after the Second World War, and secondly, in connection with the problem of industrial pollution.

Let's look at the first question: Why had there been no

international revolution against capitalism in those countries where, according to the Marxist thesis, the economic system had developed to a point where it could no longer be regarded as progressive? Why had the revolution in backward Russia not led to revolution in the advanced countries of Europe and the predicted historic advance of the European economy according to the Socialist model? The answer given during the thirties by the Trotskyist movement was the following: The failure of communism in the advanced countries of Europe was due to the victory of communism in backward Russia, for it was in fact the backwardness of Russia which had placed at the head of the international proletariat a bureaucratic caste, led by Stalin, which was both politically incompetent and faithless to the interests of the working class. This Trotskyist answer led, however, to a further question: Was the international proletariat really a revolutionary class? For if so, how was it still being led by bureaucrats who were disloyal to it? The middle classes in the European revolutions had not been led by traitors or scoundrels, though in France some of the revolutionary leaders—Danton, for example —had been charged with dishonesty and treason. Nevertheless, even if one accepted the accusations brought against Danton and others, nobody would claim that the entire leadership of the French middle class during and after the French Revolution was composed of men who were traitors to the interests of the bourgeoisie. So the idea that the proletariat was revolutionary, but badly or traitorously led, could hardly convince anyone after the Second World War. And there was something else which made it unacceptable: Until the defeat of Hitler, the Soviet Union had been a single, isolated state, trying out a new collectivised economy in a world economic system dominated by capitalism. As the Trotskyists put it, the Stalinists were committed to socialism in one country; this was in fact a reactionary ideology which had led to inhibiting the revolutionary potential of the working class in other countries. But directly after the war, the Red Army occupied eastern Europe and very soon the Soviet Union's economy was not the only collectivized one in Europe. Poland, Yugoslavia, Hungary, East Germany, Romania, Bulgaria, Latvia, Estonia, Lithuania, and finally, Czechoslovakia, were brought into the same "socialist" economic system. And in 1949, the Chinese revolution toppled the Chiang Kai Shek regime, and communism was triumphant in the most populous country of Asia. So the Soviet state was no longer isolated. How was it, then, that capitalism still remained extant in western Europe, in South America, and in the United States? New reasons had to be given.

One reason set forth by the Frankfurt school of radicals in West Germany, led by Adorno and Horkheimer, was that the very development of technology in the West which had created the *objective* conditions for an economy of plenty under a social-ist politics, had, on the other hand, so warped the human *subject* that the spiritual health needed for political action by the prole-tariat was no longer there. The old Marxist view had been that increased control by man over nature would lead to weakening the control of man by man. The domination of nature, it had been thought, would lead to political freedom. This position the theorists of the Frankfurt school disputed. The domination of nature by man, they said, leads to *increased* domination of man by man. The reason for the failure of socialism as a political goal was to be found not merely in human inadequacy but mainly, and first of all, in the success of our technology.

I have gone into this matter at such length here because this idea, I believe, is the important notion which has stimulated and which justifies, if one accepts it, the many protests against the use of nuclear energy for industrial purposes. Obviously, the question as to the utility and safety of nuclear energy is a techni-cal one which can only be judged by experts in the field. Granted that these experts are human beings who may make mistakes of judgment. On the other hand, their judgments can only be adequately corrected by the scientific community. There is, in fact, no other collectivity competent to do so. From this it would appear that we should follow the judgments of experts on the matter of nuclear energy. But against this view there is the argument of the Frankfurt theorists, to wit: Our technological prowess is the source of our spiritual and political weakness. If we cannot set up a good society, the main reason is our industrial success.

44

So the idea that there must be a human nature unspoiled by money (capitalism) or by technology (science) is still with us, as the demonstration at the Battery against nuclear plants, addressed by Ralph Nader, Jane Fonda, and Tom Hayden, and attended by two hundred thousand people, attested. (How Nader, Fonda, Hayden, and the rock singers who entertained the demonstrators can be thought to represent an unspoiled human nature is beyond me.) I must add here that the influence of the "Greens" in West Germany must be due in part to the effect on West Germans of the thinking of the Frankfurt theorists.

BUT I must leave the present and return to the thirties, when the idea of a group or class of the still unspoiled led John Hermann to try to recruit to the Communist party farm girls in the Iowa cornfields. Admittedly, he and people who thought like him were exceptional in that period. Most of the persons I knew who became interested in politics did not think of an unspoiled human nature but, rather, of the right party to join. Which was it to be?

I had one friend at that time, a writer, who had so far expressed himself only in verse, but believed in preaching to his friends, and who changed his sermon to them from week to week. For one week he would preach art for art's sake, and the next week advocate joining the Communist party, then, for the week following that, revert to his former view. After some six months of reversing himself in this way, out of some longing to be more resolute, he ordered his wife to join the Communist party.

There were those, though, who had already joined the Party and were thinking about how to make an exit from it in some way that would not be inglorious, that would not tarnish convictions which they still wanted to think of as revolutionary. How to get out of the Communist party once one has become a member? No doubt the one who found this most difficult to do was Whittaker Chambers, who, "in the awful daring of a moment's surrender," had joined a Red Army military intelligence unit that operated in the United States. How he broke from his Communist affiliations and saved his own life he himself has told in his autobiographical work, *Witness*. The people I knew in the Village, though, who were in the Communist party and were beginning to feel uncomfortable about it were quite different from Chambers, being much less romantic. Philip Rahv and William Phillips, to whom I had been introduced by Harold Rosenberg, were, when I met them, individuals regarded by the Party as experts on questions relating to ideology and literature, and they had been entrusted by the Party (in fact by Alexander Trachtenberg, who was Rahv's political mentor) with a magazine, *Partisan Review*, which at the time I met them was a Communist organ paid for by the Communists, though to all appearances in agreement with the Communist line only insofar as the editors *happened* to agree with it. And the editors were beginning to disagree. Hitler had come to power in Germany and had liquidated the largest Communist party in Europe. He had seized the Rhineland, the Saar, set up fortifications there, and sent the German unemployed into the munitions factories on a program of German rearmament. Leon Trotsky, writing in *Harper's*, warned that Hitler would next try to split the British from the French, and it was soon clear that Trotsky was right. For the British showed sympathy with the German Fuehrer's programs, and lent a deaf ear to the objections of the French. But Trotsky not only warned against Hitler, he warned the West against Stalin, too, and he attributed Hitler's victory in Germany to the fallacious theory of social fascism (which held that Socialists were really Fascists) promulgated by Manuilsky under Stalin's direction, and repeated constantly in the Communist party presses throughout the world. To intellectuals editing a literary-political review, the question of Communist responsibility for Hitler's victory was a very serious matter. What if one had oneself written articles describing Social Democrats as Social Fascists, or published articles by others making that assertion? There were intellectuals who rushed to pen such statements, but in general they were written by persons without any political flair. Kenneth Burke, for instance, wrote an article for the *New Masses* in which he described

46

American democracy as a form of "naïve fascism," and there were many others who expressed like views. But Rahv and Phillips did understand something about politics. They agreed with Trotsky's judgment about Stalin's responsibility for Hitler's victory, and yet there they were editing a literary magazine paid for by the Communist party, and they were required, if they discussed the matter at all, to say the contrary of what they believed. They were both deeply troubled, and they used to come and visit me (we all lived in the Village) to discuss their problem and also politics generally.

By that time I was fairly persuaded of the Trotskyist political line, and when Rahv and Phillips came to visit me this was what we talked about most of all. All of us had jobs on the Writers Project (I was first on the New York Guidebook, then on the Creative Project), and our political conversations embraced Roosevelt's policies, the new turn of the Communists toward Popular Front-ism, what was likely to happen in loyalist Spain, and, finally, the fate of *Partisan Review*. They were already planning to decamp from the Communist movement, taking a Party-created institution, *Partisan Review*, with them. I doubt whether this ever happened before or since to any Communist institution. But Phillips and Rahv did not tell me what they were going to do. They talked in terms of possibility only. Suppose they were editing a review—not *Partisan Review*—independent of Communist party support? Who would write for it? "Well, after all," I remember arguing, "there *are* non-Communist magazines filled with articles, poems, and short stories. Maybe you could publish some of those!" "But," countered Rahv, "we don't want to publish such writings. We want to publish writers who are committed to communism, but whose political thought is not controlled by the Communist party. And," he added gloomily, "except for us there are no such writers." In fact there were some: There was Jimmie Farrell, whose *Studs Lonigan* had been highly praised in the Communist press, but who had since then taken an independent line in the judgment of literary works, and who was critical of the Communist political line. There was Eleanor Clark, who was already sympathetic to the Trotskyist views, and who was known to be serious about writing though she had not yet produced any of the works for which she is known today. There was Mary McCarthy, who was known to be sympathetic, and there was Delmore Schwartz, who had just come on the scene and who was anti-Stalinist. Around such writers could not a review be formed? Dreams, dreams, said Rahv. And he called me a *luftmensch* for thinking that what actually did occur was at all possible.

What we were agreed upon was this: The Communist party line was wrong; the judgment that Social Democrats were to be combatted as if they were Fascists, the line summed up by the slogan raised in Germany before Hitler's triumph, "Beat the Social Fascists where you find them," was wrong, and had led to the defeat of the working class in Germany and the advance of reaction throughout Europe. We also thought that the new Communist line of Popular Front-ism was wrong, that it would lead to the defeat of the Spanish Republic and finally, to war, which indeed came within only a few years' time. Yes, we agreed on all these judgments of the Communist party, but the question for Rahv was not the correctness or incorrectness of the Party line. What he wanted to know was this: When would the Party's errors be so gross as to be widely perceived? When would it be quite safe to call the Party to account for disasters to the working class, to Europe, to culture, to human freedom? How enormous would the next catastrophe caused by the Communist party have to be for even a few more writers like ourselves to perceive the Party's responsibility? This is what Rahv wanted to know. He wanted to know the future, which was still to be revealed.

In the dark days of the Spanish civil war, when the arms embargo, which Roosevelt and Blum had agreed to, was strangling the Republic's military efforts, I said to Rahv: "If Spain is conquered by Franco, don't you think people will realize that the Party is responsible?" Rahv wasn't at all sure. "Look," he said, "the Communists are not the only ones responsible. People can point to the arms embargo and blame the French and American governments. With the propaganda machine at their disposal, the Communists can get out of almost any defeat." This judgment, as we know, was by no means unrealistic.

Rahv thought then, and on this too, I think, correctly, that only a successful revolution led by some other group besides the Communist party could weaken the Communist party's hold on liberals and intellectuals. The trials of the old Bolsheviks had begun; the first was in 1936, the second in 1937. They were obviously unfair. The accused, when they tried to defend themselves, were scolded by the court. These show trials, of which I shall have more to say later, seemed designed to provoke those intellectuals who concerned themselves with political matters to the severest condemnation of Soviet justice. But the result was quite the contrary. Intellectuals vied with one another in finding formulas to justify Moscow, and in fact the only real break in the power of the Party to influence came with the first secession from the Soviet ranks by Tito after the war, to be followed in the late fifties by the secession of China. These were the events that weakened Communist influence over intellectuals. The only one who had foreseen them in any important sense was Trotsky, who in 1940, the year he was assassinated, asserted in one of his last articles, "The USSR and the War," that if the Communist party came to power in other countries, the Stalinist system would not be able to mediate the inevitable conflict of these countries with the USSR. . . . In any case, the defections of Yugoslavia and China have made the criticism of the Soviet Union and of Communist party policies if not easy, in any case not too jarring. Such criticism was not at all easy during the thirties. Rahv even suggested that it was just impossible.

Yet it must be said to Rahv's credit that he finally undertook the very kind of criticism of Communist policies which he himself had asserted it was impossible to make. Yes, indeed. Philip Rahv undertook to do what he thought was impossible! (I have reread my own sentence and can hardly believe what I have written!) Of all the people I have ever known, the one person least likely to take any kind of risk—intellectual, physical, or social—was Philip Rahv. And yet, there are the facts. He broke with the Communist party in the period when its appeal in America was at its height—when the Communists were the allies of the New Dealers against the Republicans, and working with the union organizers in forming the first big industrial union, and when they were conducting appeals for Loyalist Spain. At one of these meetings Louis Fischer, calling for aid to the Spanish government, declared: "We have a very good army in the field." By "we" Fischer meant American left-wingers and intellectuals, influenced by the policies and ideas Rahv wanted to combat, thought it impossible to fight against successfully, and did finally fight against with a certain success. When he decamped from the Communist party with *Partisan Review,* it must have been with a continual feeling that what was probably the greatest action of his life was his very greatest mistake.

In 1937, Philip Rahv and William Phillips took the *Partisan Review* from the Communist party which had set it up and put it under their control, and made of it an independent intellectual review open to the criticism of Communist policy. There was no other such review in the country at that time, and for several decades that followed, *Partisan Review* was to become the leading journal in this country, due to a unique combination of political as well as literary sensitivity in its editing. Rahv and Phillips added Dwight Macdonald, Clement Greenberg, and Delmore Schwartz to their staff, and, after some years, William Barrett, and the review prospered.

Here I want to express myself more personally about Philip Rahv, who played a leading role in this whole affair.

Philip was tall, powerfully built, and handsome, not in the way movie stars are, but rather as a prizefighter might be, with a square jaw and a nose flattened not of course by an opponent's blow but by whatever genetic forces have been Asianing noses in the Ukraine, where, as it happens, Philip was born. He was not highly imaginative, but he was very intelligent, in fact one of the most intelligent men I have had the luck to be acquainted with. So I still remember my surprise when, just a few years ago, Harold Rosenberg, who had introduced me to Rahv in 1935, brought him up in speaking about the Soviet Union, which Rosenberg had visited on an art mission, saying, "It's a dumb country, quite as dumb as Philip Rahv." I remember replying, "But Philip Rahv is not dumb. He's the last person in the world

I would say that of." To which Rosenberg countered, "I mean Russia is as dumb as Philip was before he read Henry James." From which I understood what Harold had in mind. At our very first meeting, which was before he had read Henry James, Rahv had said to us, that is, to Rosenberg and me, that he thought Mike Gold—whose review of Thornton Wilder's *The Bridge of San Luis Rey* had just appeared in *The New Republic* and created something of a sensation—was a much greater writer than Paul Valéry. No doubt it was because he had heard judgments of this type made about art in the Soviet Union that Harold was willing to call Russia, with its wealth of talented people, a dumb country. And it was for this judgment of Valéry by Rahv that Rosenberg could derogate Rahv as he did. But however wrong Rahv's literary opinions were at an early stage of his political and literary career, he was always intelligent, and he had something else too, which I think he alone of all the intellectuals around *Partisan Review* had: political flair. His extreme political cautiousness—some have called it cowardice, though I think it should not be called that—came from a keen grasp of political realities, an understanding of them which was much greater than any idealizing impulse he could find in himself. So his caution could be explained either as due to his being overly intelligent or to his lack of will, depending on whether you were for him or against him. In any case, for all his caution, he behaved with extreme audacity intellectually and socially in crossing his political mentor, Trachtenberg, and decamping from the Communist party with *Partisan Review*.

(Incidentally, I do not think the estimate of Mike Gold, as compared with Valéry, made by Rahv in his youth, one that it is right to call "dumb." It is not a judgment I share or ever could have shared, and it was certainly ideologically motivated. But just as wrong, in my opinion, and just as ideologically motivated, is the estimate made by Valéry, and by those who followed him, that the sonnet of Oronte which Molière ridicules in *The Misanthrope* is superior to the folk song Alceste preferred. I think Valéry's judgment wrong, but I would not call it "dumb" either. Here we are involved with matters that cannot be decided by intelligence alone.)

William Phillips was more boyish than Rahv, mischievous, catty even, quite witty, and with a gift for subtlety. But he did lack Rahv's driving forcefulness, and will to power. It was Rahv who took the initiative in almost all serious matters and William who made the jokes at Rahv's expense. I think, too, that they depressed each other, and I must say for my own part I would not have ever wanted to venture on any enterprise with either of them as a main collaborator. All the same, they did manage to cooperate in a masterful coup at the expense of the Party and in the editing of a really brilliant review, which opened its pages to the best that was being written here and abroad in literature and in those other disciplines that have some bearing on it.

Rahv, Phillips, and Rosenberg were employed, as I was, on the WPA Writers Project, though after a while Rosenberg opted for the Artists Project, a decision which may have affected his subsequent career, many years later, as an art critic. Philip, William, and I stayed on the Writers Project, which was directed by Henry Alzburg, the translator from Yiddish of *The Dybbuk*, and whom I used to meet regularly for drinks at the Jumble Shop on MacDougal Street, where we would argue about "Charlie Marx."

I was put on the creative program by the New York administrator of the writing projects, Jimmie McGraw, who had been selected for that post by Henry Alzburg, and McGraw also came nightly to the Jumble Shop.

I mention these facts because of what happened on the Project. It was 1936, the year of the invasion of Ethiopia by Mussolini's armies, and by this time I had joined the Trotskyist faction in the Socialist party, which the Trotskyists now adhered to. I was the spokesman for the Trotskyists in the Writers Union, which was formed by the workers on the Project. So I was involved in continual rhetorical brushes with the Communists, who would have liked to see me off the Project. It was at that time that the announcement was made in the press that the Soviet Union was selling oil to Mussolini, oil needed for the campaign against Ethiopia, and many leftists were shocked by this move by the Soviet government. After all, the Communists

were the very ones who had been insisting on action by the
British and French governments to halt Mussolini, and they had
been scandalized by efforts of these very governments to assist
him. Now the Russians were helping him. Taking cognizance
of these protests, the Soviet government, in a move of typical
political ambidextrousness, sent the Italian imperial government something described in the press as a "sharply worded
note" against its invasion of Ethiopia, while still continuing to
sell the oil it needed to sustain this invasion. At just that moment, the Party faction on the project decided to demand my
dismissal from it by Jimmie McGraw. And they sent him a
delegation with this demand. Now, Jimmie McGraw had been
reading the press, and he was also a personal acquaintance. He
heard them out and then said to them: "I'll tell you what I'll do.
I'll do what the Soviet Union has done against the Italian Fascists. I'll send Abel a sharply worded note!"

When I first got on the Writers Project I worked on the
Guidebook with Ralph Manheim, who sat at the same desk with
me. (You got to know other writers during the thirties by getting on the Writers Project.) By 1937, though, I was "advanced"
to the Creative Project, for which one had to do whatever one
felt like doing. And I felt like writing verse. One did not even
have to report to the project office more than once a week, when
one received one's check. As a matter of fact, I had been told that
on the Artists Project there were painters who refused to make
even that concession to the government in return for their
weekly wage. One painter even said: "My signature is going to
be worth a great deal of money some day. The government can't
expect to get it from me every week for a tiny salary." Finally
he was prevailed on, though, to append his "valuable signature"
to the necessary government papers, but only after he had won
the right not to go down to the office to do this, and had had the
papers brought to him.

As to the verse I wrote on the creative project, I shall cite
one poem (it was published in *American Stuff*, the anthology
which the project got out), and not for its value as a poem, but
rather for its interest as a document. If one wants to get some
sense of the politics of the period, consider the fact that to write

this poem and others like it, I was being paid a weekly wage by the United States Government! Here it is:

How Comrade the Present Addressed Our Party

> *I could stand it*
> *no longer*
> *I kicked my*
> *chair over*
> *cried, "No, no,*
> *why should I sit*
> *elbows*
> *on the table,*
> *dreams idle*
> *gone gray*
> *with coffee*
> *and butts,*
> *while Comrade*
> *the Future*
> *with billions*
> *of poems*
> *stuck out of*
> *his collar,*
> *his shirtsleeves,*
> *his every*
> *pants pocket,*
> *is published,*
> *established,*
> *and looks like*
> *a dandy?*
> *Why should I*
> *for my few*
> *poems,*
> *have to live*
> *like a bohemian?"*
> *I expected*
> *expulsion.*
> *The Central Committee*
> *rose, applauded:*
> *"Comrade Abel*
> *has accomplished*

a Marxist
and also
a poetical feat!
getting Comrade the Present
to speak at our meeting!"

In an essay of mine published by *Dissent* in 1963, I said of New York City that in the thirties it went to Russia and spent most of the decade there. For, in the spiritual life of the city during the thirties, the important question discussed was whether to defend the Stalin government against those who criticized it, or to join the critics of that government's policies, the most important of whom was Leon Trotsky. So the Trotsky-Stalin controversy became the most bitterly discussed and violently argued issue wherever radical politics were discussed, and they were discussed in the city streets and cafeterias, in the unions and at the universities. They were discussed in the offices of the leading reviews published at that time in New York City. But the climactic event, I think, of the whole city's trip to Russia was the mass meeting at the Hippodrome when Trotsky, then in Mexico, was scheduled to deliver his defense against the accusations made against him in Moscow, over long-distance telephone, which, presumably, through loud speakers, would then reach the audience.

Some six thousand people crowded into the Hippodrome that night, and very few in that crowd were political supporters of Trotsky. So I think for the most part the audience was composed of people who were either simply curious about the kind of defense Trotsky would make against the sensational charges brought against him in the Soviet courts, or who had come to confirm their faith in Stalin and the Soviet system by noting at first hand the inadequacy of Trotsky's arguments and his inability to explain away the evidence brought against him. No doubt, of course, there were plenty of people in New York who had followed the Russian trials and had not made up their mind about Trotsky's guilt or innocence, but I do not think that many in that frame of mind went to the Hippodrome meeting. The people who were there had come because their passions were involved. They had not come just to satisfy their curiosity, or in a disinterested pursuit of truth. They had come out of an impulse like that which sends masses to see an execution, a *corrida*, a contest which ends in somebody's death. Of course no one was going to be hung at the Hippodrome that night. This could not happen even in the New York City that was already in Soviet Russia, but it was going to be proved that evening— this is what almost everyone in the audience *did* think, or hope —that somebody deserved hanging, and who would this one be? Would it be Trotsky or would it be Stalin? That was the question which was to be answered. So I went with great excitement to the huge, shapeless building on Eighth Avenue, whose name may call up one of the heaviest of animals, and if it does was properly named for an event as heavy as this one was bound to be, though nobody back in 1936 used the word *heavy* in the sense it is now used. Max Shachtman of the Trotskyist group appeared on the Hippodrome stage and announced that Leon Trotsky would talk to the audience in English from a prepared text; there was great expectation, people were asked to be silent, they were silent for some minutes and the voice of Trotsky was not heard. Max Shachtman came forward again and gave the explanation. The telephone connection with Mexico had been cut, sabotaged. He indicated who he thought the culprits were, and then announced that the interference would be unavailing, since he had a copy of Trotsky's speech and would deliver it himself.

I recall that when he announced that the connection with Mexico had been cut, a great cheer went up from most of the audience, a cheer from persons who had come presumably to hear Trotsky speak. In fact they had come to see him proved unworthy and culpable. And the first sign of his unworthiness was the interference with the arrangements to have him speak to them. Somebody shouted from the audience that it must have been the electrical workers union which had silenced Leon Trotsky, and proposed a cheer for those workers. But the rest of the audience would not accept this resolution of the matter. For there were many who, hating Trotsky, still wanted to hear him speak. They didn't just want to hate him, they also wanted to be able to take his justificatory arguments apart; but to do this they would have to hear him out. So there were shouts, "Let's hear the speech!" whereupon Max Shachtman, who was himself a remarkable political speaker, gave the performance of his life, and held the whole crowd spellbound, reading Trotsky's text, "I Stake My Life," as if he had written it himself.

If today one reads the speech Trotsky was to have given that night, one is not likely to be as affected by, or as admiring of it, as those who heard it delivered by Max Shachtman. It does not, I think, have the force of summation Trotsky made of his case before the investigating committee headed by John Dewey, which, I am told, Ernest Nagel thought a marvel of forensic logic. Yet it was powerful, biting, clear, and impassioned, and Max Shachtman rose to his highest powers of oratory in delivering it. He didn't merely deliver it, he became the person who had written it! Trotsky, the Old Man, the Bolshevik leader, the Red Army commander, the right hand of Lenin, the taker of the Winter Palace. Shachtman actually became the living presence of Trotsky in his greatest actions, and even the Stalinists, who composed a major part of the audience, must have been taken by his performance, for they sat absolutely silent through what amounted to a powerful assault on all their deepest political convictions. Were they convinced? Oh, but that was a different matter. Perhaps many of them were, for the moment. But this did not mean that they were going to quit the Party and seek membership in the Trotskyist organization. And there is always the pleasure of willfulness, the pleasure in rejecting a position that seems logically sound, for reasons you do not feel required to make specific. If there is a pleasure in marshalling logical arguments, there is an equal, and perhaps even greater, pleasure in simply refusing to be persuaded by the best-presented case. After all, did not Descartes argue that will is superior to intellect, so that God could make two-and-two equal to three or five, if he so willed it? Maybe people even think, in rejecting a good argument, and precisely because of the soundness of it, that they are identical with the divine. In any case, if there is a pleasure, and I think there is, in rejecting what seems to you a true opinion, this is the only pleasure many of the Stalinists in the audience could have gotten from the speech delivered by Shachtman.

Not all of them, though. One whom I recognized from the Writers Project came up to me as the crowd was filing out. "You liked the speech?" he asked me. "Naturally. It was marvelous," I answered. "Didn't you?" "Oh, yes," he said. "It was forceful." "Did it convince you?" I asked him, for I had the feeling that he was humoring me and not really agreeing with me. "It convinced me," he said, "that any man who can be so wrong and sound so right, ought to be shot."

ANOTHER memory of the thirties, less political than my recollections of that gathering at the Hippodrome, but yet not without a political side to it—I have hardly any memories of the thirties that are completely untouched by politics, and this does tell us something about the period—concerns Ford Madox Ford. He had been hired by the Writers Project, as had another modernist writer, already famous, Djuna Barnes. Now Djuna Barnes never attended any of the Writers Union meetings, but Ford did come to one of them, and this is the meeting I remember. Ezra Pound, with whom Ford had been well acquainted, and who had published many of Ford's poems in reviews and anthologies, and who I think had written about his verse, was being attacked at the Writers Union for his support of Mussolini. Pound was the one leading American writer who had publicly championed the cause of Mussolini's Italy and of the Fascist form of government, and so in those days he was regularly abused in the Union and his literary ideas were denounced whenever literary values were discussed. And it so happened that on the one occasion Ford came to a Union meeting, he had had to listen to lengthy and violent denunciations of an old friend and a master of verse who, in his view, happened to have taken up some mistaken views about the conduct of government. This was the way Ford judged Pound, and it was of course not the judgment of the majority at the Writers Union, which was composed in the main of Communist party members or sympathizers, nor was it that of even the most minimal minority in the Union, for in the minorities that made up the membership the prevailing political view was anti-Fascist, and Pound had, in fact, spoken in support of Italian fascism and its policies. So nobody in the hall, on the one night Ford Madox Ford addressed them, agreed with him. I had come to the union meeting that night by chance. I did not know that Ford would be there. I did not even know that he was on the project. And I had begun to avoid general meetings of the Union, for I did not like what was being said there on most occasions, and I do not get any special pleasure out of being in a minority. There are some people who actually enjoy this; I do not. In any case, I did come to the meeting, and when I got there Ford was already speaking. I saw on the platform a very tall, dignified, hook-nosed man with a mane of white hair, and he was speaking in a high-pitched, quavering voice using the most exquisite diction of England's highest social and intellectual circles. But he was not getting through to the audience.

Apparently, Ezra Pound had been attacked, and Ford had come to his defense. But it was impossible to defend Pound in that atmosphere to that audience. After I had heard just a few of his remarks I asked someone sitting next to me, "Who's that on the platform?" He said, "Don't you know? That's Ford Madox Ford," and then added, "He's lucky if he gets out of here alive. Look what he's doing, he's defending fascism." I replied, "I didn't hear anything like that. I heard him defending Ezra Pound." "It comes to the same thing," was the reply. I listened then to what Ford was saying, with extra care, and there was a murmur in the room while his words were very quietly spoken. He was talking about beauty, about the beauty of literature. "There is this beauty, after all," he said, "and you have to care for this thing called beauty. For that's what literature is all about, and you are supposed to be interested in it, for after all, aren't you writers? You are members of a writers' union. And if you do care about beauty, you have to care about Ezra Pound's poems." "I'd like to hit him," someone next to me whispered. I remonstrated, "Ford's an old man." And someone behind me said, in what certainly was louder than a whisper, "We can tear him for his white hair," and I did not know if he was satirizing what the union member next to me had said, or threatening the speaker on the platform.

I've often wondered what prevailed upon Ford Madox Ford to address that gathering with such a message. To be sure, he wanted to defend Pound's writings, but didn't he know the response he was going to get? Would Joseph Conrad, with whom he had collaborated, and who shared many of Ford's notions about the art of the novel, would Henry James, whom he had known in London, have had the naïveté to tell an audience like the members of the Writers Union that what counted in literature was not social progressiveness, but beauty of form? That evening was somehow very Russian. It was like the party described by Dostoevsky in *The Possessed*, in which the liberal-minded Stepan Trofimovitch contends, against the jeers of the radicals, that a great painting is more important than a pair of boots.

A Russian evening. But as I have already noted, people were asking themselves Russian questions and, in fact, the whole of New York City had gone to Russia. It stayed there for an entire decade and did not come back until the fall of 1939, when Stalin signed his pact with Hitler.

≺ *Three* ≻
AS THROUGH A GLASS DARKLY

I WANT to take up here two difficult and related matters, forced on the attention of some of us at the outset of the Second World War, matters which, from the spring of 1940, we found we would have to confront again and again. And since what was at issue during those years must still in some form or other remain before us, I shall try to go back and forth between the beginning of the Second World War—even to a few years before that—and the present time.

There were two problems those of us interested in politics found difficult to deal with—intellectually and morally. The first had to do with the use of force so as to prevent or to forestall the use of force against us by others; the second with the need we felt to support powers or policies we had in the past opposed, so as to act more effectively against other powers and other policies, to which, for reasons of principle, we had come to stand in even greater opposition. While separable, the two problems are of course related when understood at a certain depth, for both may require that because of the very strength of one's convictions, one break with some conviction by which one has hitherto been bound. And after such knowledge, what forgiveness?

I mean to speak to both these problems directly, but first of all I want to describe occasions when it seemed they could not be resolved. Recalling problem number one, I am brought back to a circumstance I was caught in just before the war began, and which I can understand better now than I could while it was unfolding, which is not true in all such cases. There are events one understands fully when one is *dans le coup*, and to the understanding of which reflection afterward can add very little. But the matter to which I am referring here, if it is to be understood at all by others at this point in time, requires a certain background of fact.

The year was 1938, it was March, and the third of the Moscow show trials was just about to take place. Bukharin and Rykoff were about to stand in the prisoners' dock, even as had Radek, Pyatakov, Zinoviev, Kamenev before them, also other Bolshevik leaders judged guilty in the first two trials. Moreover, the third trial was to be covered by Walter Duranty, whom the Trotskyists called the GPU (Soviet Police) journalist of the *New York Times*, and whom the Stalinists described as the one honest voice of the bourgeois press. He had reported the first two trials to be normal in appearance, orderly, and in thorough accordance with Soviet law. There was no indication from his account that the defendants, as he perceived them, had been unduly harassed—defendants, mind you, whom Khrushchev, in his 1956 speech against Stalin, claimed had been made to confess by the method of "Beat! Beat! Beat!" The confessions of the accused had made it hard to defend them, and it was also difficult to defend Leon Trotsky, charged by the Soviet court with having been their teacher and the main organizer of their "counterrevolutionary" deeds.

American intellectuals, by now suspicious of Stalinist justice, had formed a committee that sent John Dewey with several other politically nonaligned intellectuals—mainly labor journalists—to Mexico to question Trotsky, so as to make some independent assessment of his guilt or innocence. This committee, which Sidney Hook organized after the first of the Moscow trials, immediately became the object of Stalinist vituperation and attack. Members of the committee were regularly awakened in the middle of the night by telephone calls demanding they give no further assistance to an enterprise that "hurts socialism and helps fascism." Some were ordered to resign at once from the committee, and warned of further harassment if they did not. One member told me that his telephone rang every ten minutes from midnight until six in the morning for almost a week. I must say that at this sort of operation the Communists were expert. They certainly knew how to keep one awake all night.

For those who distrusted the Soviet courts, and who could not believe that Trotsky had conspired with Hitler, and who noted, too, that the judgment of the press was reflecting Stalinist opinion on the matter to an alarming degree, the time was a very difficult one. It became painful to read journals like the *New Republic* and the *Nation,* and, in view of Walter Duranty's coverage of the trials, it became almost as painful to read the then respectably bourgeois *New York Times.* And there was another difficulty for Trotsky's defenders. The English Stalinist lawyer, Pritt, pointed out that if one rejected the verdict of the Soviet court, one was not merely saying that the accused were innocent, but also that their accusers were guilty of a frame-up. And among the accusers there was Comrade Stalin. Now, to charge Stalin with frame-up at that point in time, one had to have already made a pejorative judgment of the Soviet state, something few liberals had done or were prepared to do. It seemed almost impossible to declare Stalin guilty unless one had previously decided not merely on Trotsky's innocence but also on the correctness of his political position, a position held only by the Trotskyists. Thus, it was very hard to argue with those who spoke or wrote against the accused. Finally, those of us who supported Trotsky did not know how to meet the argument that, after all, the defendants in the Moscow court had in fact confessed. And we all tried to think up brilliant explanations as to why they had confessed. But there was no explanation, however brilliant, as astonishing as the fact itself. Delmore Schwartz said to me one day, "I guess if there were no such thing as an objective world, the Stalinists would have their way. But I think there is such a world. If subjective idealism were correct, the Stalinists would be in the right, and we would be lost." But was this metaphysical reasoning all we could count on? There were other supporters of Trotsky less interested in philosophy than Delmore, and more interested in action. And it is one of these supporters—I shall refer to him as S.—who was involved in the event which I should now describe.

S. was one of those remarkable people with culture, talent, and intelligence, who have never been forced, by some special skill, by chance, or by poverty, to make the choice of a profession. And so, in a period of political radicalism such as the thirties, he became a political radical; but I shall not call him a professional revolutionary; it would be much truer to say of him that he was a revolutionary without a profession. And if he hoped his political activity would some day become professional, in actual fact it never did. Associated with the Trotskyite group and yet very supercilious toward it, as well as toward all the other radical groups, extremely competent at all sorts of clandestine—how else shall I describe them?—operations, S. was an always interesting and resourceful personality on the extreme Left, whom anyone with political problems that were difficult, dark, or deep, liked to consult. I found him socially agreeable and always liked to see him. And I particularly enjoyed his air of secrecy when on occasion he dropped in on me, for I never knew exactly why he had come.

One day he rang me up. There was something urgent, and he could not tell me about it over the telephone. I would have to meet him outdoors, not in a public place, and it would have to be after dark. And he couldn't tell me in English, we would have to communicate in some other language. What language? "Not French," he said, "too many people understand it." I replied, "In some other foreign language, I won't understand you." After a pause he yielded, and said if we could meet in a place sufficiently deserted we might talk in the language of Shakespeare. Where did he suggest? The darkest and quietest street in the village, Greene Street just off West Broadway, a street too deserted to visit safely at night in the fifties, but in 1938 it seemed a safe place to divulge a secret. "Okay then," he said, "Greene Street it is, this evening, after nine," and paused. Then he said, "there to meet with Macbeth," and hung up.

I met him at about nine on Greene Street and he told me

what was on his mind. He had been investigating a very interesting young woman, fluent in Russian, who was then being considered by the Socialist Workers' Party as a secretary for Leon Trotsky. In fact the young woman, V.,* having passed every moral and technical test, and been judged politically reliable, was just on the point of leaving for Coyoacan to take up her duties in Trotsky's household. There was one difficulty about her. She had once visited the Soviet Union and tried to smuggle a Russian typewriter into the country; she had been detected, detained by the authorities, and then expelled. But if she was politically reliable, why did this matter? "Well," said S., "that's what I brought you here to tell you. But I wish we could talk either in Chinese or Malay, because this is something that is very dangerous to talk about in English."

S. looked about him, made sure that we were quite alone, and then told me these facts: V., just on the point of leaving for Mexico, had been telephoned by a ranking member of the Communist party, who had asked to interview her. Incidentally, the young woman had been personally close to some of the more important members of the Committee for the Defense of Leon Trotsky. I suggested that the Communist party official might have called her in order to dissuade her from going to Mexico. "No," said S., "that's not it." And then he was silent. "Don't drag this out," I begged him.

Looking his most mysterious, he then told me something he expected me to know, but which I did not (I had missed the *New York Times* story): A Mr. and Mrs. Robinson—the husband, S. thought, was a Soviet agent, and, as it turned out, he was—who had gone to Russia from the West Coast in 1937, had been arrested by the Soviet authorities and were being detained. S. thought the Russians might very well try to use them as links between Trotsky and the defendants in the Third Moscow Trial. And then he said, "And if they say they know V., that would connect them with the members of the Committee for the Defense of Leon Trotsky." (The hypothesis was not absurd. "Robinson," as we know today, was Ewald, a Latvian Commu-

---

*V. was Sonia Volochova, an expert on Russian films, who died in 1980.

nist agent. He had been called back during the purge and had brought his wife, an American citizen, evidently placing his hope for safety in this American connection. When they were arrested, no less a personage than Alger Hiss, according to Allen Weinstein's *Perjury*, took it upon himself to inform the Soviet military intelligence that the United States would remain passive no matter what happened to the Robinsons.)

I said, "If they say they know V., she can deny it, she can give them the lie." "It is clear," he countered, "that you don't understand the GPU. What if V. isn't here to deny what the Robinson's say? What if V. is kidnapped? They might take her in a barrel to Moscow." I said I didn't expect this to happen. "And if it should happen," S. came back at me, "you wouldn't know what to do." I: "I guess I wouldn't know what to do." He: "Oughtn't we to think of what we can do to keep something of that sort from happening?" We had been walking up and down the dark of Greene Street; here I stopped, faced him, and I think I raised my voice. "What are you talking about?" He: "I haven't said a thing. I've been thinking." I: "I hope you're not thinking what I think you're thinking. . . ." "You're right about what you think I am thinking." I stared at him and I noticed that his face was white and drawn. I really felt quite sorry for S. at that moment, and also strangely exhilarated. I said to him, "As it happens, I have a great deal of affection for V. How do you feel about her?" He: "Oh, she's adorable, delightful. . . . If we didn't like her we'd have no right at all to think along the lines we've indicated. . . ."

I shouted at him, "*We've* indicated! I haven't indicated anything! I haven't agreed to anything!"

Anyone who has never been associated with a movement for a cause he has judged to be great will perhaps not be able to understand this; he will perhaps also not be able to understand his own potential for crime. For the prospect of committing a crime to further a cause in which you deeply believe is a very exciting one. Here is a test not only of what you believe, but also of what you are. The very fact that we knew V. and had some liking for her, which made the suggestion of a crime against her all the more odious, also made the action contemplated seem the more important. I was very shaken, too, and finally I said to S., "I think you should discuss this with someone else." "With whom?" he wanted to know. And then I saw a way out. I said to him, "don't tell me I'm the only one you've talked to about this. I'll bet you've met someone else about this right here on Greene Street." As it turned out, he had.

I must note here for any reader who in the course of this narrative may have developed some concern for V. that she was neither kidnapped nor assassinated by S., and was at the last moment not accepted as a secretary for Leon Trotsky—her lack of skill with firearms was the reason for this; a secretary for Trotsky was also supposed to be a guard. I must add, too, that one of the secretaries taken in her stead to Mexico, Sheldon Hart, was kidnapped by the Siqueiros group in their unsuccessful attack on Trotsky's villa and killed by them.

The second problem we faced in those days had to do with the necessity to support powers and policies judged dangerous or evil, in order to overcome powers or policies we judged to be still more dangerous, still more evil. The beginning of the Second World War, especially the victory of the Nazis in the Battle of France, presented this issue to us in the most drastic way. Many of my best friends simply would not face it honestly.

Those of us who had been at the extreme left of the radical movement found it particularly difficult to deal with a situation in which the only alternatives seemed victory for the Nazis and nazism, or support—and real support—for the British and American war machines. I was at the time quite unable to make this kind of choice. In the middle thirties I remember arguing with a Communist against supporting LaGuardia for mayor of New York City. Now in fact, there was no one else to vote for in that election, and it may be that LaGuardia was the best mayor New York City has ever had, or will have. Yet I argued with my Communist friend—he wasn't a friend, of course, being a Communist, except in the sense that he too wanted to argue about politics—in much these terms: I: "Do you mean to say you're going to vote for LaGuardia?" He: "I've done much worse things politically." For my part, I could hardly think of doing anything worse than voting for a man who turned out to be the best mayor New York City has ever had.

When Hitler's army broke through the French lines in April of 1940 I was living in Chicago. The defeat of the French army was just a stunning surprise. Our press had built up the impregnability of the Maginot Line and the strategic thinking of the French and British. Moreover, we thought of Germany as a country whose population was kept in line almost entirely by the police. I think it was not generally realized to what extent the mass of the German people supported Hitler. The only intimation that some outcome of the war was possible other than victory for France and England came from Leon Trotsky. In the winter of 1940 he published an article in *Liberty* magazine, in which he foresaw that in the spring of the year, the Danish, Dutch, Belgian, and even the French governments might be in London, in exile. Among the reasons he gave for the possibility of a Nazi victory was the *disciplined* population of Germany. A disciplined population! I remember how surprised I was at the phrase. Disciplined! We had thought of the German people as harried, terrified, rebellious. Trotsky's was the only voice that spoke of them as *disciplined*.

Then, in April 1940, the Germans began their assault on the Western Front. My Chicago apartment was above one occupied by a German workman—I should say a skilled worker, though I never found out or tried to find out just what trade he was in —and I met him frequently in the hall as I was going up to my flat. He spoke English with a heavy German accent and I assumed he had emigrated from Germany out of distaste for the Hitler government. How wrong I was about this I only knew after the Nazi breakthrough, for after that the sounds of *Deutschland über Alles* and of the *Horst Wessel* song broke through into my own apartment and occupied it even as the Nazis were marching on Paris. If I was depressed by the victory of Hitler, my working-class German neighbor evidently was not. The next time I met him in the hallway he said to me: "You know I killed many Frenchmen in the First World War." "A lot of Germans are going to be killed in this war," I said in reply. "And who's going to kill them?" he asked sarcastically, "the dead Polacks? Or the Frenchmen we've taken prisoner? Are those the people you're counting on?" I wanted to say—sometimes what you *want* to say seems very important—"We will, we, the Americans." But I couldn't say this, for at that time I was still committed to the Trotskyist view that under no circumstances should one support a capitalist government, even against Hitler. I was suspicious by then of the Trotskyist political line, but I was not yet ready to discard it.

On the University of Chicago campus I knew two persons who thought the Trotskyist political line on the war ridiculous and said so openly. One was Nathan Leites, who after the war assisted Harold Lasswell in Freudianizing American political theory, and the other was Edward Shils, the sociologist, then at the outset of his career. We used to walk up and down the Midway, arguing about the war, and the question I tried to answer could be formulated thus: Was there any help against Hitler except by way of Washington?

But I wanted to know more directly what people of my general persuasion were saying in New York, and I made a trip there just to find out. In those days, by the way, train travel from Chicago to New York was very pleasurable. You had drinks in the parlor car, played cards, enjoyed the time, and looked at your watch much less often than you do on an airplane run nowadays. But this particular trip I took was not for pleasure, but to find some expression of political authority, and I thought I might find it in New York. As I got into the train, I heard the Chicago newsboys shouting: "Hitler pitching! Pétain catching!"

At the outset of hostilities, Trotsky had described the conflict as a continuation or prolongation of World War I. His judgment on this matter was backed by both factions of the Trotskyist movement, which had split into Shachtmanite and Cannonite wings.* (There are still some Trotskyists and ex-Trotskyists who to this day see nothing wrong with this judgment of the war, and have criticisms mainly for those in their ranks who did not continue to hold it.) But I found when I got

---

*The Cannonites, following Trotsky, maintained that however degenerated, the Soviet Union was still a workers' state; the Shachtmanites denied this, judging the Soviet Union to be a new historical formation with a new kind of economy, which they termed "bureaucratic collectivism."

to New York City that at *Partisan Review,* Philip Rahv, who had been politically influenced by Trotsky even as I had, thought this particular judgment of the Bolshevik leader absurd. He related it to what he called the "lollipop" theory of revolution, putting his criticism thus: "The Trotskyists think that if they don't support this war, the workers, when it is over—but who knows when it will be over if the United States won't enter it, or who may be the winner of it—will realize that the Trotskyists did the right thing in opposing the war, and will give them power as a reward, like a lollipop." He also accused the Trotskyists of counting on the capitalists to deal with Hitler while they themselves preserved their revolutionary purity by writing articles attacking all capitalist governments.

After some talk with Rahv, I went directly to the offices of the Cannonite Trotskyists at Thirteenth Street and University Place. And I asked those in the office, most of whom I knew quite well, what their program was for France in view of Hitler's military success.

I must say they seemed to me a cheery lot at that moment of catastrophe. They did not even admit to seeing a real problem. "We have the same program," they said, "as we had before Hitler broke through. And you know what that program is. You know it as well as we do." I recall saying in reply, "Just state it for me, please. I don't think I know it *quite* as well as you do." "For one thing," they said, "we would like to start some mutinies in the French army." I showed my surprise. But why? Wasn't Hitler the problem? The answer came: "He is a problem the French army has been unable to deal with." "And you think," I said, "that mutinies in the French army will terrify Hitler?" "Not at first," they granted, "but if these mutinies spread, he might have to face mutiny in his own ranks." "Are you," I asked, "also in favor of mutinies in the British navy?" "Of course," they said, "we are just as much against the British Empire as we are against Hitler." And, looking at me suspiciously, someone said, "Maybe, like the liberals, you prefer England to Hitler." I replied with some vigor, "Yes, I prefer England to Hitler. Also, France, Czechoslovakia, Poland, Norway, Belgium, Holland, and the United States! I prefer all of them to

Hitler." With some alarm they said, "Read our interparty documents," and they gave me some.

The justification for using force was made (indirectly to be sure) by Charles Saunders Pierce when he pointed out that there is more than one way of fixing a belief, one way being to hold perseveringly to whatever belief one has already held. Tenacity is a means, and a means often successfully relied on, to arrive at satisfactory opinions. From which it can be seen why force often has to be employed. For if one's opponent thought he was wrong, or if he were not tenacious in thinking himself right, he might not call upon force, and one would not have to call upon force to defeat him. What Pierce's view maintains is that no one is finally wrong until he is defeated, and from this it follows that it is often only in battle that there can be adjudication of the right and of the wrong. If we did not fight against Hitler, we would be allowing him not only to assert and to strengthen his case, but to give at the very least *a kind of proof* that he was right. And that is why he had to be fought with whatever weapons there were at hand and alongside whoever was prepared to fight against him.

But to support a war such as the United States and its allies were to wage meant giving one's support to the very ideological positions most of the intellectuals I knew had always opposed: capitalism, militarism, nationalism. Could one support such positions and yet continue to make the criticisms of them one had previously made? One had to learn to think all over again, and this some of our best intellectuals refused to do.

Clement Greenberg and Dwight Macdonald even argued in *Partisan Review* that to defeat the Nazis we would have to become like them, and in many important respects. And this was the position taken by Leon Trotsky, though in fairness to him it must be said that he had only seen the beginnings of the war, whose nature he so misunderstood, and might have changed his view of it had he lived beyond August 1940, when he was assassinated. Trotsky had declared in the *Militant* that the democracies allied against Hitler would have to be supported, if in fact it was possible for them to defeat him. Trotsky did not believe that the democratic powers could defeat Hitler, and this was one of the main justifications he gave to his followers for not supporting the war effort of the United States. On this point, Trotsky, like the intellectuals he influenced, was certainly in error. Hitler was in fact defeated, and the states that won out against him are today more democratic in their structure than when they entered the war against him. One has only to think of the vast changes in the British Empire, now a commonwealth, and in the United States. In addition, there has been at least a certain trend toward democratization within the Soviet Union.

But once again, what was wrong with Trotsky's view of the war? It came down to this: There was no way to defeat the Nazis other than by armed struggle, which enabled the democracies to use the weapons of fraud and mass violence, which the Nazis hoped to monopolize, and which, without going to war, the democracies could not have called upon. War made the peoples of the democratic nations militaristic enough and efficient enough to defeat the Nazis, but yet politically distinguishable from the Nazis in their support for free institutions. Yet, to make war in 1941, if one was a Socialist, one had to learn to think darkly.

AFTER the war, too, many of these questions remained unresolved. Hitlerism had been defeated, but the Communists, with whom we had been allied, were, with the aid of the Soviet armies, coming to power in the states of Eastern Europe. We had the atomic bomb and the Soviet Union did not, and some intellectuals, like Bertrand Russell, even advocated the use of the bomb against Russia. Others advocated a declaration of war against the Soviets unless they relinquished their military hold on Eastern Europe. I was even told at the time by an Italian newspaperman, enlisted in the American army, who had been with the first American division to contact the Russian forces along the Elbe, that if the American government then had insisted on Soviet withdrawal from eastern Europe, Stalin would have yielded at once. Of course, this was just a presumption, and there is no way of testing whether or not it was true. In any case, the Communists came to power in the European countries through which the Red Army passed and where it remained. And then Americans became aware of Communist penetration of the unions, schools, the press, Hollywood, and even the armed forces.

In line with these discoveries was another we made (also in 1947) when we read Jean-Paul Sartre's essay *Portrait of the Anti-Semite.* The effect of the essay was quite sensational; I think it was more talked about than any other intellectual effort of that period. Edmund Wilson even compared Sartre, on the strength of the essay, to Voltaire, but his judgment here is wide of the mark, for in many ways the attitude of the new French writer, as will be seen, was quite the opposite of Voltaire's.* What Sartre had to say about the anti-Semite was very simply that he was a murderer and not someone with a set of opinions that could be discussed and argued about, analyzed as true or false. Now in one respect Sartre was certainly correct. Anti-Semitism, at least since the First World War, has been connected with mass murder.

But on the other hand, Sartre was not writing just about anti-Semitism in the twentieth century, but about anti-Semitism as such. And in other historical periods, men noted for their anti-Semitism could hardly be called murderers. Dostoevsky was anti-Semitic; was he a murderer? Belloc and G. K. Chesterton had been anti-Semites; could they have been called murderers? And there was another difficulty. If you call the anti-Semite a murderer, are you not asking for his execution? Or asking, at least, that he be sentenced to prison for life? And can one be punished in such drastic ways merely for expressing views? But such views, said Sartre, indicate the nature of the anti-Semite's project, which is, in fact, murder. When I was introduced to Sartre I had just read his essay, and I asked him, "Aren't you advocating the murder of anti-Semites?" He did give me an answer. All I can recall of it now is that it was very complicated

---

*But let me spell it out: Voltaire was anti-Semitic, and in favor of tolerance; Sartre was pro-Semitic, and favored intolerance towards anti-Semites. Incidentally, in defense of Sartre's thesis, I must note that murderousness was not absent from the literary anti-Semitism of the nineteenth century. In *My Heart Laid Bare* Baudelaire declared himself "For the extermination of the Jews."

and did not satisfy me. I wrote an essay against Sartre's essay for Dwight Macdonald's *Politics*. And as I recall, too, Harold Rosenberg wrote something against it in *Commentary*.

But the point that Sartre made in his essay remains with us as a problem to be considered after all the arguments and all the polemics: Suppose someone asserts that it is right to kill members of a certain group and holds tenaciously to this opinion, argues for it, tries to spread it, will not admit himself mistaken in holding it? Fundamentally, what can you do against such a person except put an end to his social existence by death or imprisonment? In other words, the tenacity of your antiliberal opponent forces a certain degree of antiliberalism on you. To act, whatever your commitment to clarity, you may have to begin to think *darkly*.

When the Communists seized the government of Czechoslovakia, murdering in the process Jan Masaryk, the son of that republic's founding father (they said he had committed suicide —but their story is not supported by any fact, and is quite unbelievable), and when with this development in eastern Europe it was revealed that Klaus Fuchs had transferred knowledge he had obtained in working on the atom bomb project to the Russians, the stage was set for the entrance onto the national political scene of Senator Joseph McCarthy of Wisconsin.

EVEN today it is difficult to write with full objectivity of Senator McCarthy. The emotions his career excited, the passions he himself deliberately inflamed in his often talented anti-Communist orations, his tactic of sullying by accusation, and when necessary (to his purpose) by slander, have made of the senator a figure toward whom one can hardly take a neutral stance. But, on the other hand, it is simply not the case, as some liberals have claimed in their recollections of the period, that there was no justification whatever for the positions Senator McCarthy took, for instance his claim that there was Communist influence in many areas of American life. If one judges—as do I—that McCarthy was a political opportunist without deep conviction of any kind, then surely he must have been presented with a historic occasion especially suited for exploiting the particular convictions he claimed to hold. He could not have been as unnecessary to the American political process as some of his opponents claim he was, or, I submit, he would not have had even the limited success he enjoyed for the period when his power was felt in the State Department, in Congress, in Hollywood, in the universities, and finally in the Army, which did not fail to retaliate, and in a way fatal to McCarthy's aims.

Something had to be done about the Communists, nationally as well as internationally. Now giving power to Senator McCarthy was not, of course, the right way of countering Communist influence. But the weak point of some liberal attacks on McCarthy was the claim that there was no problem—that he was the problem in fact, and not communism—in those areas of American life where it had become strong. The liberals were quite right if one concentrated entirely, as some did, on the havoc McCarthy was causing in the school system and among our career diplomats. And we must consider, too, that internationally the Soviet Union was far weaker in that period than it is today, also that the United States, before Vietnam and Watergate, was much stronger than it is now. So everything considered, the argument of the liberals was a strong one, and it finally prevailed with the top brass of the Republican party, which staged the Senate hearings on the McCarthy Committee, and destroyed the senator's power from then on.

But there can be no doubt, for this observer at least, that the appearance of McCarthy on the scene and the growth of his power were properly read by the Soviet leaders as warnings of what they might expect if the split between Russia and the U.S. deepened. Moreover, someone had to warn a rather complacent America of that period about the penetration of the Communists into American institutions. Unfortunately, the only one entirely willing to take on himself the task was Senator Joseph McCarthy. One can only say here, "The offense must come!" and also, "Woe to him through whom the offense cometh!"

Curiously enough, during those days the ones who defended Senator McCarthy, at least in private conversations, were often former radicals, ex-Stalinists, or Trotskyists. Some would say, "So he wants power. What's wrong with that? Doesn't Eisenhower want power?" This was from an ex-Stalinist, who had supported arguments equally as bad for the Moscow trials. But I found, to my surprise, that friends who had been or were hoping to remain Trotskyists in their general outlook found some virtue in the Senator. During the early days of the McCarthy committee hearings, they pointed to the fact that McCarthy was making a fool of Senator Stuart Symington, and that Roy Cohn had successfully replied to Welch's interrogations, which the press at that time even called "brutal." One ex-Trotskyist said to me: "The world the liberals are defending is gone forever and Senator McCarthy knows it. The liberals don't."

What disturbed many left-wingers and also liberals about Senator McCarthy's tactics was his evident disregard for accuracy to fact in making his wholesale accusations. He was quite willing to make the most drastic charges on the basis of the most ambiguous evidence. Whatever the political objectives of the senator, such tactics could hardly be endorsed morally, and they often led to the severest consequences: blighted careers and ruined lives. On the other hand, there is this incontestable fact: many of those who objected to Senator McCarthy's actions saw nothing objectionable in such tactics when pursued by the left.

For example, Jean-Paul Sartre, who pilloried the United States for yielding to McCarthyism, saw nothing objectionable in the charge made by the Communists in 1952 that the United States was guilty of using germ warfare in Korea. Admitting that the charge was unsupported by any kind of evidence, Sartre nonetheless reproached French workingmen for not having supported Communist demonstrations at which the charge was made. To be sure, there is a difference between slandering individuals and slandering a great national state, which can hardly be destroyed by false charges. All the same, the willingness to back slogans one knows to be false is hardly better, morally speaking, than the making of accusations against persons without regard for their truth.

The comparison I am making here between Senator Joseph McCarthy and Jean-Paul Sartre is justified, I think, by other (and comparable) policies they followed. The policy advocated by the senator toward Communists and those suspected of communism was not so unlike that advocated by Sartre toward the anti-Semites. Sartre had asserted in his essay that we *should not* think clearly about the anti-Semite. If we tried to understand him, we might forgive him, and we should not forgive him, for he, said Sartre, is a murderer. And the senator from Wisconsin was asking: How could we deal with such unprincipled opponents as the Communists if we ourselves insisted on being principled? Now this was very like the question raised by radicals during the war: How could we defeat Hitler without becoming like the Hitlerites?

Did we in fact become like the Hitlerites in defeating Hitler? The prediction that we would become like the Hitlerites, made at the outset of the war was, however, scarcely noted as proved or disproved once the war was over—or at least not in the years immediately following it. But by the sixties, when the moral judgments made during and directly after the war, having lost much of their urgency, lost some of their force, actions of the United States and its allies during the war became again subject to criticism. And at this time it became possible to compare, morally, the bombings of Germany, as well as the Hiroshima and Nagasaki bombings of Japan, with the mass violence of the Nazis, even with their organization of murder camps.

DURING the sixties Hannah Arendt published *Eichmann in Jerusalem*, a review of the trial of Adolf Eichmann, which gave rise to a spirited and at times furious controversy in which I myself participated. But I do not want here to go again over the arguments that were hurled between those who disagreed about the meaning and validity of Miss Arendt's discussion of Eichmann. What concerns me here is only one of her ideas, but it is the idea she herself singled out as the main contribution of her book, the idea of the "banality of evil." This idea is supposed to describe a process for which no particular social group in modern times is responsible, and by means of which actions that in past times would have been considered unusual for their malignant intent

77

are converted into the most banal happenings.

According to Miss Arendt, modern civilization has set in motion forces that regularly transform the unusually evil into the regularity of the humdrum, so that the evil as such is often not even remarked. Now according to this view of modern times, it was not at all necessary for the Nazi leaders to have been especially morbid or malignant in their political goals for them to have set up the murder camps that so scandalized the West. And if Miss Arendt did not herself point up the British bombings of Dresden and Leipzig, and the American bombings of Hiroshima and Nagasaki, as operations morally equivalent to the setting up of human crematoria, many of her supporters did.

I do not believe that it is right, or can ever be right, to regard evil as "banal," no matter what processes are at work in society, for I do not think we can properly designate anything as *evil* unless we can point to an *intent* to do evil: An earthquake that took as many lives as went up in the smoke coming from the Nazi crematoria would not make us morally indignant, or cause us to indict the earth. The Nazi violence against the races they described as inferior was preached before the war began, and carried out during it. The American bombings of Hiroshima and Nagasaki, however frightful in their effects, had, after all, the purpose of bringing the slaughter to an end. We did not desire the death of a single Japanese victim of the Hiroshima and Nagasaki bombings; the Nazis, on the other hand, clearly desired the deaths of all those dispatched in their annihilation camps, and of many more besides. So our actions and the acts of the Nazis, even when equally violent, have to be distinguished morally. I say *have* to be distinguished, but many do not feel the necessity of this, as can be seen from Marcel Ophuls's film *Memory of Justice*, which I want to discuss in some detail.

OPHULS's *Memory of Justice* occasioned much controversy when it was first shown. On April 23, 1977, I went to Philadelphia to see the film, which was being given a single showing at the Walnut Street Theatre. The film began at three o'clock and there was a dinner break at six. At seven, the showing was resumed and went on until about nine-thirty or ten, after which Marcel Ophuls and Susan Sontag appeared on the stage and answered questions from the audience.

Ophuls's film has many faults, some of which were properly pointed up by Harold Rosenberg in the *New York Review of Books* and by Dorothy Rabinowitz in *Commentary*. In fact, their criticism was for the most part repeated by Susan Sontag from the platform of the Walnut Street Theatre, and Marcel Ophuls, seated next to Miss Sontag, was not able to meet the critique as formulated by her. What Harold Rosenberg had said violently Miss Sontag repeated sweetly, and what Miss Rabinowitz had said angrily Miss Sontag stated as if motivated by the most earnest friendship, and thus Marcel Ophuls was not able to call upon the anger that had served him rather well in replying to Harold Rosenberg in the *New York Review of Books*. The main criticism of Rosenberg, Rabinowitz, and Sontag was this: The introduction of film shots of the aerial bombardments by the American air force in Vietnam, of the bombing of Dresden by the British, and of the atom bomb exploding over Hiroshima tended to give the impression that the enemies of Hitler had committed crimes like his. Ophuls, of course, denied that he had intended to give any such impression. The bombings of Dresden and of Hiroshima, he said, were war crimes rather than crimes against humanity. However, *Memory of Justice* does not make this distinction clearly, and we do have the impression at the film's end that the court at Nuremberg represented powers guilty of crimes like those the court was called upon to judge.

In fact the film is a trial of the judges and prosecutors at Nuremberg, rather than of those who were found guilty there. Thus I cannot accept Marcel Ophuls's statement—he made it from the platform in Philadelphia—that he was *for* the assizes at Nuremberg and *in favor* of the judgment rendered there. If the film is, indeed, as I claim it is, a trial of the judges and of the judgment they rendered, then how can it be a statement in favor of their judgment? We do not require of a question profoundly put that it be an answer too, but only that what it asks be asked probingly and fundamentally. Certainly one should not require of a film such as *Memory of Justice* that it make a statement in favor of the Nuremberg decisions. Any artistic treatment of the event is entitled to question that decision. The real issue, then, is whether Marcel Ophuls's film is sufficiently insightful in its questioning of the decision reached at Nuremberg.

I am not sure how responsible the filmmaker, Ophuls, is for the fact that if there is a hero in *Memory of Justice*, that hero is undoubtedly one of the accused Nazis, Air Marshal Goering. Compared with him, the American prosecutor, Robert Jackson, cuts the figure of a rather dull, self-righteous, not-too-bright American, whereas the Nazi air marshal is subtle, unexpectedly candid, Mephisthophelean, disturbing, and profound. There is another American important in this film and associated with the prosecution as an assistant, General Telford Taylor. He is certainly more sympathetic than Robert Jackson, and he does not seem unintelligent. But his way of expressing himself is even more likely to induce a distrust of Americans, and in fact of what might be called the American spirit, than the heavy-handed moralism and downright stupidity of Jackson. For in Telford Taylor one sees the inconsequentiality of intelligence, and this is what Europeans are prone to see even in intelligent Americans, whom they think of as not being concerned to follow where their intelligence would lead them if they allowed it to. In any case, General Telford Taylor strikes one as inadequate to the Nuremberg Trials and it is on him that the camera is most often fixed.

One of the very striking revelations of the film—and perhaps it is a revelation that only the film medium could make this powerfully, for on the screen we see the faces of the principals themselves—is the genuine astonishment of some of the Nazi leaders at the evidence of the concentration camp horrors they all certainly knew about, and each in his own way had a certain responsibility for. At times one could see that they were appalled at the sickening details of what was in fact their own agreed-upon program toward resisters to Hitler and most especially toward the Jews. The explanation for this peculiar fact is perhaps best made by Simone Weil, who died during the war, before the Allied victory and the setting-up of the Nuremberg Tribunal. Now Simone Weil, whom Conor Cruise O'Brien in the *New York Review of Books* has called nonpolitical, was one of the few intellectuals in the prewar period who showed some depth in assessing the stature of Hitler. In fact I would say she was one of the few intellectuals who wrote as an intellectual about Hitler, and not as a partisan. She was not interested in calling him names, but in understanding him. And one of the things she said about him was this: "He strikes directly at the imagination." There is no doubt that this is true, but she is also right in noting that adversaries of Hitler who tried to imitate him in this respect were never able to do so successfully. But let us go back now to the Nazi leadership in the courtroom at Nuremberg as they are confronted with the filming of concentration camp atrocities. As they watch these films, we see them aided only by their own devices of imagination, reflection, and justification. Hitler is dead, and he can no longer strike their imagination with the goals he had proclaimed, as he had done in life. Hitler was the reason they had not seen, and could not have seen, the concentration camp details with the horror they have for us. Hitler was not in the courtroom at Nuremberg to astonish them as he had while he lived. What did astonish them now was what they themselves, under his command, had done.

Now, in response to questions from the audience, Marcel Ophuls remarked that while Nazi officials could be charged with guilt for inhuman actions—assuming of course that such charges were proved—he could only support charges of guilt against Nazis as individuals, he was against any charge of collective responsibility for acts during the war that can be described as mass executions and mass murders. Now, can mass executions, mass murders, be properly attributed to individuals? It is hard to see how. Only a collectivity can organize collective murder.

When one considers further that one of the main charges at Nuremberg was the charge of crimes against humanity, the attribution of guilt for this to individuals becomes even more difficult and complicated. Can a single individual commit a crime against humanity? No doubt the possibility that this may happen exists. I have heard at least one person say, though I doubt that it was seriously meant, that he was ready to throw the bomb which would destroy the race. Equipped with a dooms-day instrument, a single individual, alienated from his fellows, could no doubt destroy them and himself, and certainly this would be a crime against humanity, though if successful there would be no one left to describe it in those terms. But without such a lethal instrument, how could a single—individual—act be described as a crime against humanity? The brutality of con-centration camp officials, even of the murder camp experts, was directed against those they were assigned to torture or kill. Criminals though they certainly were, their acts can hardly be called crimes against humanity.

Once again, what is a crime against humanity? At Nurem-berg it was decided that genocide, the attempted extermination of some human collectivity—the Jews and the Gypsies were marked for extermination by the Nazis—is a crime against hu-manity. Note that the number of persons killed or whose death was projected is not a factor here. What counts is the aim of utterly wiping out an entire group of humans. I suppose what we have here is a recognition of the biblical idea represented in the story of Noah, that every animal species found on the earth has to be preserved. Thus we are told that Noah took two of each species, male and female, with him into the ark. And in fact even to this day, anyone who destroys the last member of a still-existing species is subject to punishment. An American hunter who killed the last remaining buffalo would be punished as an enemy of nature, though for this crime no one yet has devised a satisfactory penalty.

No doubt the Russian Communists under Stalin killed many more persons than did the Hitlerites. Did they also com-mit crimes against humanity? But they never announced it as their intention to extirpate entire collectivities of human beings. So then an act aiming at genocide is a crime against humanity, no matter how many or how few the actual victims. Now I take it that genocide can hardly be an individual aim. It is an ideologi-cal aim, and there has to be a collective responsibility rather than individual guilt for the carrying out of such an aim. If this responsibility does not extend to the whole German nation, and I would agree with Marcel Ophuls that it does not, or extend to every single member of the Nazi party, and I would accept this judgment too, though I am less sure of it than of the qualification I have already made—yet certainly some definite responsibility falls on the entire leadership of the Nazi party, which accepted Hitler's program for extirpating whole peoples, most specifically the Gypsies and the Jews.

Here again, I find some of Simone Weil's ideas illuminating. I quote from Simone Petremont's *Simone Weil, a Life:*

A new book by Bernanos, *Les Grands Cimetières sous la lune*, had just been published. It dealt with the Spanish civil war, which was still going on. Bernanos, who had lived in Majorca, had seen what had happened on the Franco side of the war. A Catholic writer, a royalist, an admirer of the reactionary Drumont, he should have been sympathetic to the revolt of the Spanish generals against a republican government. But he had been appalled by the regime of terror that the fascists had established in Majorca, and the great number of senseless executions that had taken place on that island, where nothing could justify such severe measures. In his book he denounced this mad intoxication with death.

Simone felt impelled to write to him about the analogous experience she had had on the opposite side. In this letter she describes some of the events she had seen or heard of when she was in Spain. These events, though they never reached the utter ignominy described by Bernanos, suffice to show, she says, that a certain atmosphere reigned equally in the two camps. Bernanos thought that fear had caused all these useless cruelties.

Simone says: "Yes, it is true that fear played some part in all this butchery; but where I was, it did not appear to play the large part you assign to it. Men who seem to be brave—there was one at least whose courage I personally witnessed—would retail with cheery fraternal chuckles at convivial mealtimes how many priests they had murdered, or how many "fascists," the latter being a very elastic term. My own feeling was that when once a certain class of people has been placed by the temporal and spiritual authorities outside the ranks of those whose life has value, then nothing comes more naturally to men than to kill. As soon as men know that they can kill without fear of punishment or blame, they kill; or at least they encourage the killer with approving smiles. . . . The very purpose of the whole struggle is soon lost in an atmosphere of this sort. For the purpose can only be defined in terms of the public good, of the welfare of men— and men have become valueless. . . .

Simone Weil's observations here surely make clear just what it was that the Nazis did that could be called a crime against humanity. They had created an atmosphere in which whole collectivities became valueless and were consequently killable. But surely they accomplished this not as individuals, but as Nazis, as supporters of an ideology that justified, precisely, the exclusion of certain collectivities from valuation as human beings. Can one say the same for the anti-Fascists in the Aragon militia with which Simone Weil found herself in the Spanish civil war? Here the answer has to be qualified. Whatever the behavior of the anti-Fascist militiamen—and I would accept Simone Weil's description as accurate—they had not consciously formulated a set of ideological notions with the express aim of rendering whole groups of persons, whole collectivities even, valueless so that they could be killed. And I think not even the Stalinists did this. But the Nazis did. This was in fact their crime, and this crime is hardly even alluded to in any direct way during the five or six hours of Marcel Ophuls's film. We meet some of the master criminals and we see exhibits of their cruelty, but we are never informed in moral-political terms of what it is they did.

I have considered *Memory of Justice* in so much detail because it expressed, with the vividness and force of modern film technique, some of the ways by which the political actions of the democracies during the Second World War can be shown to jibe with, rather than differ from, those of the Axis powers. Typical of this film, as of other efforts to involve the Western democracies in the evils they claimed to be combating, is the method of admitting differences between the democracies and the Axis, and then denying such differences by emphasizing similarities.

One can barely consider going to war in modern times

without accepting the necessity to do many evil things, and after a war is concluded, it is always possible for a list to be made of all the wrongdoings of those who justified it. But these lists of errors, evils, mistakes, and vile actions that the presses continue to bring forth hardly help us to resolve the difficulty of the problem I mentioned at the start, or suggest any way of dealing with it. What general criteria are there for justifying force and especially "force to the uttermost"? for that is what one may have to exert in modern war.

Serious consideration of the circumstances under which the use of force may be justified has been the subject of much thinking, but I myself know nothing better on the subject than an essay by the German literary critic Walter Benjamin, "Toward a Critique of Violence," in which the critic shows both sophistication and depth in treating one of the great questions of our time.

In his essay, Benjamin points out that there are two ways of judging violence; it may be looked at from the standpoint of *natural law* and also from the standpoint of *positive law*. He writes:

> If natural law can only judge each existing right by the criticism of its goals, then positive law can only judge a right in the process of establishing itself by the criticism of its means. If justice is a criterion of goals aimed at, conformity to law is a criterion of means employed. Natural right tries to justify means by the justice of the goals aimed at; positive law tries to guarantee the justice of the goals aimed at by the legitimacy of the means employed.

What if there is a contradiction—there often is—between the means that natural rights regard as legitimate, in view of the goal aimed at, and the rejection of these means by positive law, insofar as they are violent? In such cases, how is the matter to be judged? Here Benjamin holds that ". . . one must find a point of view external to the philosophy of positive law, and also external to that of natural right. . . ." He suggests that only the philosophy of history can supply such a criterion.

Perhaps philosophy of history can supply a criterion, but it will not be a clear criterion. It will prove in many instances a "dark" concept, like the one I suggested Jean-Paul Sartre was relying on when he described the anti-Semite as a "murderer." I say it is a dark concept, because philosophy of history requires us to claim a knowledge of the future that in fact we do not have. We can predict, we can prophesy, we can guess what the future will bring out of the darkness. But it is from the darkness that the future comes. How little this criterion can serve becomes apparent when we consider the attitude of the Trotskyists to the Second World War, in which they refused to participate on the side of the nations united against the Axis powers. This refusal was termed, after the war was over, "mad," by one of their own leaders, Max Shachtman. But how is it that he, certainly sensible and very well informed, could support a policy on such an important matter, which after the war he himself would designate as mad? How could this have happened?

Let us look at the Trotskyist program at the outset of the war, as it related to the values of natural right and to positive law. I must say neither value was especially honored by the Trotskyists. Positive law could be denied where it went counter to the interests, as understood by the Trotskyists, of the proletariat; natural right they often regarded as a bourgeois shibboleth insofar as they had accepted Trotsky's *In Defense of Terrorism*, which justified even the shooting of hostages. The one value they called upon in denouncing the support of the Allied war effort by liberals they derived precisely from their philosophy of history, which, it can be seen now, clearly had misinformed them about what the results of the war would be.

Having rejected the more-or-less clear concepts by which violent actions may be judged, they relied entirely on a "dark" concept with the results we know. On the other hand, insane though their policy may have been, they had no alternative but to persevere in it, for the ideology they held required them to place the deliverances of the philosophy of history far above those of natural right and of positive law. They were in a position in which it was just as reasonable to follow an insane policy as it was for others outside their movement to urge them to break with it.

CAN we come to any definite conclusion after these varied recollections and observations? Is there any definite conclusion we can state about force and the use of force? I would hold to the notions Benjamin has advanced. There are occasions when in the name of natural right it will be right to use force in unexpected ways and even against existing law. On the other hand, Benjamin insisted, any such use of force in the denial of existing law can only be defended if it *aims at founding some new law.* What about such matters as the taking and killing of hostages, supported by Trotsky in his *Defense of Terrorism?* Such actions are purely nihilistic or utilitarian and cannot be defended, and the work in which Trotsky tried to defend them is the very poorest of his writings. One can only defend such actions by relying entirely on what I have called "dark" concepts, and while concepts of that sort cannot be totally excluded, it is certainly best not to rest one's whole case on them when one is about to commit a violent deed or to urge it on others, or when one refuses to participate in acts of violence that the rest of society finds necessary. Witness the fate of the Trotskyist movement after World War II. Perhaps they would not have been so trusting of the "dark" concepts embodied in their philosophy of history if they had had a little more respect for natural rights and the existing laws they so often dismissed as bourgeois illusions.

≺ Four ≻
THE SURREALISTS IN
NEW YORK

I VISITED Meyer Schapiro one summer night in 1942, and found him engaged in conversation with a slender, well set-up, quite handsome young man, with blond hair falling in pale, flat lines across a high forehead. This was Robert Motherwell, then only up to the prolegomena of what has been a brilliant career.

Motherwell, enrolled at Columbia had followed some courses by Schapiro. And he had studied the aesthetics of the American philosopher, David Prall, whom, during the evening, he frequently cited. Apparently blind to his own rather Saxon blondness, he stressed that evening the fact—to him, it seemed a fact—that Anglo-Saxon painters lack pictorial imagination. Certainly he would not speak that imprecisely today. His own writings on art are quite precise and often elegant. He was probably expressing the influence over him at the time of the surrealist painters, mainly Latins, who were then in New York, and most particularly that of Matta, with whom, as I discovered later, he was deeply involved.

I said he seemed young to me then. To be sure, he was younger than I. Delmore Schwartz, as I recall, lamented just a few years before he died: "There was a time when I used to think Dwight Macdonald was so much older than I—and I can't feel that way any more." And then Delmore was gone, while

Dwight, whom he had thought so much older than himself, was still sociably shouting down those of his dinner guests who happened to be in the right against him. (Dwight, too was gone in 1983.) Probably the reason I was so struck by Motherwell's youth that evening was a certain lack of ease he showed in conversation. It was that of a man not yet fully in touch with himself. Some years later, Motherwell noted this aspect of his personality in a piece in *Possibilities*, a review he edited with Harold Rosenberg, even characterizing himself there as at times "inauthentic." Unhappily, the review was limited to just one issue, and the reason, as Rosenberg told me with some glee, was that Motherwell had decided to undergo psychoanalysis, and his analyst had found Rosenberg bad for his ego. It struck me that someone who would drop you for the sake of his ego would have to be someone who had taken you up for his ego's sake.

Now on the night I met him, Motherwell made a request of Schapiro which in a way expressed his peculiar lack of contact with what I have come to recognize to be a very real intelligence. He wanted Schapiro to tell him of some encyclopedia about the class struggle, so that he could read up on it. Schapiro replied at once: "Fortunately there is no such thing. You can't just read up on class struggle. . . . If you're laid off a job, or have to go on strike, you may find out about it. . . . Also you have to read the radical press . . . regularly." And I think he recommended the paper *Labor Action*, put out by the Shachtmanite faction of the Trotskyists. (Recalling that paper, one realizes that there is no such thing as a radical press today.) "In any case," said Schapiro, "you can't just open a book. . . . To learn about class you have to struggle yourself." Motherwell saw at once that he had been imperceptive, and blushed.

He had come to ask Schapiro for advice about working with the surrealist painters then in New York, and he particularly wanted to find out how to deal with their leader, André Breton, with whom questions relating to the class struggle were bound to come up. I think it was Schapiro who suggested that Motherwell take me along with him on his next meeting with the surrealist leader.

After that encounter at Schapiro's I saw a lot of Mother-well. I was living on Irving Place in Greenwich Village then, he on Eighth Street, right smack across from Macdougal Street. Those were days when people would drop in on one another without first telephoning. Happy days! I think Motherwell must have liked this sort of bohemianism; he was anything but formal then, in fact there was something quite unbuttoned about him. I can hardly remember any time between the summer of '42 and the fall of '48 when he didn't have a little paint on his face or even on the tip of his nose, and his shirt always hung out over his pants—this was long before university students had made this their most typical attire. Anyway, it was with a bit of paint on his nose and his shirt hanging out that Motherwell took me to meet André Breton, the most courtly person I have ever known.

But before that I had met Matta, to whose apartment on Twelfth Street between Sixth and Fifth Avenues I was taken by Schapiro only a few days after I had seen Motherwell. As I remember, it was a warm summer afternoon and on the way to Twelfth Street from his own apartment on Fourth, Schapiro told me something about the painter I was going to meet. Matta was of Basque origin, but born in Chile, and he was a member of the surrealist group. In talking about Matta, Schapiro could not help but tell me something about himself. He had been shown two surrealist paintings, one by an American, Gordon Onslow Ford, and the other by Matta, and he had remarked, pointing to the Matta, "The painter who did this was born in the country. . . . the other in a big city." And it turned out that Schapiro had been right. "But how did you know Matta was born in the country?" I asked. "From his exuberant color," was the reply.

We went up to the apartment. As I remember, it was a three- or four-room place, quite modest, but comfortable, and not without elegance, qualities which are not often found to-gether in the apartments available in New York City today.

Matta welcomed Schapiro warmly, and I was introduced. The painter was very youthful, under thirty, and he was nerv-ously alive, with deep brown eyes and wonderfully straight black hair. (He did not at all resemble the young Rimbaud, as the late Julien Levy has claimed in *Memoir of an Art Gallery*. Rimbaud, from the photographs we have of him, was a very blond, very Nordic Frenchman, and Matta is swarthy and dark-haired, like the Latins of the wine country.) He laughed a great deal and his laughter immediately engaged you. It trilled and trilled, going up, up, upward, on soprano wings. Having heard Matta laugh, you wanted to say something to make him laugh again, but as it turned out, it was Matta who said the things which made *you* laugh, and him, too. For like most intelligent men I have known, he was accustomed to making himself laugh and he liked doing this, providing both the cause and the effect, humor and the exemplary enjoyment of it.

He introduced his wife, Ann, a young woman still in her twenties, from Lincoln, Illinois, of which I believe her father had been the mayor. Julien Levy has described her as unobtrusive. Now Ann Matta was certainly not forward, and she was not very articulate either, but she could not be called unobtrusive, for she was quite beautiful, with rather wild eyes and an expression I can only describe as one of infinite regret. But regret for what? For being married to Matta, who was so amusing, so charming?

We sat down and Matta produced a bottle of absinthe. He announced: "This is not anisette . . . this is the real thing." So we, who thought we were the real thing, had a drink of the real thing. I had no inkling at the moment that for the next few years Matta would be one of my closest friends.

WHAT I valued most in him during those years was his sense of fun. Not many painters have humor, and Matta is one of the best of those who have. In his paintings and drawings he can be as funny as Miró or Magritte. And when you got to know him, you began to depend on his humor and didn't feel quite up to par when he wasn't around. But there were also occasions when his humor represented a certain danger. An example: I had collapsed a lung and had to lie on my back for six weeks until it inflated. Matta came to see me, as did other friends, but he was the one who made me laugh, and this was what I was not supposed to do, that is, if I wanted to recover. But I didn't just want to recover. I also wanted to laugh, at things Matta said.

One day I was visited by Nicola Chiaromonte, one of the most interesting of the Italian intellectuals in exile here. He was my good friend, too, a wonderful friend. I can honestly say I've never known anyone I've liked better or respected more. While Chiaromonte was with me Matta arrived, bringing with him all sorts of good things: food, drink, and a tape recorder, so that I could do some work while I was recovering. But what meant most to me then was not his intention, however generous, but the manner in which he transformed the atmosphere of my place with a few words that set us laughing. Matta did an imitation of Harry Truman—this was the first year of Truman's Presidency—flying through a snowstorm to meet his mother in Missouri, how he embraced her when they met, just which cheek of hers was kissed, and their dialogue after kissing. Then he went on to develop one of his ideal projects. He was going to arrange a musical concert for dogs at Madison Square Garden. The musicians would play notes too high for humans, but which canine ears could catch. So the concert would be just for dogs. They would all come in limousines, dressed up for the occasion, their owners reduced to the roles of chauffeurs and attendants. And Matta performed the whole concert. He imitated the dogs barking their applause when it was over, and the dogs leaving the Garden filled with music and contentment. I laughed throughout the performance, but Chiaromonte grew more and more somber, finally looked at his watch, and left. Afterward he told me: "I felt I couldn't say anything to amuse you or interest you while he was around."

Once we were well acquainted, Ann Matta told me how she had met her husband. She had gone to Paris in 1939, an art student—I think she was on a tour which was to include Florence and Venice, and in the Parisian *pension* in which she stayed she met Matta. Her story went: Matta, on being introduced, had stared intently at her, then seized hold of her and lifted her in the air over his head. "Let me down!" she exclaimed. "What are you doing?" Matta replied, "I'm trying to sweep you off your feet." But he did set her down, and then when she told him that the next day she would be in Florence, he said "I'll see you there." When she got to the *pensione* in Florence, there was Matta waiting for her. The same thing happened in Venice. They returned to Paris together, were married there, and shortly after took off for the United States just before war was declared.

A happy, a romantic beginning. But the continuation was hardly that. Matta called Ann *pajarito*, "little bird," and she evidently did not like being called that. "He's trying to make me smaller," she said once, when someone asked her why she objected to the name. But I have heard other, more violent explanations of why that name should have been disliked, and why that name was chosen by Matta. In any case, their life when I got to know them in '42, was already one of bewilderment, frustration, and sadness for the young woman Matta had swept off her feet.

Why people who have been in love separate is to me one of the most interesting of all questions, and I know of no instance in which it can be answered fully. But my reason for dwelling on what happened to the Mattas is that what I saw happen to them, and I saw most of it, was also happening to other people I knew. I hardly think I am making of their fate an "instance of *all* fate," to quote Wallace Stevens's expression. But yet the fate of many other people was told in clearer, sharper, and more painful strokes in the life of the Mattas than in the lives of others I knew. Once again, how is one to explain this? The desire to give another pleasure ceases to be a joy and then becomes a form of pain. And pain continued under these circumstances is certain to become hate. . . .

BUT I must come back to the summer of 1942. Motherwell, as he had promised, took me to André Breton's apartment on Eleventh Street, and Breton, as he came forward to greet me, took us both with him into the eighteenth century. The movements of his hands when he talked were graceful, his voice musical, his diction perfect, and his sentences always in syntax: he never failed to take the subjunctive as required. Powerfully built, he gave the impression of a certain effeminateness; in fact he looked rather like Oscar Wilde, though he was, I think, better looking than Wilde, his features being more finely drawn. In revenge, as the French say, his hands were very large, and his fingers huge enough to seem quite monstrous. I often thought —influenced no doubt by his resemblance to Wilde—that those huge fat fingers had absorbed into their substance any feelings in him that were brutal, or in any case indelicate. Maybe these were the very fingers that had painted the portrait of Dorian Gray. . . .

In his apartment on Eleventh Street between Fourth and Bleecker Streets, the walls were covered with paintings by surrealist painters. As you walked up and down the living room conversing with Breton, those paintings looked at you from two sides of the room. Maybe some calculation had gone into this. Perhaps he thought you could not walk with impunity between the rows of surrealist paintings, as, it has been said, you cannot under the palms. Reserved, always grave even when playful, very courteous yet capable of sudden extraordinary rages, Breton was, in my very short acquaintance with him, always likable and always compelling. Alfred Rosmer, the Anarcho-syndicalist, Communist, early Trotskyist, member of the Third, and then the Fourth International, became acquainted with Breton by chance during the late forties; his closest neighbor on the Côte d'Azur happened to be Breton. Rosmer told me in Paris that he found Breton to be so good and noble a person that he often deeply regretted never having been interested in the theories of surrealism.

Was Breton really noble? In appearance, certainly. His voice had a noble music to it, and there was nobility in his manners and in his feeling for gesture. But more fundamentally? Certainly there is something noble about his prose, and I, for one, find his poems beautiful, as in his farewell to the painter Arshile Gorky, who hanged himself in his Connecticut studio:

> *How high you are*
> *In the air*
> *Less than in what you leave us*

Less than in your name
Aimed at the great storms of my heart

And he held ideas that are certainly romantic: he held for instance that true lovers could reach orgasm by simply listening to each other's heartbeat.

But there was another aspect to André Breton. When Violette Nozières, a Parisian schoolgirl, killed both her parents by putting rat poison she had obtained from the Pasteur Institute in their soup, Breton hailed her deed and placed her as a heroine above Jeanne d'Arc. And he celebrated her deed in a poem:

With all the curtains of the world
drawn over your eyes
It's no use whatever
In front of their breathless mirrors
Their stretching the cursed bow of
ancestry and posterity
You no longer resemble anyone living
or dead
Mythological to your fingertips
Your prison is the mooring buoy they
try to reach in their sleep
They all come back to it, it burns
them

"Mythological to your fingertips." Why? Because she had murdered her parents? But was Breton in favor of parent-murder? And how is one to understand this assertion in *The Second Manifesto of Surrealism:* "The simplest surrealist act consists in going, revolver in hand, into the street and firing as many shots as possible at random into the crowd"? "This sentence has, of course, been too much quoted," writes the French philosopher Ferdinand Alquié in his book *The Philosophy of Surrealism.* He grants this much, though: "The fact remains that Breton wrote it."

And I associate with Breton's definition of the "simplest surrealist act" something else which I think in an even clearer way expressed his decision to put an end to further searching for the sacred, with some assertion that it had been found. In the fifties, Alberto Giacometti told me that at one time in the thirties, known as the heroic period of surrealism, Breton had asked him to sculpt an idol which the surrealists could worship. Giacometti, an honest atheist and anarchist, though attracted to the surrealists because of their approach to art, refused.

A PROBLEM of moral ambiguity came up constantly in the surrealist movement and in all dealings with Breton, and I think it was allied to an ambiguity about spontaneous creation which the surrealists, under Breton's influence, refused to try to clarify. They claimed to write automatically, that is, suspending the intervention of reason. But were their writings automatic? When Breton showed me his "Ode to Charles Fourier" (written in his hand), there were many corrections in the text. I should say much of it was probably written automatically, but still there were corrections.

However, that is not the important point. The important ambiguity in their behavior and their thought lay in their insistence that they were not interested in art or in literature, while at the same time they were striving to succeed, even as artists and writers who were not surrealists, in literary and artistic careers. At the Eighth Street Club during the fifties, Max Ernst, speaking for the surrealist expression in painting and literature, said that surrealists were not interested in creating beautiful works or proving that they were talented in the use of pictorial or verbal forms. What were they interested in? In discovering something about the subconscious. Had not the French philosopher Jean Wahl defined poetry as "consciousness of the unconscious"? All the same, Ernst's statement implied that surrealists were not interested in being described as artists. I answered from the floor that they were. Why, I wanted to know, did surrealists exhibit their paintings, why were they interested in reviews of their work? Didn't they like praise as much as the abstract painters did? Ernst was a man of great charm, and he replied thus: Yes, they liked praise just as much, but they didn't want to earn it. But this was patently untrue, as became clear when I asked him if he would say that they hadn't earned praise, and he was unwilling to answer roundly that they hadn't.

Ambiguity in moral matters and ambiguity as to the right use of deliberation in writing and painting, these are the two aspects of what could be called the surrealist pact (with the devil?). But the moral ambiguity is the one that interests me here. I recall a meeting of the group at Breton's, in which the latter, yielding to one of his unanticipated rages, this time against Max Ernst, insisted that he leave, even opening the door so that he could do so more quickly. As Max Ernst made his way down the stairs, Breton shouted after him, "You are a monster of egotism!" Whereupon Matta went up to Breton and said, "But André, aren't we all monsters of egotism, and isn't that what you want us to be?" I do not recall that Breton answered "No." And I do not think he could have answered Matta's question unequivocally.

Breton incarnated his movement. I use this word because when, in 1950, the French surrealist youth, led by an American expatriate named Patrick Walberg, informed Breton that he was no longer a surrealist (in his absence they had voted to expel him from the group) Breton replied with this shout (and right he was this time to shout): "*I am surrealism!*" And he *was* surrealism, what was left of it, when, after the fall of France, he came to the United States. But the lively and creative period of this movement was over. The advanced positions Breton had taken—his support for the writings of Lautréaumont and the ideas of Freud —had been widely accepted. The painters and poets he had backed were all by then famous. On the other hand, some of the surrealist ideas were now discredited—and most particularly by the political successes of nazism. It was hardly revolutionary to praise sadism while Hitler's agents were practicing it; and in fact the support for Sade was dropped during the war years and only revived much after the war—this time, curiously enough, by people persuaded of Marxism, people like Peter Weiss, the German playwright, and the Parisian structuralists.

In any case, Breton, in New York City, past middle age, a cultural hero and also a hero of anticulture, a successful revolutionary, widely suspected by his followers of now wanting to profit personally from the revolutions he had promoted, wary, disabused, alert to everything, and yet with an incredible capacity to become naïve at a moment's notice—that is, if he had to —cut the figure of a leader in a time of cultural shocks: a man who had come, not unscathed but not deeply wounded, through any number of volleys of slings and arrows. In fact, as early as 1932, in *Communicating Vases,* he had announced: "Beauty will be convulsive—or it will not be."

BRETON had visited Mexico in 1939. He had been with Leon Trotsky a guest of Diego Rivera's; thus Breton had had many conversations with Trotsky. They signed a joint declaration on art and literature which appeared in *Partisan Review* in 1940. Naturally they did not agree on all matters, and sometimes their differences led to serious arguments. One bitter argument, according to Breton, was over their different evaluations of Zola and Jules Romains. Trotsky had been reading Romains's portmanteau novel, *Men of Good Will*—everybody read it during the thirties. I had friends—I won't mention names—who would not go out with girls unacquainted with *Men of Good Will* (what could one talk to them about?). And Clifton Fadiman, then the literary critic for the *New Yorker,* had made this pronouncement: "We shall be remembered as the generation that read Jules Romains." Well, today nobody reads *Men of Good Will,* though it is, in fact, a very readable book, civilized, engaging, and full of gossip, political and literary.

Now, Trotsky had put Romains above Zola as a novelist, and Breton would not accept this judgment. Not a doubt of it, Breton was right on this matter. The interesting question is why Trotsky should have been so mistaken in his judgment. For Trotsky was often an excellent literary critic. His essay on Céline, written right after the publication of *Journey to the End of the Night,* is still the best assessment of that writer. Why was he mistaken about Romains's novel? Here one can only speculate. In one of his articles on the Moscow trials, Trotsky made a brilliant comparison between the manner in which the GPU obtained confessions and the manner in which Strigelius, the poet in *Men of Good Will,* who I think represents Romains's understanding of <u>Paul Valéry</u>, went about creating a poem. Actually, I doubt very much whether Valéry wrote poems in accordance with the method of Strigelius,* but it is very likely that the GPU put together confessions in that way. Perhaps Trotsky overrated Romains's novel because it had enabled him to understand certain things that were taking place in Russia. But here, I think, he was generously confusing his own depth with Romains's sophistication. In any case, he told Breton that Romains was a greater novelist than Zola, to which Breton replied that no one had even succeeded in writing a novel since Huysmans's <u>Là bas.</u>

There was another conflict. About this Breton has written himself in his essay, "Prolegomena to a Third Manifesto of Surrealism or Else." In this account, Breton did not reveal, as he did to me, how violent his dispute with Trotsky had been. Apparently there was a dog with Trotsky at Rivera's villa in Coyoacan. Trotsky was fond of it, and as he sat conversing with Breton in the garden, the dog came up, asking to be stroked. Trotsky complied, and stroking the dog's head, he said to Breton, "This is my friend." "My friend!" Breton was shocked. As he wrote in his "Prolegomena," if one is going to call a dog a friend, then what is to prevent one from calling a lobster retrograde, a mosquito reactionary? He went on, he told me— he is less explicit in his article—to object to what he considered a sentimental rhetorical indulgence on the part of someone who had been as tough-minded as Trotsky during and after the revolution. He had said of the Kronstadt sailors, "We'll shoot them down like partridges." Did not one have a right to expect a greater rhetorical self-control from a man whose nervous hands had held the levers of history?

---

*Strigelius, starting with an image which did not quite satisfy him, would try to derive from it another more to his liking, and then, with a number of such critically purified images in mind, would construct out of them a coherent whole. Trotsky thought that the GPU had similarly obtained confessions to all sorts of things from the prisoners in their power and then used these first confessions to extort more damaging ones. From a great number of disparate statements of guilt, the GPU would then construct, by logically refining each of them, the outlines of a criminal conspiracy.

This was the substance of Breton's complaint, and it seems Trotsky for his part was shocked that anyone should be shocked at his calling his dog his friend. As I remember at the time, Harold Rosenberg, to whom I showed Breton's "Prolegomena," and to whom I told what Breton had told me, was sympathetic to Breton's position, and the two of us went through the whole affair again, I taking Trotsky's view and Harold Breton's, and though it wasn't our argument, we too became quite violent in our assertions and denunciations.

The third argument was the worst. Breton had been reading William James, and he came upon the idea that maybe, like parasites on some huge animal, we are all inside or parts of some tremendous organism which we cannot even see. Breton thought that in this notion of James's there might be the basis for a new myth. And he said as much to Trotsky, who was simply outraged at the idea. We did not need new myths, but additional clarity, Trotsky shouted at him. He had not rejected the Third International in order to announce his belonging to some gigantic animal not known even to Breton, or to James for that matter, or to any American idealist. I do not know what Breton said in reply, but in his "Prolegomena," he proposed "The Great Invisibles" as a new myth for the surrealist group.

It is interesting to note that there could be such differences between revolutionary leaders—even when they agreed politically. Paralleling the differences between Trotsky and Breton with regard to the value of reason and myth was one quite as sharp on a less elevated matter, that of intoxicants. The German scholar and literary critic, Walter Benjamin, whose radicalism has struck a chord among contemporary intellectuals, hailed the achievements of surrealism in 1929 thus: "To win the energies of intoxication for the revolution—this is the project about which surrealism circles in all its books and enterprises. *This it may call its most particular task*" [my emphasis]. Benjamin does try to qualify such acceptance of intoxicants somewhat by noting that ". . . to place the accent exclusively" on them "would be to subordinate the methodical preparation for a revolution." All the same, even as so qualified, his attitude is quite different from the one Trotsky expresses in *My Life*, in which he praises Markin, an obscure Russian sailor in the Baltic Navy, a gunner, and a Bolshevik, through whom, according to Trotsky, "the October revolution was victorious." Why was he so important? Apparently during the Petrograd insurrection there was much looting of the rich wine stores by the rabble. According to Trotsky, Markin instantly sensed the danger and went to fight it: "He guarded the wine stores: when it was impossible to guard them, he destroyed their contents. In high boots, he would wade to his knees in precious wines. Revolver in hand, Markin fought for a sober October." This man, Trotsky claims, "beat off the alcoholic attack of the counterrevolution." To make the issue still more complicated, it should be noted that for some observers of the October events, without the alcohol there might have been no insurrection, no revolution at all.

SOME weeks after our first meeting, Matta invited me to a party at which he was to exhibit a new painting of his, and publicly name it. It was to be something like a baptism but not too much like one. Among those present were the painters Chagall, Masson, Tanguy, Seligman, Motherwell, the composer John Cage, the dealer Pierre Matisse, and of course André Breton. At one point in the evening Matta produced his painting and gave it a name, which was, "The Earth Is a Man."

It might have had any number of names, and I remember asking Breton: "Is there a definite surrealist theory about how a picture should be named?" "Oh yes," he said. "We have such a theory." What was it? I can't remember the words he used exactly, but the purport was that the name given to a surrealist painting would have to be such that the picture would remain forever nameless. "Well," I asked him, "take Matta's painting, 'The Earth Is a Man.' Is it nameless, now that he's named it?" "Yes," said Breton. "It is now nameless, because the title, 'The Earth Is a Man,' is completely independent of that painting." (It most certainly was.) "You can think about it without looking at the picture at all. You could type out that title, 'The Earth Is a Man,' and hang the typed letters up by themselves on the wall and they would have some effect on you." "And I suppose," I replied, "you could hang the painting up without the title." "That's just what I meant," said Breton. "But couldn't that have been done before he invited us here to give the painting a title and called it 'The Earth Is a Man'?" "That would have been more difficult," said Breton, unsmiling—he was always grave. "Because, had he shown it to us without having named it, we would have thought it lacked a title."

As for Matta, he was quite happy with his title. In fact I've never in my life seen anyone so excited as he was that night. And he made a little speech about painting and his notions about painting. He said, "There will never be a recognizable object in a picture of mine. Never. Not one object, not the shadow of an object. No object is good enough to be in a picture of mine. No woman is beautiful enough. Let her hair be green, purple, or pink. No fruit, no bottle, no table, no tree. I will not put them on canvas. Never. I swear it."

What were Matta's paintings like during the years of the war? Schapiro used to say that what Matta painted were *éclats*—bursts—not necessarily of color, though he painted these *éclats* in color, and not in his line drawings of that period, in which there were generally organic forms, often very comical. Now Matta had said that he didn't paint anything, that he would not represent anything in his pictures. On the other hand he would not say that he was painting nothing. He did not claim, as Ad Reinhardt did years later, that he put everything into his paintings by leaving everything out. I think what Matta must have meant was that the "bursts," or explosions, which took place on his canvases, were set off in the act of painting itself, and not calculated in advance. He was an automatic painter from the outset, with all the advantages and disadvantages that implies. I'm speaking of his work, of course, before Gorky came on the Surrealist scene, for Gorky's appearance there was to change everything.

To be sure, the notion that a purely plastic "happening" not rehearsed in advance, but which occurs, so to speak, spontaneously in the act of painting—the notion, I say, that such a happening is an "act," is to me a strange one, and so far I have not been able to find much justification for it. But perhaps action was meant in the weak sense rather than the strong sense of the word. Action in the strong sense has to destroy something, and it is hard to see what a pure plastic happening could destroy, any more than one can see how a burst of sunlight through a window could move around the furniture in a room. I note that Harold Rosenberg in his little monograph on Gorky, comparing that painter to Matta, says that the medium, the combination of paint, brush, and canvas with which Gorky worked, became a "mind" creating plastic ideas. But this is hardly different from the assertion that language itself creates ideas rather than providing a vehicle for expressing them. We are still a long way from action, at least in any strong sense of the meaning of that word.

It was Rosenberg who fathered the notion of "action" painting, and I do not want to drop that idea without some further examination of it. Evidently the term meant something to many painters, and so one cannot just dismiss it, even if in Rosenberg's own writing there does not seem to be sufficient justification for its use. What meanings could it possibly have? It could have the meaning of the acting out of a fantasy or an impulse, of a convulsion or a spasm in connection with a canvas. As a matter of fact, Lee Krasner, the widow of Jackson Pollock, years ago implied this meaning to the term when she explained a mural Pollock made for Peggy Guggenheim by saying that Pollock's physical movements in making the painting were expressed in its brushstrokes, so that the painting was an action painting insofar as the physical actions involved in painting it were an actual part of its content. This notion of action painting does have meaning, though here too I think it involves the weak meaning of action rather than the strong one.

(Some may question whether the *strong* meaning of the term action necessarily has to involve some destructive content. The argument might be given that a lifeguard's rescue of one in danger of drowning is certainly an action, and in the strong sense of that word. Is it, though, really, if the lifeguard happens to be powerful and a skilled swimmer? Compare the quality of this action by a lifeguard with the heroic deed of Joe Delaney, the star halfback of the Kansas City Chiefs, who, scarcely able

103

to swim himself, tried to save three drowning boys, and saved two of them at the cost of his own life. Here, to be sure, is action in the strongest sense of the term.)

Is drip-painting action painting? But the method of dripping paint on canvas was invented by the surrealists, who were interested not in action, but in dreaming, so once again, I do not think the term *action* proper for describing the method Pollock took over from the surrealists, and which he used more powerfully than they.

I think there is something else which connects the abstract expressionist school in New York with the surrealist painters. Recently I came across an essay by the French literary critic Jean Paulhan (he has also written on painting) in which there is a sharp insight into the workings of the modern artistic consciousness. Paulhan referred to some lines of Homer in the fourth book of the *Iliad* in which the body of Menelaus, who has been wounded, is compared to ivory being dyed purple. Of this comparison the French critic remarked that it would be wrong to think Homer had any difficulty in hitting on the image of ivory being dyed purple; very probably he had had this image in his mind all the time. His real difficulty may have been to keep fixed before his mind the bleeding body of Menelaus. Was this true of Homer? It does seem true, if one looks at his lines in the fourth book of the *Iliad,* but what is of interest here is the pertinence of Paulhan's notion to the thinking of modern poets and painters, for it may be fairly said that a general tendency in modern painting and in modern poetry has been to restrict the work of imagination to presenting images like ivory being dyed purple, while making no move whatever to locate mentally anything like the reality Homer associated with his image: the wounded body of a Greek warrior.

But what made abstract expressionist paintings something new and different in modern art was the fact that Pollock, Gorky, de Kooning, Kline, Rothko, and Vicente (I have in mind his fiery collages of the fifties) did try to connect their abstract forms with realities not at all abstract, and quite comparable to the wounded body of a warrior. What were these realities? In any case they were not unlike the content looked for by the surrealist painters in the recesses of the unconscious: psychic wounds, stark urgencies, inner disturbances. The painters did not describe these, nor can I, but one may feel the impact of such realities in their paintings.

In any case all of this is certainly not best summed up in the term "action painting." And if "action" in the strong sense really has, as I have argued, a content of destruction, then, I think, we should call Picasso and Duchamp action painters, for their works have been most destructive of the symbols once found sacred to religion, to literature, and to art.

In the fall of 1942 Breton asked me to help edit the new surrealist review he was preparing, *VVV*, and we got out one issue together (Breton's "Prolegomena" appeared in this issue). But our relationship only lasted for about the length of time, a few months as it happened, needed to get that issue out. People used to say to anyone who said he knew Breton, "Do you know him well enough to have had a fight with him?" I can say I knew him that well.

Two things I learned from Breton. After I had introduced Harold Rosenberg to him—Rosenberg contributed to the first number of *VVV*—Breton said to me: "I know you think Rosenberg is very intelligent. But tell me this. Do you think he's an artist? This is *very* important." I said I thought Rosenberg was an artist, but what really struck me was my own surprise that it should be important to be able to answer this question about someone affirmatively. But if it wasn't important to be an artist, then why were we getting out a magazine devoted to art? I think my difficulty was that I thought of art as something produced by someone we then called an artist because of what he had produced. I did not think of the artist as being himself an expression of his productive life. In other words, I wasn't used to thinking of the artist subjectively. Curiously enough, I had thought of him too behaviorally, as if he were merely the foreman of his factory rather than its main and most significant product. I had thought of art in terms of making, and not in the terms Valéry expressed in his formula: *"Faire, et en faisant, se faire*" ("Make, and in making, make oneself").

Then there was something else I got from Breton. At *VVV* we had received a manuscript from the French critic and scholar René Étiemble—it was an attack on Jacques Maritain. I did not care for the article and I wanted to reject it. I had met Étiemble in 1940 in Chicago and Breton knew that I was acquainted with him. When I said I wanted to reject his article Breton asked me, "What about the man? What about Étiemble? Do you reject him?" "No," I said, "I only want to reject his article." "Well," said Breton, "if you don't reject the man, then I think you'll take the article, especially in view of the much finer articles which you know that he can write." I do think that Breton was quite right about this, and that a magazine should be edited in that spirit.

And now I think it is only right to warn my readers that certain unpleasant things will necessarily be told. They deal with the increasingly cynical view of sentimental and sexual relations which developed in a very few years' time among the surrealists generally, and then took on an explosive violence in the life of Matta. First of all, Matta broke off with Ann, and under these circumstances: still a young woman, Ann told him she wanted to have a child. He agreed, but on the condition that she agree to a divorce. He suggested this as a quid pro quo. He would produce a child with her, if she would obtain a divorce from him. And this is how it happened. They remained together until she became pregnant, and after she gave birth they were divorced. Only nothing of this kind takes place exactly as planned. She did not give birth to just one child, but to two, twins, identical twins, and after one year, Matta left her. Shortly after that he remarried. His new wife was Patricia Connolly, a wealthy New York girl whom he had met at Gloucester.

But I referred to cynicism in the whole surrealist group, and there are no doubt some who will deny that the surrealists stood for cynicism in sentimental relations. Now there was one who certainly did. This was Marcel Duchamp, the artist of whom Gorky said that he had the most sarcastic profile of any person he had ever known. Duchamp's was the willed headstrong cynicism of a man who at some point in his life must have been unbelievably romantic, and he expressed his cynicism with an irresistible verve. He used to argue with me—and this is twenty-five years before structuralism—that there were no values, only differences. Instead of insisting on the original design of every snowflake, he made the point that every light bulb was different from every other, thus ready-mades were unique. And he delighted in reducing the human body (in painting) to its mechanical conduits for foods and fluids. Who else but he would have thought of entering a urinal into an exhibition of sculpture? "The Bride Stripped by Ferocious Bachelors"—that was his image of sexual relations, and he had great prestige and influence among the surrealists, especially with Matta.

Of Breton, for example, it is said by Mary Ann Caws in her book on him that he expressed reverence for women. This, no doubt, because of the love lyricism in works of his like *Nadja* and *L'Amour fou*. In addition to which, there were those signs of nobility in him which I have already indicated. But I am not sure that it extended to those moral matters in which sex is involved. He once boasted that no woman had ever seen him nude when not "pricked out" for women's pleasure, if I may here use Shakespeare's expression. How different is this though from the attitude expressed in Paul Éluard's beautiful but hardly noble line of verse: "Only your kisses are to be kissed." What about the rest of the woman? Is that to be thrown away, obliterated, forgotten? When one looks closely at Breton's love lyricism, one finds what is certainly a noble tonality, but I think it is a dream of the woman that makes the writer sound this note, and not any real woman with her actual problems. Walter Benjamin has seen this too. In his essay on surrealism he writes: "The lady, in esoteric love, matters least. So, too, for Breton. He is closer to the things that Nadja is close to than he is to her."

Breton insisted on the importance of games. He had said that whenever humanity suffers a catastrophe—and he was in New York City during the time we were undergoing the catastrophe of World War II—games are going to be invented, and in any case ought to be played. He particularly liked "Truth or Consequences" and he liked to set consequences, as for example: you have to be my slave for this evening, or you must never read

anything you wrote for the next year. But I must say that whenever Breton was present and "Truth or Consequences" was
played, the game did not get out of hand or become uncivilized.
I had played the game with others of his group when he was not
present, and then it almost always did get out of hand. I remember being given this consequence for refusing to answer some
question truthfully: "Your penalty is this: you must kiss my
wife, and right on the mouth." This sort of thing was typical.

HAVING remarried, Matta took a house on the Palisades and used
to drive there for weekends, for he maintained his apartment in
New York. It was in the New York apartment and in his home
on the Palisades that we together planned and brought out a
little review, *Instead*. When people asked what the title represented we replied that it meant "instead of all the other reviews." Matta made up the format of the magazine and selected
the drawings to be represented and I edited the literary material. With each issue we published—*Instead* did not come out at
regular intervals—we threw a party, and at these parties made
the magazine up. And so it must be realized that it was not made
up by people who were entirely sober.

Matta designed the review in such a way that it was hard
to find the continuity of most of the articles. You had to wind
your way from page to page hoping to take up again something
you had begun to read. He said he wanted the review to be a sort
of labyrinth. At the time readers did not appreciate this, but
Matta held that if they didn't know how to make their way from
page to page they were not intelligent enough to be readers of
Instead. I think we lost a lot of readers because of this. But since
the sixties when taste changed and when absurdism became a
kind of faith (I think absurd), people who saw the old issues of
Instead developed a kind of taste for it. Today a review made up
like that would probably find a public.

To get back to the unpleasantness which I announced, at
that time many people broke off with each other. Patricia Connolly, so recently married to Matta, expressed her shock that
Pierre Matisse was going to leave his wife, Teeny, to whom he
had been married for over twenty years. I had no idea when she

confided this to me that she was at that moment planning to divorce Matta and marry Pierre Matisse herself, and that the whole thing had been arranged between the two of them. For his part Matta, who was quite sensitive to the breakups that were taking place or threatening around us, began to say that this was a time of hemorrhages, and in accordance with the language game favored by the surrealists, he broke up the word "hemorrhage" and spoke instead of the "Age of Hemorrh"—in fact he made a painting, a bleeding, threatening, engulfing painting which he called by that name. I think it was one of his best. I remember when he showed it to me. "You know I never talk about my work but this is something special." I think it was.

In back of Matta's place on the Palisades there was a kind of dollhouse which he used as a playroom for his two sons, and as a bedroom too when they stayed over on weekends. I mention the dollhouse because it came up one day when we were talking with Marcel Duchamp about a party for the next issue of *Instead*.

Duchamp made this suggestion: why didn't we have a masked man in the little house, and why didn't we announce to each woman who came to the party, even as she entered, that just as there were foods to be eaten and liquors to be drunk, so there was a man in a mask in the children's house to serve any purpose a woman might have? Matta was delighted with the idea and at once agreed. The only problem was where to get a man whom we could count upon to make good what we were ready to promise. Then Duchamp maliciously asked Matta, "What will you do if Patricia goes into the children's house?" I think he must have known then about her and Pierre Matisse. Matta replied, "I don't want her to." "Why not?" asked Duchamp. "Because," Matta said, "I love her and she loves me." "I think you're stupid," said Duchamp. "All you had to say was that you love her." Even to have said only that would have been to have said something false.

In all the struggles among married couples that were taking place perhaps the most unpleasant to think of then as now was the struggle between the painter Arshile Gorky and his wife, Agnes Magruder, who was called Mougouche. Here Matta was deeply involved.

Gorky had been known as a painter in New York for many

years; many were aware of his outstanding qualities but I think his present fame was due to his discovery by André Breton who first knew how to appreciate him, and singled him out from all the painters in New York as the one to be most admired. Also he owed something to Matta; there is no question about this. Meyer Schapiro in his introduction to Ethel Schwabacher's *Arshile Gorky* has sensitively stated what this debt was. Gorky, previous to meeting Matta, had imitated Picasso and Miró (he did not, however, have Miró's sense of humor). I remember going to a show at the Whitney at which one of Gorky's paintings covered an entire wall and talking to him about it afterward. It was an analytical piece of cubism which Picasso might have painted himself, and it was as well painted as any Picasso. When Gorky asked me what I thought of it, I indicated that I thought it was a wonderful painting, but that it was not *his* painting. Gorky replied, "You mean it's a Picasso." "Yes," I said, "though painted by you." "Well," he said, "I think Picasso is right, so why should I paint differently?" But if he had not begun to paint differently his would not be a famous name in painting today.

However, he did begin to paint differently, and he did this after he had met Matta. As Schapiro has indicated, when Gorky imitated Picasso or Miró he was like a son imitating a father, but when he imitated Matta he was like a brother imitating a brother. Matta could paint a Matta and Gorky could not quite paint a Gorky, but Gorky could paint a more beautiful Matta than Matta himself was able to produce—though I must say there is a certain energy in Matta, so that even his poorer paintings are not quite dead and there is a certain lack of tension in even the most beautiful paintings of Gorky. In any case, at the time I'm speaking of, Gorky had met Matta, tried to assimilate his "bursts" into a style of his own, and was making some of the wonderful paintings that thrilled André Breton, and at that point he developed cancer.

I went to see him at about that time. It was just after the war and I was on the point of getting out a French issue of Dwight Macdonald's magazine, *Politics*. I asked Gorky to contribute a drawing to it, which he did, a beautiful color drawing in a new technique he had invented but which could not be used for the review; it would have been spoiled in black and white. I went to see Gorky to return the drawing to him but he would not take it back and urged me to keep it and then he told me that he had cancer and something, just something, of his other difficulties as a result of having cancer. And then he said, but without any sentimentality or self-pity that I could notice, "Well, maybe I'm like Job."

THOUGH Gorky was to die a suicide less than a year after that conversation I had with him, he was always the painter, the almost perfect painter, in the formalist sense, and never the poet of that distress in which he and we all lived. There is a vast difference between the formalist conceptions which determined Gorky's art at its most abstract and the assertion of Matta, "There will never be a woman on my canvas, not even one with green hair." I think Matta, if the lesser artist as a painter, was on the other hand a poet of our distress, as a surrealist indeed he had to be.

I should like to quote here from an interesting statement in Heidegger's essay, "Why Poets," which I did not read until some years after the events I am describing, but which does apply to them. It is from Heidegger I took the term "time of distress." But here are the philosopher's own words:

> Long is the time of distress of this world's night. . . . In the middle of this night, the time's distress is greatest. It is then that the indigent epoch no longer even feels its indigence. . . . To be a poet in the time of distress . . . is to try to seek the traces of the gods who have fled. . . . Not only is the sacred, insofar as it is a trace of divinity, lost, but even the traces of that lost trace are almost obliterated. . . .

Heidegger also makes the point that it is useless in such a time, and I think he implies even wrong, to use violence so as to make the sacred appear. The spirit must blow where it lists. Now if the surrealist movement in its criticism of "the paucity of reality" in modern life, and in its criticism, too, of conventional morality and conventional art, stimulated those artists attracted to it to be poets of the time of distress, members of the group, and André Breton particularly, often did try to start up the sacred by some act of force.

But I think the great thing about the surrealists is that they were attuned to the distress of their time—a distress which continues into ours, and to which the American abstract artists, including Gorky, were not attuned. There is one single exception—Jackson Pollock. But this is a complicated matter, too complicated a matter for me to treat here with the fullness it deserves.

Does the representation of real distress, such as ours, involve a compact with the devil?—who perhaps asks nothing more of us than to claim to have seen God when we have not. How many have refused to make such a compact? "And I have seen what men believe they see," exulted Arthur Rimbaud in his poem "The Drunken Boat." But later, in "A Season in Hell," he conceded, "I had declared sacred the disorder of my brain."

So much for the spiritual differences between Matta and Gorky. Complicating all this was the fact that Mrs. Gorky, a bold, handsome, and engaging woman, was attracted to Matta and he to her. And then Gorky went driving with his dealer Julien Levy and other friends; there was an accident, in which no one was hurt but Gorky, but he seriously. His spinal cord was affected and his right arm partially paralyzed. He was told by the doctors who attended him that he would recover the use of his arm in time, but he did have reasons to fear that he might not, and in this state, afflicted with cancer as he was, the right arm which produced all he could be proud of useless, he was visited in the hospital by Matta and Mougouche.

It was late summer in 1948; I was living in Sag Harbor, Long Island. Someone called me and told me that Gorky had left the hospital he had been brought to after the accident, gone to his place in Connecticut, and hanged himself in his studio.

Beyond these facts all that I know was told me by Matta.

He came from New York to see me a few days later and told me he was on his way to Maine where he was going to join Gorky's wife. He had seen Gorky, though, just before the latter's suicide. Here is how it happened.

Gorky had called him from the hospital and asked him to meet him in Central Park. (This was 1948 and Central Park on a Sunday in those years was a very different place.) According to Matta, he had tried to dissuade Gorky from leaving his hospital bed, but could not, and so he consented to the meeting. They met in a deserted spot agreed upon over the phone. Gorky, who was quite tall, well over six feet, carried a heavy cane in his left hand and had a leather collar around his neck (which had been near-broken in the automobile accident). He said to Matta, raising the cane in his left hand, "I'm going to give you a good beating. You are very charming, but you have interfered with my family life." He raised the cane in his left hand, and holding it upright, added this: "Besides, whatever your talents, you don't understand work. Like the Soviet Union. You don't understand it." (Gorky was, during the war, pro-Russian. Once he said to me, "The Russian peasants are beating the German mechanics." And when I remarked, "Why should Stalin say anything about art when he's not interested in it?," Gorky replied, "If he were, he wouldn't be in the Kremlin, he'd be on Fifty-seventh Street." But Gorky never joined the Communist party, and I believe Matta after the war did, and that he supports the Communist position today.)

But on that Sunday in Central Park, there was Gorky threatening to chastise Matta for not understanding the Soviet Union and work. He raised the stick, and Matta ran. And Gorky ran after him. And Matta said he was afraid of only one thing, that Gorky would fall and that his head would come off. So Matta ran out of the park, and at some point Gorky stopped chasing him, got in a cab, and went to his Connecticut farm. There he hanged himself.

Anyway, Matta told me, the surrealists had always exalted suicide, they had made heroes of the writers Jacques Vaché and René Crevel, who were suicides. They could now make a hero of Gorky, a moral hero, but in fact they were making a villain of him. Matta. He did not try to conceal his excitement and I must submit here that it did not seem to be hysterical; he admitted no guilt toward Gorky. His love for Mougouche, he said, was beyond what he had felt for any other woman, and he seemed to claim that she, in her turn, felt that way about him. The dead Gorky was a sacrifice which had made possible their present ecstasy. He was aware of what was being said of him. Breton had even called him a murderer, and hung up on him; many other former friends had cut him on the street. The American artists whom he had influenced now had a pretext for ignoring or attacking him. Pierre Matisse had made public his intention to marry Matta's wife, Patricia, who now asked Matta for a divorce. Moreover, Matisse dropped him from the painters regularly exhibited in his gallery.

So his misfortunes were mounting, but he told me with an exuberance I could not but think was genuine that all these things mattered nothing to him compared to his feelings for Mougouche. Had he felt that way before Gorky's suicide? As a matter of fact, he had not, he said. I did not spare him, but asked: did there have to be a corpse? He did not answer this directly; his reply was that the surrealist movement had taught sadism and even insisted on it. The question was not whether a person happened to be sadistic, but whether he had gone into sadism deeply or superficially, as if it were some discipline, like folklore, or architecture, or ancient languages. He said, didn't Breton tell us the Marquis de Sade was a greater man than Christ, and that he, Breton, who hated any reference to God, was still willing to follow Swinburne's example and call the Marquis "divine"? And he brought up the matter of the simplest surrealist act, the emptying of a revolver into as many passersby as possible. "Could anyone who subscribed to that idea," he asked, "attack me?" Now the surrealists subscribed to that idea and also attacked him. I must note, too, that in 1950 I read in *Combat* an apology by the surrealist poet, René Char, *for not having carried out the simplest surrealist act*; he had not fired at a single passerby, let alone as many as possible, and the implication was that he should have done this.

Despite his exuberance, I had to have some doubts about

what was in store for Matta, and in fact, a few weeks later, he and Mougouche had broken off. Their love was as dead as the husband who had been humiliated, and when I next saw him (a few months later, in Paris) he was close to a nervous breakdown. Evidently there was a difference between the support for sadism as an ideology, and a dependence on sadism in fact. Certainly he had found out something about himself he had never taken cognizance of before his great moment of exhilaration.

I must note here that in his little book on Gorky, Harold Rosenberg took what seems to me a very slanted view of the tie between the artist he favored and Matta. Rosenberg's judgment here, based, as he admitted in his text, on gossip, is arbitrary, unconvincing, and I will go as far as to say willful. Matta no more wanted to destroy Gorky than to be destroyed by him.

I THINK that the year 1948 may have marked the end of surrealism as a movement.

⊰ *Five* ⊱
SARTRE REMEMBERED

IN the fall of 1948 Jean-Paul Sartre, lecturing at Carnegie Hall, made his second appearance before a general public in New York City. (On his first visit here, in 1944, he had spoken publicly, but he was not then widely known.) Prominent among his auditors in 1948, was Marcel Duchamp, who had told me he would not attend the lecture and urged me not to go either. In his most winning way of appearing—I think he really was—cynical, Marcel had this to say of Sartre: "One of those chaps the *école normale* turns out from time to time, who can write fifty pages for you on no-matter-what over the weekend." Then he amended the remark, "I mean *good* pages." But the effect was not a bit the less perjorative. All the same, when Sartre gave his talk at Carnegie, there was Marcel in a box seat. Taking his cue from Valéry's Monsieur Teste, he observed the audience more closely than the speaker on the stage, and then, with a gesture enveloping the others with him in one box, and the crowd below, too, exclaimed (in the tone of a tourist guide): "We are now before Sartre Cathedral!"

Chartres still stands, Sartre Cathedral is no more. But was the word *cathedral* ever appropriate to the expectations built by those who already knew something of Sartre in 1948? In point of fact, he had made no direct appeal to the religious feelings of those his works addressed; the interests to which he had spoken had been exclusively moral and intellectual, and he held this stand until late in his career when, in the middle fifties, he began to indicate that he had become somewhat less concerned about what was moral and what was not. (His moral indictment of the United States in the sixties for "genocide" in Vietnam was directed, he himself said, exclusively towards those of the petty bourgeoisie who were susceptible to "moral" forms of propaganda.) By then he had espoused Marxism and even denied many of the existentialist views he had himself advanced. He may in the end have wanted us to regard the ideas he expressed more than thirty years ago as among the follies of that time. Should we?

Sartre, of course, has a great many readers today. There are those who waited over these years for his latest pronouncements on philosophy, psychology, politics, and literature; on the other hand, nobody expects anything of promise or importance to result in philosophy from the ideas he set forth, and he himself claimed to have completely expressed his thought. But let me here give some indication of what was once expected of him. Claude-Edmonde Magny, writing on Sartre's *Being and Nothingness* in the late forties, judged that work to be the herald of many new developments in French philosophy, for no work of like scope had appeared since Bergson. Have her expectations been fulfilled? I think not. Sartre's phenomenological ontology, like the philosophical writings of his colleague and friend, Maurice Merleau-Ponty, have led to few significant discoveries in French thought, which is perhaps even more barren today than it was in the late twenties, when still dominated by the ideas of Bergson and Braunschwig. French philosophy has little to show today which can compare with the work now being done by our own American logicians and epistemologists, with the British followers of Wittgenstein and Austin, or with German social theorists like Habermas, who continues the work of the Frankfurt school. French structuralism is, of course, an important intellectual tendency, but it is not part of, nor does it have significant implications for, any of the traditional disciplines of philosophy. And it was inspired basically, not by Sartre's writings, but by those of his rival social theorist, the anthropologist Claude Levi-Strauss.

What about the moral expectations of those who listened

with admiration to Sartre in 1948 and found in his writing a stimulus to renew their own moral or political interests? Who were the supporters or followers of his existentialist ideas during the late forties and early fifties? I think they were in the main intellectuals who had been convinced, or at least partially convinced, by Marxist views, and then been disillusioned in these by the manner in which the Second World War had terminated. Many remembered Trotsky's pronouncement that if the war which began in 1939 did not end with the revolutionary overthrow of the capitalist system, then the Marxist outlook would be exposed as the very opposite of what it had taken itself to be. Its socialism would have to be called utopian, and *not* scientific at all. Other programs would be advanced and other ideals set up. And in the advancement of these other programs the individual would count for more than he had in the Marxist schema.

I HAD met Sartre before I heard his lecture at Carnegie Hall. *Partisan Review* had arranged a luncheon for him at a French restaurant on West Fifty-sixth Street, and I was invited to it along with Hannah Arendt. William Phillips and Philip Rahv came to welcome the visitor to New York, and to ask him to write for their review, but since neither of them spoke French they could only communicate with Sartre through Hannah or through me. But any difficulty in communication was due entirely to the language barrier, for we all saw at once that there was nothing whatever uncommunicative about Sartre. You wondered, once you heard him speak, whether there could be any kind of situation in which he might be at a loss for words.

The man I saw at that luncheon was short, stocky, thickwristed and broad-chested. The thrust of his shoulders gave one a sense of physical power; his speech was sharp, crisp, virile, while his complexion was an unhealthy gray; even his sandycolored, straight-falling hair seemed gray. In fact, his face was all grayness and animation, and you could not look him straight in the eyes, for each eye turned in a slightly different direction past a small, finely wrought nose in the center of a round face which, because of the nose's position on it, seemed all the rounder. Not at all handsome, he had what I judged to be one of the most interesting of modern faces (as one can see from the excellent photo of him in *Obliques*). I have often thought, after that first contact with Sartre, about the very special kind of virility evident in his style of speaking and in his attitude generally. One conclusion I have come to is purely speculative, but I shall set it down for whatever it may be worth. Sartre was haunted, I suggest, like most philosophers since Plato, by the idea of eternity. (I could document this judgment with quotes from *Being and Nothingness*.) Now what connection would there be between the idea of eternity and the attitude I have described as virile? I am reminded here of a gym instructor who used to say whenever some student hurt himself on the bars: "The pain won't last forever." His was a virile attitude towards pain, and I think Sartre took a like attitude towards most problems. But perhaps I would not have thought of him in just this way on the basis of his writings alone. His style of speaking, his physical forcefulness, even the set of his shoulders, conveyed the attitude.

As I remember, the editors of *Partisan Review* asked Sartre a great many questions and he answered all of them; his answers were never lacking in definiteness or detail. Philip Rahv wanted to know what he thought about Camus, who was already well known in the United States for his novel *The Stranger*. Sartre replied at once that Camus was a friend, a fine writer, a good stylist, and not a genius. This judgment, that Camus was no genius, simply delighted Rahv, and also Hannah Arendt, who, earlier in the conversation, had volunteered the view that in Camus' novel *The Stranger*, which we all admired, there was "a crack." But the reason Sartre had chosen to criticize Camus with such finality was in order to prepare us for his judgment of Jean Genet, the writer he said was the one real literary genius in contemporary French literature. And then he took my breath away, saying, "Genet has the style of Descartes."

What were our expectations of Sartre after that luncheon? I think Philip Rahv and William Phillips expected him to support in France the very positions, literary and political, which they themselves had advanced and defended in *Partisan Review*. But from what they said to him at lunch, I guessed then that they expected Sartre to attack Stalinist influence in Europe's intellectual circles. Hannah Arendt's expectations, as she expressed them to me, were quite similar. She expected him to do battle with the totalitarianism she herself was then engaged in defining and describing in her major work, *The Burden of Our Time*, which she was to publish a few years later. For my part, I don't know what I expected of him, except to be different from the French intellectuals and writers who had excited my interest before the War. And clearly Sartre was different from other French writers I had read or met. In 1948, I already knew something about his plays, and of his interest in the theatre, and I suppose I expected him to use the stage as a "factory of ideas," even as had Bernard Shaw. As it turned out, Sartre addressed none of these tasks, which, it must be granted, he may not have set himself. Back in Paris, he proceeded to attack, not totalitarian Russia, but the United States. He attacked the French workers, even, for not supporting the communist-led demonstrations against General Ridgeway's military operations in Korea. In 1954, when the Rosenbergs were executed, he called the American government which had executed them "Fascist." And then he abandoned the theatre and the novel almost entirely, to pursue the intellectual journalism which made his magazine, *Les Temps modernes*, the outstanding review in Europe.

I must note here that Sartre *did* satisfy the most contradictory expectations. For instance: During the thirties, in this country at any rate, but I think it was also true in England and in Germany (until Hitler came to power), there were serious prolonged intellectual efforts to bring Marxist ideas in line with an informed and nondogmatic discussion of literary works. The models for such efforts were the essays on literary topics by Lunacharsky, by Trotsky, and most especially by Georg Lukàcs. But I think nothing done in this way in the United States was equal to the analysis Sartre made in his brochure *What Is Literature?*, so that I remember thinking, as I read it, of how delighted Trotsky would have been to read literary judgments so subtly made which yet took into account the class influences on the writers treated. So if there were those, and there must have been such, who expected of Sartre a more subtle and more refined kind of literary analysis, this expectation he did fulfill, and I must add here that in the essay he gave us on Tintoretto, he made a similar kind of contribution to art history, once again taking his cue from Marxist notions.

But on the other hand, one of Sartre's important contributions to the political discussions of that period was to lay the theoretical groundwork for the assertion that it was possible to be a Communist *without being a Marxist*. This view was surely different from, if not exactly contrary to, the one advanced by Sidney Hook in this country during the early thirties, that one could be a Marxist without being a Communist. Hook was asserting that it was possible to think along Marxist lines without joining any particular group, or assuming responsibility for any group's actions. Sartre was asserting that revolutionary political action could be justified in other ways than those laid down in Marxist theory, and in taking this stand he can be said to have prophesied as early as 1949 the adventurous revolutionary perspectives and tactics of Castro, Guevara, Debray, and others. And he can be said to have achieved these contradictory results: to have upheld the Marxist view in literary criticism, where the relevance of such views is still questionable, and to have vindicated the abandonment of Marxist theory in revolutionary political action, the domain where it would seem to be pertinent. Sartre achieved all this, not in successive periods of his career, but from 1949 through the early fifties in the essays on literature and politics he published in *Les Temps modernes*.

But it was already clear in 1949, when Sartre began the publication of his essay "What Is Literature?" in *Les Temps modernes*, that the program he held out for other writers was in no sense a new one. He had already made a contribution to the criticism of literary works, but the only program he had to suggest for writers in *What Is Literature?* was the use of their literary skills to win a mass audience for radical ideas. In the theatre this meant the kind of left-wing Broadway attitude toward writing represented in the United States during the thirties by Harold Clurman and by Clifford Odets. And in the novel it meant the abandonment of the kind of writing which had won Sartre admirers for his novel *Nausea;* also it meant support for the kind of intellectualized soap opera he himself had given us in *The Age of Reason,* which so disappointed many of his readers that he did not even complete the novel. Here, I should say, Sartre made one of the worst mistakes of his career,* for which Adorno, comparing Sartre's plays unfavorably to those of Beckett, has already called him to account. A literature of commitment could not be promoted in the name of literature, it could only be justified politically; but Sartre's own political judgments were neither clear nor sure, as was to be revealed during the next two decades. Every man has a right to be mistaken in his political judgment, but then not every man can be the leader of other men, and Sartre made too many mistakes in politics to be a guide for others in determining a relation of literature to politics. All the same I think Sartre did manage in this period to write one fine political play, <u>Dirty Hands</u>. However, he himself did not take the play too seriously and, when in '49 I made some criticism of it to him (I had translated it for Knopf), he said to me, "Perhaps you're right, but the theatre is vulgar; if one wants to be subtle, one should write a novel." I remember I thought it strange at the time that a man who had called on writers to be responsible should blame the medium he had worked in for faults I found in his work. I said to him in reply, "Well I don't think the theatre *has* to be vulgar; I don't think Pirandello is, not to speak of Molière or Racine." As I remember, he did not argue this point, but went on to say that he thought plays were essentially myths constructed for *la grande publique* (mass audiences), and not artistic works designed for the happy few; they, he thought, needed guilt feelings rather than additional happiness.

Here I want to add one further fact which is not directly pertinent. Merleau-Ponty and Hannah Arendt were very enthusiastic at that time about an essay on *Hamlet* by Harold Rosenberg which Merleau-Ponty planned to publish in *Les Temps modernes,* and which did appear there in 1951. Harold told me that his essay on *Hamlet* had been the inspiration for Sartre's politi-

*Sartre's worst political mistake was his letter to Kosygin, published in 1966 in *Les Temps modernes,* urging the USSR to risk nuclear war with the U.S. to prevent an American victory in Vietnam.

cal play. When I asked Sartre about this, he answered without
hesitation and with his customary generosity, in the affirmative.
Yes, he said, he had been influenced by Rosenberg's essay in the
writing of *Dirty Hands*.

Suppose we turn aside now from what was expected of Sartre
as a philosopher and try to respond directly to this question:
What did he, as a philosopher, achieve? Here we will have to
look at the situation of philosophy when Sartre appeared on the
scene.

Modern philosophy, when Sartre produced his first philosophical work—I think it was his thesis, a phenomenological
study of the imagination—had become extremely technical.
What is now called philosophy of language had not yet done
more than indicate a few of the alterations and revisions it has
required of the language of philosophers. It seemed at the time
impossible to treat any of the real problems of life as instanced
in morals or in politics, or to describe the data necessary for
treating such problems, in terms technical enough to satisfy the
philosophically scrupulous. Perhaps the best way to grasp the
language problem posed for philosophers before the fifties is to
note its effects on Bertrand Russell, who had little in common
with Sartre philosophically, but later joined with him in attacking American political action in Southeast Asia in the war
crimes trial that was held in Stockholm. The noted British logi-
cian, mathematician, metaphysician, and publicist had, since the
beginning of the century, produced philosophical writings of
the most uneven character. On the one hand, he had come forward with works of logical analysis, like his essay "The Theory
of Descriptions," now a classic; on the other hand he had turned
out journalistic homilies on sex, education, manners, and morals
which in their glibness, superficiality, and lack of rigor could
not but shock any of his readers who were also familiar with his
expert analyses in difficult areas of thought. Could it be that the
serious questions of life were not to be examined with the same
care as the technical questions of logic and theory of knowledge?
Here Edmund Husserl had already, earlier in the century, sug-

gested a solution—one, in fact, put forth by Aristotle. (But as
Gide remarked, everything important that was once said has to
be said again, otherwise it will be forgotten.) Husserl noted that
not every discipline is capable of the same degree of precision.
And to this idea he added another of his own: There *was* a
definite way of being rigorous in investigating and conceptualiz-
ing any subject matter: marriage, morals, and sex—just like
space, time, and causality—could be studied phenomenologi-
cally. And to do this the philosopher would not have to exchange his own precise terms for the vaguer terms of journalists.
Following this lead of Husserl's, Sartre, in *Being and Nothingness*,
published in 1943, managed to bring off a philosophical treatise
on the human condition in which the questions as to whether
human action is free or determined, values are created by men
or situated in some heaven of ideas, action is conscious or unconscious, were dealt with in a language aiming at psychological
accuracy and logical refinement. One thing must be granted this
work of Sartre's even today: it was an immense effort to give
logical form to the treatment of problems which had been
treated either without logic or against it, and to do this in terms
of the most sophisticated concepts available to the theorist at
that time. While the groundwork for such an effort had been laid
by Edmund Husserl, and though Martin Heidegger, in *Being
and Time*, published as early as 1927, had done something very
similar, Sartre's *Being and Nothingness* is probably the most complete effort that has been made in modern times to deal in a
philosophically precise manner with questions which, by their
very nature, had seemed to condemn the theorist to inexacti-
tude.

What can be said about *Being and Nothingness* in this regard
today? Can it be said to have a rigor comparable to what we have
come to expect in contemporary philosophy? Or does one indeed breathe in a purer intellectual atmosphere when reading
Chisholm or Putnam or Kripke on the technical problems of
theory of knowledge than when reading Sartre's analyses of the
human condition in *Being and Nothingness*? I think it is clear that
the language of philosophy has been altered during the last
thirty-five or forty years in terms of rigor, for what was techni-

cally precise in 1943 would not pass muster for many American and English readers of philosophy in 1980.

When Professor Arthur Danto defends Sartre in a charming and eloquent little book devoted to the French philosopher,* he takes what is obviously a protective attitude toward Sartre's ideas, at times defending them with arguments Sartre might not have had the logical sophistication to call upon. And while Professor Danto is sympathetic to Sartre's work, one cannot help but feel there is something disparaging about his attitude toward it. Why should a philosopher need any other protection than that afforded by his own ideas and his own arguments for them? Surely something must have happened in the language of philosophy between 1943 and the present time which made Professor Danto feel that Sartre's ideas could no longer speak convincingly for themselves and now had to be spoken for more logically by him.

What happened in philosophy since 1943?

At about the time Sartre was writing his *Being and Nothingness,* another major effort was being made in philosophy of quite a different, though related, kind. If Sartre was trying to treat the problems of life—matters of morals and politics—with a precision like that already achieved by philosophers in logic and theory of knowledge, Ludwig Wittgenstein in England was trying to do almost the exact opposite, that is, to treat the most complex problems of logic and theory of knowledge not in technical, but in natural, that is to say, in ordinary language. This development in modern thought, sometimes referred to as ordinary language analysis, also subjected to a very severe criticism the *theory* of language on which the better philosophical writings of Russell had been based.

Now, suppose we are asked to decide which was more interesting, more important, more valuable, the discussion of the problems of life in technical language, or the discussion of technical problems in ordinary language, what would our answer be? Here I do not feel required to give more than an indirect answer. In fact, the two efforts were in some sense parallel.

*Published by Viking in 1975.

Clearly, if one can talk about technical problems in ordinary language, then one can talk about morals or politics without having to mathematicize these disciplines. I must add here that when Sartre wrote his first great work, French philosophy, unlike Anglo-American, had resisted the effort to make it dependent on formal systems. So that a critical operation like Wittgenstein's was perhaps less needed in France than in England and the United States. I must add, too, that the yield of ordinary language philosophy has not been as great as was expected. "There's gold in them thar hills," announced John Austin. There was some gold, no doubt, but rather less than he thought.

I IMAGINE some of my readers may be thinking that I have merely commented on Sartre's language and said practically nothing about what he employed that language to assert. Moreover, Sartre himself showed little interest in philosophy of language; this interest was, however, cultivated by his friend and colleague on *Les Temps modernes,* the philosopher, Maurice Merleau-Ponty. The latter made frequent trips to London, influenced some of the Oxford philosophers and, influenced in turn by them, made a major effort to connect phenomenology and existentialism with ordinary language analysis. During the late forties and early fifties I ran into Merleau-Ponty fairly regularly in Saint-Germain-des-Prés. He was often accompanied by the beefy, though beautiful, Sonia Orwell, later Sonia Pitt-Rivers. Merleau-Ponty, with the pink cheeks of a provincial, was supremely sophisticated, and he tried to give you the impression when you got into an argument with him that he knew what you were going to say before you had actually said it. This is a very effective device. I remember once taxing Merleau-Ponty with not being able to use it against me. We were discussing an article of his which I believe Dwight Macdonald had republished in English in *Politics.* It was a defense of a sophisticated kind of Marxism and an attack on vulgarized Marxism. When Merleau asked me if the position he had taken appealed to me, I told him it did not. And then I asked, "Can you guess what I'm going to say against it?" "I suppose I can't," he replied, smiling. "Otherwise I would have taken it up in the article." My objection, which in fact he was not able to meet, is the following: I do not think one can defend the ideas of a mass movement by stressing a sophisticated version of them. For in a mass movement, ideas are necessarily going to be vulgarized. If you want to defend Marxism ideologically, then you must defend it *as vulgarized*, against the vulgarizations of rival movements. Incidentally, Sartre was much keener about matters of this kind than his friend, though he claimed to have been the pupil of Merleau-Ponty in politics.

But if Sartre was the keener here, this was—I would hazard the guess—not because he was the better, but because he was less purely the philosopher. For there was always a good deal of ideology in Sartre's philosophical writings, and not a little of the psychologism which his teacher, Husserl, had condemned. Husserl was opposed to the use of philosophical concepts for the presentation of any *Weltanschauung*, or view of the world. Out of his very love of wisdom, he thought, the philosopher should not try to show us that he himself is wise, and this he could not avoid doing in trying to tell us what the actual world is like. Here, Jean-Paul Sartre did not follow his philosophical teacher. He tried, in *Being and Nothingness*, to combine both wisdom and rigor—philosophy as a precise science, and philosophy as a coherent picture of the world. Now I do not think this is the proper place to set forth and argue about the merits and demerits of Sartre's philosophical assertions. Moreover, there is a content to Sartre's philosophical writings which can be discussed without becoming over-technical. Sartre argued eloquently in *Being and Nothingness* for a very definite view of the world, and again for a very different view of it some twenty years later in his *Critique of Dialectical Reason*. These works are both highly ideological, and may be regarded as ideologies of and for modern man.

The denial of God's existence, a position one can hardly establish by rigorous argument, is very important in both these works of Sartre. Very much to the point here is a comment made about him by George Lichtheim some years ago when the political writer was editing *Commentary* in New York City. The value

Lichtheim said he found in Sartre's existentialism was due to Sartre's peculiar kind of atheism. For the usual denial of God's existence tended to encourage people to expect a rationality in human affairs experience is likely to contradict. Religious belief, as Lichtheim saw it, had been a protection against a too-great expectation of reasonableness, a protection men in the past had benefited from, and which contemporary man, insofar as he has lost his traditional faith, has had to do without. Sartre's existentialism, said Lichtheim, was, of all the varieties of atheism which had been presented, the only one which prepared us to experience the irrationality of the world. It is interesting to note here that Sartre, an atheist, should in *No Exit* have written a play plotted about the punishment of sin after death. An atheist of the eighteenth or nineteenth centuries would have simply denied that life continues after death and denied, too, that there is any judgment of sin or wrongdoing after one's life is over. Of course, in his play Sartre is not saying the contrary. But he has no objection to *imagining* the contrary. An eighteenth- or nineteenth-century atheist would have had such objections.

Let me here try to indicate in what respect Sartre's *Being and Nothingness* and *Critique of Dialectical Reason* may be regarded as ideologies of modern man.

Modern man is, as Sartre has presented him to us, man torn from his traditional group, traditional religion, his traditional metaphysics or ethic. He is the spiritually unaccommodated man, and nothing is impermissible for him. He must decide himself just what it is he forbids himself to do. Modern man would, in fact, like to belong to some other time. He would like to be some other kind of being: a Christian, a heretic, a libertine, a sensualist. He would like to be unmodern, though modern he is, without knowing exactly what it means to be that. For being modern is precisely not having to be anything with true "resolute decision." He thinks of communism and at times would like to be a Communist, but not finally. He may try to be a Communist, but with results that he knows in advance. If he has children, he does not know what he wants them to become. To resolve the problem of generations he has to change into some other kind of man than he is, send his children to a church he does not attend himself, to a synagogue of which he does not care to be a member. What kind of a man is this who has to be an entirely different kind of man just in order to have a family? It would be best of all, perhaps, not to have any children. But this would be to give up the only fundamental consolation men have found in growing old. Whatever else he is, modern man knows this: he is not pure. He knows he is impure of heart. "The pure of heart," said Kierkegaard, "think only one thought." This is the very kind of thought a modern man cannot think. Plato told us that musical purity required an instrument limited to only three strings. Modern man will not be so musically abstinent. He needs the fiddles, pianos, bassoons, and tympanum, and even these are not enough. He needs electronic wailings, the music of sounds that don't seem at all musical, and even then he isn't satisfied, nor can he be, for essentially he is dissatisfied with his mode of hearing, and not with the sounds he hears. What paintings please him? All sorts of paintings, but only to a limited extent. He looks at the golden forms of Tutankhamen's tomb on exhibition, admires them, but thinks, even as he admires, not merely how beautiful they are, but also this: "Why did I ever see anything else that diverted me from concentrating on beauty such as this? Why did I ever have to see Greek sculpture, Michelangelo, Donatello, Rodin, the Bodhisattvas, Brancusi, the sculptures of Ankhor Wat?" For every great form of art suggests to him a deliverance from his state as a modern man. It suggests such a deliverance, but the suggestion is never made good. Unstable, constantly facing the collapse of his most recent conclusions, modern man hopes to be supplanted by human beings more successfully adapted to the time, though he himself takes no little pride in his inadaptation to it.

As moderns, we are aware of the great difficulty—if one begins with the self—of proving the existence of other selves. And, swinging to the other side, the difficulty, if beginning with the others, of ever getting back to ourselves. So we no longer expect decisive arguments from philosophers on whether there are or are not other selves. But since we are moderns, we want to hear some argument, and an argument that appeals to us, that sympathizes with us, that tells us something of what the world is without denying what we ourselves are. And we want to hear an argument that even takes account of our social situation, for however well situated, we do not like to think of ourselves as members of a ruling class. The sweetness of life that ruling classes once knew, we ourselves shall never know. And we may even say that such sweetness of life belonged to a period when one could yield to an argument for the existence of others which was not a lower-class argument. But a lower-class argument is what we want to hear today, and that is what Sartre provided us with in *Being and Nothingness.* Certainly it does not persuade us that there are others (which we never really doubted anyway), but it does identify us, separating us from past generations who were interested in the problem and in other solutions to it. How does one know, according to Sartre, that there are others? When one is seen. The other's gaze freezes the movements of one's mind into a stillness like a stone's, and one's powers over words into silence. (One actually helps the other in this operation, for one has a secret wish to be a thing anyway, and escape from the pain of conscious life.) In any case, stared at, one becomes the object of the other's glance, and one knows one is not sovereign in this situation. One's *I* is deposed, and this can only be by an alien *I*. So the experience revealing that there are others is modeled on the kind of revolution in which a monarch is put down. It is also suggestive of the French Revolution to which, if we are moderns, we cannot but relate our feelings, our thoughts and all our hopes. And the gaze of the other has a keenness like that of the guillotine, lopping off one's self-awareness like the head of an aristocrat which, as Hegel has it, falls like a cabbage. It has been said that Sartre's real genius and originality is best instanced by his argument for the existence of others. And I think this is quite true though it would not convince any philosopher; it does not even convince us. But it does something else which is perhaps just as important. It tells us what we ourselves are, and this is certainly something both literature and philosophy are supposed to do.

Perhaps Sartre is not in the front rank of modern philosophers, who were his contemporaries, though there are some who still rank him with Wittgenstein and Heidegger. In any case, he is probably the best writer among contemporary philosophers, and certainly the best philosopher among contemporary writers.

In his various works, Sartre did try, I think, to keep philosophy and literature separate. They were, for him, quite different projects and he wanted to excel in each of them in terms he himself had set. Yet the effect of his success in both endeavors has been to create a confusion about the boundaries proper to philosophy, proper to literature. We have, for example, the lecture of Roland Barthes about how he would go about writing a novel were he indeed to write one, and the lecture is presented as the commencement of such a novel. And we have Jacques Derrida's philosophical writings which, as Richard Rorty rightly indicated, have more to do with *writing* philosophy than with philosophizing. We already distinguish between doing philosophy and talking about it, so Derrida may possibly have achieved something new: not the doing of philosophy *or* the talking about it, but the *writing* about the *writing* of it. Now Sartre, when he wrote *Being and Nothingness*, was doing philosophy, not talking about it, and not writing about the writing of it, if that is indeed something different.

All the same, Sartre's conversation was always that of the man of letters. I remember a lecture he gave on American literature in Paris under the auspices of UNESCO. As it happens, I did not greatly admire his talk. He described American literature as fundamentally optimistic, and how can one call men like Melville, Hawthorne, or Faulkner optimists? The lecture was given to a very small audience and I happened to be sitting in the front row. I mention this because the next time I ran into Sartre, I told him I was critical of his talk. In reply he said, "And I know what you were critical of." "How do you know?," I asked. He said, "I was watching you while I was talking." And then he proceeded to tell me exactly what my criticisms of his talk were, almost point by point.

LUNCH with Sartre meant argument and still more argument. I remember one occasion especially. We had an appointment for lunch at noon, but just before noon Nicola Chiaromonte and Ann Matta dropped in on me at my hotel. At noon Sartre appeared with Simone de Beauvoir and at once invited Chiaromonte and Ann Matta to lunch, too. He brought us to Chez Lipp and we were taken upstairs to the room sacred to luncheon talks on the second floor.

We lingered over lunch for a long time and the conversation touched on many subjects. Sartre was interested at that moment in the suit for libel of Kravchenko, the Russian defector, against the French Communist party, and what amused him was that the Communist party lawyers accused Kravchenko of all kinds of things, including drunkenness, but did not accuse him of the one serious crime of which, in Sartre's eyes, he was obviously *guilty*, namely, treason. This drew very strong objections from Chiaromonte. Why was it treasonable to desert the Soviet bureaucracy and criticize the Soviet state? Sartre replied that Kravchenko had done more than that. He had also revealed information which had been entrusted to him by Soviet leaders who thought him loyal, and whom he had encouraged to think of him as loyal. Sartre's criticism of Kravchenko would not apply, of course, to the criticism of dissidents who had openly challenged the regime in Russia. And as a matter of fact I have myself heard very unsavory things about Kravchenko since. At a party in New York he said to a friend of mine who spoke Russian, pointing to the other guests, most of whom—it was a New York party—were Jews, "I don't consider the people here the real Americans. In fact I think there are very few real Americans in New York City." "And where are the real Americans to be found?," my friend asked. "In the South," said Kravchenko. "They're the people who once owned the big plantations." What he meant was, the people who had owned slaves.

Simone de Beauvoir said very little at our luncheon. She watched Sartre intently throughout the discussion like a spectator at a play or better still, like a substitute player on a football team, watching a star player and wondering whether an opportunity will arise to substitute for him. I do not mean to suggest by this that Simone de Beauvoir is lacking in conversation. On the contrary, in all my meetings with her I always found her lively and communicative. But with Sartre there, engaged in some argument that had meaning for him, she was without initiative and took her cue from him, entering the discussion only when he signalled her to do so. She certainly did not behave like an independent woman. The author of *The Second Sex* on this occasion, at least, was very much a feminine supporter of the male lead.

I said that Sartre was the best writer among philosophers, the best philosopher among writers, and if this is true, there should be some feature of his writing to which one could point which would illustrate a specific union or fusion of the literary and the philosophical. And in fact we can point to such a trait, illustrative of what Saint-Beuve might have called "a master faculty." As poets have shown their purely rhetorical or literary power by many discoveries in similes and metaphors, so philosophers have shown their peculiar insight into our use of words by turning up tautologies, our different ways of expressing a single meaning. Now Sartre, in his various literary biographies, but I am thinking most especially of his biographical work on Genet, *Saint Genet, Actor and Martyr,* is given to piling up tautologies in an ecstacy of analysis even as modern poets pile up images and metaphors. No doubt Sartre's famous prolixity is due to this aspect of his writing, but we should also note that through it his prose attains a great rhetorical value. When we have been told the same idea some twenty-five times in twenty-five different ways, we are clearer, first of all as to its meaning, and in addition we feel the intense interest in it of the writer, who has found so many different ways of communicating it. In piling up tautologies, Sartre has found a way of giving rhetorical force to the emotions he feels for the ideas he wants communicated. And the reader feels his emotion too. So we can say he has invented a rhetorical and literary use for a philosophical habit of mind.

Sartre has many talents, there are many sides to his personality. How is one to find an image of him that will do justice to all of them? Probably not by looking directly at the man, but at a particular problem of his, one that faces intellectuals generally, especially in this part of our century.

First of all, we must ask what is an intellectual? There are, of course, the positive definitions like, for instance, that he is someone for whom truth is always relevant, even when its practical importance is minimal, or someone who is interested in ideas as such, again without regard to what may result from holding them; there are also negative notions like, for instance, Heidegger's suggestion that the intellectual is the one in whom the primary experience of handling tools has become inauthentic and whose indirect inspection of objects lacks the genuineness of experience found in those who deal with objects directly, masterfully. Which of these judgments is correct? Incidentally, Sartre seems to have been inclined to the negative judgment, for he supported Heidegger's notion, for instance, that one uncovers or discloses the nature of a hammer not by inspecting it but by using it.

To such contemporary notions about the intellectual as such, I prefer the more concrete, dramatic terms suggested by Turgenev in his famous essay, "Hamlet and Don Quixote." These characters, Turgenev wrote, are the ". . . twin anti-types of human nature." He also thought Russia had too many Hamlets and was in need of more Don Quixotes. The Russian intelligentsia responded to the request for Don Quixotes in 1917, with the results we all know.

But to go back to Turgenev's distinction. Are Hamlet and Don Quixote really antitypes of human nature? Only of human nature insofar as it is reflective. In a way, Turgenev concedes this himself, for he notes the relation of Hamlet and Don Quixote with the "ordinary man," "the man in the street" and in this connection points up Hamlet's relationship with Polonius and the relationship of Don Quixote with Sancho Panza: the Danish prince ridicules the King's counselor even as the Spanish knight is ridiculed by his own squire. Now Polonius has nothing in him of Hamlet; Sancho Panza, nothing of the knight he serves. So Hamlet and Don Quixote are not antitypes of human nature, but antitypes of the intellectual.

So let us consider yet once again—the comparison has been made many times before this—what it means to be a Hamlet, and what to be a Don Quixote. Hamlet is the easier figure to describe, and by describing him, we can better understand the Spanish hero, his very opposite. Hamlet is that kind of intellectual who constantly sees the hiatus between the meaning of any of his actions at a particular moment and the meaning the same action will probably have on the final horizon of his days. The horizon of the moment and the horizon of the end are not at all the same. He cannot ever bring them together. He begins to insist on their difference, and in this insistence lies the paralysis of his will to action. Don Quixote is the very opposite, though he begins with the same problem. He sees the difference between the meaning of a particular act on the horizon of its accomplishment, and the meaning of that act on the final horizon of his life, but his response to this perception is not paralysis of will, but resolution and decision. He will blot out the meaning of his act on the horizon of the moment and substitute for it the meaning he wants it to have on the final horizon of his life. Don Quixote, the intellectual, is not so different from Loyola and from Lenin. Whether they knew it or not, he was their model.

Let us note here too what is not Hamlet, what is not Don Quixote. That is to say, what is not the intellectual: the man of ordinary consciousness who lives by deliberately blurring the meaning of any act of his on the immediate horizon with its meaning on the ultimate horizon of his life. This, which the ordinary man does constantly, the intellectual must at all costs avoid ever doing.

Now what shall we say about Sartre in this regard? What dramatic model did he follow? During the Spanish civil war, according to all reports, he was paralyzed like Hamlet, while he saw the fellow intellectuals he most admired, like Malraux, for instance, go forth—what place was more appropriate than Spain?—to fight Franco, even as the mournful knight hurled himself against the windmill. By this I do not mean that the civil war in Spain was necessarily lost from the outset. If true, I do not know this to be true, and I do not think those intellectuals who went to fight in Spain, like Malraux and my old friend Nicola Chiaromonte, thought the war was lost. For Nicola it was the last good cause. But what I mean is that to go and fight in Spain one had to transform oneself into a fanatic. This Malraux was quite willing to do. Though not a member of the Communist party himself, he worked with the Communists, and refused to testify for Trotsky when the latter was charged in Moscow with collaborating with Hitler, and on a piece of evidence which Malraux personally knew to be false. But the Hamlet model had too great an attraction to Chiaromonte for him to sustain a fanatical pose in Spain. Chiaromonte was in the same air squadron as Malraux; in fact, he was the bombardier in the plane in which Malraux was the machine gunner. They were good friends and almost always saw each other at officer's mess. One day the French Communist party's contact with Malraux's squadron came for lunch. It was a melancholy day, as Chiaromonte told me about it, for him. There had been several casualties in their squadron just that morning. The Communist party man, Marcel Cachin, however, was full of self-satisfaction and optimism. He smacked his lips over lunch and when he was told of the losses that morning to the squadron said, "Oh, that's nothing, we can replace them." Chiaromonte, enraged, brought up the matter of the anarchists, like Durutti, whom the Spanish Communist party had had shot, and also the fate of Andreas Nin, the Trotskyist leader of the POUM. Cachin responded by calling Chiaromonte's political accusations "idle," and then said, "Let's be serious and have some more pork chops." Chiaromonte shouted at him, "To celebrate our fallen comrades?," and called Cachin a butcher and a blackguard. Afterwards, Malraux took Chiaromonte aside and said to him, "After your outburst, I don't think you can stay in our squadron. I suggest you shift to the Abraham Lincoln brigade." Chiaromonte knew that the Abraham Lincoln brigade was controlled by the Stalinists, from whom he could expect no mercy. He went back to Paris, but in Paris one could do little towards the victory of the Spanish Republic; one could only be ironical about its chances of success.

By remaining in Paris, Sartre escaped the exultations and ignominies of fanatical action in the Spanish civil war. But apparently he could not bear his isolation and inactivity, and after the defeat of France, having returned from a German prison camp, he commenced that furious and uninterrupted literary and intellectual activity which only came to a full pause recently after the publication of the third volume of his biography of Flaubert. After which Sartre's failing eyesight made it impossible for him to follow events as he once did. He announced that he would do no more writing and from then on would just give interviews. Let us now ask what dramatic model he followed in the period between the ending of the Spanish civil war and the late seventies, during which time he claimed to have said all he had to say.

In my judgment, Sartre was an intellectual through and through and he was always that. His hesitation never was between Hamletism and the consciousness of the ordinary man, or between that consciousness and quixotism. His hesitation was between Hamlet and Don Quixote, and he tried out the postures of both, the first during the Spanish civil war, and after World War II the second, when he tried to take communism away from the French Communist party in the radical grouping of *rassemblement* he started with David Rousset. And then when this venture failed and the *rassemblement* was dissolved, he took up the various extreme political positions, for the most part supportive of the USSR, which Merleau-Ponty characterized as "super-Bolshevik;" for instance, as I have already noted, in his essay entitled "The Communists and Peace," he denounced the French working class for not rallying to the Communist slogan that General Ridgway had used germ warfare in Korea, though he openly admitted the accusation against Ridgway was a false one. He broke with his former friend and comrade in the resistance, Albert Camus, in the main over the latter's pointing up of the Soviet concentration camp system, and he broke with his comrade in the *rassemblement,* David Rousset, on the same issue. All the same, he was continually attacked in the press of the French Communist party, so that even in this period of quixotic procommunism, he was occasionally forced to take refuge in an attitude of irony. In the early fifties, attending a public function called by the Communist party, he ran into a Party member who extended his hand in greeting. (The French always shake hands on meeting or on taking leave of one another; they also criticize

Americans for not being sufficiently devoted to the custom.)
Sartre looked at the hand extended toward him and asked the
Party member, "Do you agree with everything in the editorial
columns of *Humanité?*" "Yes," said the Communist. "Well,
Humanité says that I'm a bastard," said Sartre, "so why do you
want to shake my hand?"

Ever since the Russian Revolution and until recent years,
quixoticism, the intellectual attitude based on Cervantes's hero,
in its political and ideological form at least, has been procommu-
nist. Not for nothing had the Russian Revolution declared war
on Hamletism. What we must recognize, though, is that the
Revolution supported and furthered an equally extreme intellectual posture and, in fact, for most of this century was able to
recruit a goodly number of those ready to impose on the moment the meaning they hoped to give history at its close. There
were exceptions, of course, and two immediately come to mind.
There was T.E. Lawrence's effort to lead the Arab revolt during
the First World War, and there was Malraux's support of General de Gaulle at the end of the Second. But these expressions
of quixotism were in a way limited and parochial. The passion
for some ideal political solution to all our problems carried most
intellectuals into the Communist camp or to a position of favoring the Communists, or of favoring Russia against the United
States. I believe all this came to an end with the publication of
Solzhenitsyn's *Gulag Archipelago,* and the revelation of the struggle of the Soviet dissidents against the state, which Western
intellectuals of first rank, like Sartre, had favored over American
democracy. This much Solzhenitsyn and the other Russian dissidents, but he, most of all, achieved: they put an end to the long
identification of communism as a political goal, and quixotism
as an intellectual attitude. Even Sartre had to yield on this point,
and after the publication of *Gulag Archipelago* attacked the Russian state and the Russian Communist party in no uncertain
terms, though not with the violence he employed in Stockholm
at the war crimes trial when he attacked the United States.
When I read, in the last brilliant pages of his biography of
Flaubert, Sartre's very finely drawn assessment of the relationship between Flaubert and Napoleon III during the war and

after the defeat of 1870, in which Sartre shows how Flaubert tries to qualify, after the defeat, the regard he had had for Napoleon III before the catastrophe, I cannot but compare it with Sartre's own effort to substitute a certain lack of candor for the enthusiasm he had previously shown when commenting on the Communist world of eastern Europe. Surely he was finally as compromised by his political support of the USSR and of North Vietnam, by the way, as Flaubert was in his acceptance of the emperor and by being received by the princess at the Tuileries. And when one makes this comparison, the advantage is entirely with Flaubert, for we remember Flaubert not for his political attitudes but for the artistic purity of his work, which those attitudes did not invalidate. Sartre never placed his own art that high, nor can we. He placed politics above art, and his attacks on Flaubert's politics do not serve to justify his own.

I called Sartre's first major philosophical effort, *Being and Nothingness*, an ideology for contemporary man. Let me specify further: It is an ideology for contemporary man insofar as he wants to intellectualize his experience, and to reject the Communist faith. One can say of the Sartre who wrote *Being and Nothingness* exactly what he said of Flaubert in '48: "From the point of view he adopted—which is at once that of immediate lived experience and its metaphysical meaning, without regard to any social consideration—it is evident that his skepticism goes deep." But Sartre also wrote another philosophical work, *The Critique of Dialectical Reason*, and this, too, is an ideology for modern man, but from the very opposite standpoint. It is an ideology for the modern who wants to be a Communist. So we can say that Sartre created two distinct and different ideologies from opposite viewpoints and involving the very opposite goals. There are, of course, carry-overs from one ideology to the other, or thoughts, if you will, presented in the first which could appear in the second, and in the second which might have appeared in the first. But let us be clear about it. These two works are divergent. They are not like the two versions of *Sentimental Education*, which could both bear the same title. To make the parallel with Flaubert hold, we would have to change the title of his first version of *Sentimental Education* and call it *Unsentimen-*

139

tal Education, while leaving the title of his second version intact. But there are thoughts which would fit either text. For example, when Sartre, in *Being and Nothingness,* wants to prove the existence of others, he gives what I have called a lower class argument for this. *And this is the first time in the history of philosophy that something like the feeling of class inferiority was introduced as an argument at an epistemological level.* Now surely this argument would not have been inappropriate or out of place in *The Critique of Dialectical Reason.* In that work, Sartre describes the degeneration of the group once its moment of revolutionary activity is over, and along with this, the serialization* of the individual, something which occurs in any society—even one resulting from the overthrow of the capitalist state. Developing such ideas, Sartre thrusts us back into the atmosphere of *Being and Nothingness,* with its Flaubertian pessimism, which no more denies itself "the delights of irony" than did the Flaubert Sartre describes in his biography.

The very opposite values are set forth in, and very fundamental to, the two distinct ideologies Sartre has created. In *Being and Nothingness,* the main value, I should say, is freedom and man as a moral agent, with the freedom to be a moral agent, the freedom also to construct the moral law which he himself decided will constrain him. In *The Critique of Dialectical Reason* the main value is man, but not as the determinant of his own freedom, rather as a historical agency in historical situations he has not himself invented. In this second work, the emphasis is not on morality and not on freedom. It is on political action and the constraints within which this can operate. To give just one example: To act historically, according to Sartre's critique, the individual must yield up his liberties to what Sartre calls *the group in fusion,* to which the individual grants the power to take his life. As for morality, it is relegated to a general insignificance, after having been raised, in the previous work, to the highest point. What Sartre has to say about morality in the light of his announced conversion to Marxism was perhaps best and

---

*An instance of serialization, according to Sartre, occurs when an individual has to queue up to get into a bus.

most clearly expressed in his biographical study of Genet, *Saint Genet, Actor and Martyr*, composed just before he set to work on the *Critique*. I quote from Bernard Frechtman's translation:

> Either morality is stuff and nonsense or it is a concrete totality which achieves a synthesis of good and evil. . . . The abstract separation of these two concepts [good and evil] . . . expresses simply the alienation of man. The fact remains that, in the historical situation, this synthesis cannot be achieved. Thus, any ethic which does not explicitly profess that it is *impossible today* contributes to the . . . alienation of men.

This is from the same author who, in *Being and Nothingness*, conceived of the individual as free to act morally in any situation, even under torture.

As the creator of two distinct and quite different ideologies, full of insights into the complex mysteries of social and individual lived experience, Sartre has to be taken for what he has already been judged to be, one of the dominant figures of this age. That he constructed two ideological systems and not just one, is itself expressive of our age: Heidegger had two different periods in philosophy, though only the first of these is important, and Wittgenstein produced two different and distinct philosophies, though both are important and also deeply connected. To whom, besides these moderns, should we compare Sartre? I suggest to the other great ideological writers of this and past centuries. Sartre has already been compared to Voltaire (first of all, by Edmund Wilson), and I myself have compared the view in Sartre's *What Is Literature?* to the position taken on literature by Bernard Shaw in his letter to A. J. Walkley. Moreover, both Shaw and Sartre had periods of political support for Stalinism. But I think I would prefer to compare Sartre as an ideological writer to Dostoevsky. Not that he is comparable to the Russian novelist as an artist or even as a dramatist; what makes a comparison of him to Dostoevsky possible and also right is that he made available to intellectuals of his period systematic ways of rationalizing their lives. The specifically religious value in literature has been its justification of life, and this kind of justification is made available to the individual in both of the ideologies Sartre set forth, so much so that despite the writer's avowed atheism, the mocking phrase of Marcel Duchamp, "Sartre Cathedral," does not seem inappropriate after all when applied to either of his two systematic treatises. Perhaps instead of saying "Sartre Cathedral," we should speak of Sartre's cathedrals, for there were two of them, places of reverential yet modern decision, where, surrounded by emblems of the most refined intelligence, one could force one's spirit to sustain the stress of resolute ironic dubiety, or a fanatic faith.

POSTSCRIPT

Sartre's last work, his biography of Flaubert, followed the novelist's life and career only through the first *Sentimental Education*, and stopped short of considering him during, or at work on, his two greatest productions, *Madame Bovary* and the second *Sentimental Education*, though Sartre did find occasion to comment on Flaubert's varying attitudes towards Louis Napoleon III during and after the defeat, and also towards the communards in Paris. But to treat Flaubert without discussing his two greatest novels, or showing him at work on them, would be like writing a biography of Hamlet (it will be remembered that Morgann, the eighteenth century wit, actually wrote a biography of Falstaff) and stopping short at the point where he sails for England, leaving out his return, his duel with Laertes, and his killing of Claudius. As a matter of fact, there are many things in Sartre's biography of Flaubert that could, with minor restatement, be utilized in an imaginary biography of Hamlet. Let us not forget that Kafka connected Flaubert with Kierkegaard (who connected himself with Hamlet) insofar as he felt he had to give up sentimental relations with women, for the sake of art. Sartre actually claims that Flaubert not only disliked mankind, but also his own characters, and he compares him unfavorably with Camus in this respect, who, he says, had a certain indulgence towards Caligula. But Camus' Caligula does not move us at all, and Flaubert's Emma does. Did Flaubert really despise humanity as Sartre claims he did? I will not try to answer this question directly, but instead call attention to Stephen Daedalus's remark about Shakespeare in the spirited analysis he makes of *Hamlet*. Daedalus, speaking here for Joyce, I believe, says of Shakespeare: "Man delights him not, nor woman neither." But Shakespeare's *characters* delight us. It is idle to inquire, since we can never find out, how he himself felt towards them. Let me indicate some of the common features of Shakespeare's Hamlet and of Sartre's Flaubert. Was Hamlet mad? Only by north-north-west, according to his own statement. And Flaubert? As Sartre has it, he was mad to the degree that an artist had to be mad according to the command of concrete reason between 1850 and 1900. (Sartre is never able to establish clearly what he means by concrete reason, and his whole notion of a binding prescription on artists of that period to be mad is absurd.)

All I want to show is that Sartre himself associates the kind of madness he finds in Flaubert with the kind of madness Shakespeare indicates in his hero. If Flaubert was mad, there was a kind of method to it, and certainly we can associate Hamlet's paralysis of will with Flaubert's passivity, which, Sartre says, Flaubert even "radicalized." And Sartre himself associates Flaubert with Hamlet in the mutism of his final days, which he also connects with the silence of the deposed emperor, relating "the provisional aphasia of the imperial Hamlet" to the remark to Horatio of Shakespeare's hero, "The rest is silence." A silence by Flaubert we must regret, for, as he told Maxime DuCamp, he had planned to write another novel, *Under Napoleon III*, which, Sartre says, in a passage of great brilliance, would be a study of "the vampirization of society by dreams." There is still another way Flaubert can be, in fact must be, associated with Hamlet; Flaubert's attitude toward the choice of words in writing must be associated with Hamlet's attitude toward possible action. As Hamlet notes the hiatus between the meaning of the deed it is possible for him to perform at the moment, and the meaning of that very deed on the horizon of his life, so Flaubert, working on his prose style, always sees the hiatus between the value of the word at hand which he can employ and the value

143

of that very word in the prose style of which he has imagined himself the producer. As Hamlet is paralyzed in the choice of action, Flaubert feels paralyzed in the choice of words. The right word is always the word he has *not* chosen to use, and which haunts the word he has hit upon. From his position, no *mot* is *juste*. I think the demon of paralysis which fascinated Flaubert and tormented him in the choice of words was never exorcised until James Joyce did just the opposite from his literary forebear, and, in *Finnegans Wake,* wrote a book in the *wrong* words, chosen for being wrong, for being imposed by the physical movements of the user, by the language chances of the moment, and even by the sadism of the storyteller. The wrong words of James Joyce saved writers from *les mots justes* of Flaubert, and after *Finnegan,* William Faulkner could tell his Southern tales with an eloquence uninhibited by the notion of a perfected style.

≺ *Six* ≻

READING CATASTROPHE

Between the appearance of the surrealists in New York City in the early forties, and the regular visits of existentialists to New York after the war was over, came the reports of the atom bomb explosions over Hiroshima and Nagasaki (in August of 1945, to be exact). Existentialism, to be sure, had burst on the European scene a good deal earlier. One may date its shock arrival in France with the publication in 1929 of Gabriel Marcel's *Metaphysical Journal*, with the lecture, in 1939, of Jean Wahl on *transdescendence*, or with the publication in 1943 of Jean-Paul Sartre's *Being and Nothingness*. These texts were hardly known in New York until long after the war was over. As I recall, though, there were discussions of Heidegger by André Breton and Meyer Schapiro in the early forties. For instance, when I suggested Malraux's slogan, "more consciousness," as a leading idea or slogan for Breton's new surrealist review, *VVV*, Schapiro objected on the ground that if one put forth such a slogan, Heidegger (who was then thought of as a supporter of the Nazis), could not be excluded, even theoretically, as a contributor to the review. His writings had indeed added something to modern consciousness. On the other hand, he had joined Hitler's political party (to be sure, as we now know, he resigned from it after one year's time). It is interesting to note, though, that there was a time when a review devoted to art and literature could make one of its general aims the exclusion of a writer whose worth was beyond dispute. Of course, Heidegger was not likely, in 1942, to offer a text to *VVV*.

As for existentialism, few intellectuals in New York knew of it until Jean-Paul Sartre appeared in the city in 1947, soon to be followed by Albert Camus and after that by Simone de Beauvoir. I recall, too, that in the very first discussions of the bombings of Hiroshima and Nagasaki, Nicola Chiaromonte, who had looked into Martin Heidegger's *Being and Time,* and had heard some discussions of it in Paris, remarked that in a certain philosophical sense it could be said that it was Heidegger who had invented the bomb.

Before Hiroshima, there had been talk of such a bomb, and there had been denials in the press that it was even on the drawing board. And it was held, in certain editorials, that it would be unpatriotic even to admit that such a bomb was possible. I had assumed that denials of this sort in the press were sincere and had been seriously meant; then came news of the explosion over Hiroshima. . . . We have heard much falsehood since.

President Truman announced the event over the radio; as I remember, he did not make the announcement boastfully, but dutifully, even falteringly. There was in his voice a note of what could be interpreted as dismay. And yet the bombing of Hiroshima meant that the war with Japan would soon be ended, and this, until Hiroshima, had not seemed possible.

The atom bomb was something which few of those in high places could have wanted the governments they represented to possess. We ourselves had created the bomb, but mainly because of our fear that the Nazis might make such a weapon; we did what we did not in fact want done, either by them or by us. Even the Wehrmacht must have had misgivings about the German atom bomb project—they had such a project, though it was a small one. For the bomb was going to make military science, of which the Wehrmacht elite were such masters, somewhat obsolete. And the power of the bomb was shocking in other ways, too. Georges Bernanos, the French Catholic and rightist, was shocked that Harry Truman, an American *"sans race"* should have been able to dispose of so much power.

It so happens that when news of the atomic explosion came,

I had been reading Auguste Comte,* whom people are beginning to read again (Louis Althusser said not so long ago that
Comte is the only important French philosopher since Descartes) but whom few were reading during the war. I had noted
with some surprise Comte's deliverances on the need to curtail
and limit the natural sciences in the interest of his god, which
is to say, humanity. This god, humanity, speaking through its
Comtean representatives, would say to each of the sciences at a
certain stage of their development, "Thus far shalt thou go, and
no farther." But in that case wouldn't the Comteans be like
clerics, wouldn't they be talking theology to the scientists, even
as the priests had done in their conflict with Galileo? Had the
church been right against Galileo after all? For there could
hardly be any *scientific* way of setting a limit to the growth of
the sciences.

But I was very far from any such sophisticated views in
1945. My feeling was merely one of shock that with the prospect
of victory in the Far East there was this new danger to be faced.
After the tigers of ideology, there was this new, even more
formidable creature, a dragon born of our best scientific thinking.

We talked about this endlessly, and Dwight Macdonald
wrote an article about the Hiroshima bombing in a late summer issue of *Politics*. I was living in Truro on Cape Cod then,
and read his article there. The first sentence went like this:
"What appalled us was the blast." Referring to it, Nicola Chiaromonte asked me, "Is that what appalled you?" And then he went

---

*I am really only interested in recalling what I was doing intellectually then, but
others have asked me, "What did you do to support yourself?" So here are some of the
things I did after I left the Writers Project at the end of 1940: I translated the following
works from the French for publishers: Apollinaire's *The Cubist Painters* for Wittenborn,
John Rewald's *Georges Seurat*, Camille Pissarro's *Letters* to his son Lucien for Pantheon,
and Sartre's plays for Knopf; in these efforts I had the help of Ralph Manheim. I
translated essays by André Breton for *View* and for *VVV*, a very long poem by Aimée
Cesare for *VVV*, articles by Roger Caillois and by André Malraux, and I copyedited the
translation that Norbert Guterman did of books published in Polish, Yiddish, German,
and French. Also, I wrote some books to which others appended their signatures. It is
to be noted that the economic problems writers traditionally have faced had not yet been
solved by the university system.

on to say, "Wasn't it rather that the bomb was dropped without warning on civilians not even engaged in the production of military hardware? How could Dwight have singled out the *blast* as the thing to be objected to?" And Harold Rosenberg was even more condemning. He said, "What appalled me was the article."

In general, people divided into two groupings on the matter of the bomb. There were those who held, optimistically, that what men had had the talent to make they could not but have the disposition to control. Seen thus, the problem of the bomb was fundamentally a political one, and the mere existence of the bomb was no reason for discouragement. The other group maintained that humanity had not shown a disposition to control many of the instruments of destruction which preceded the bomb. There was little reason, they said, to think that men would be able to control this latest and most potent instrument. Everyone was, of course, frightened by the bomb, but some thought that our fright might have a real function: a sufficiently frightened humanity might make some new effort to avoid war. But I do not think anyone genuinely believed this.

Dwight Macdonald, who had begun public discussions of the bombing of Hiroshima, and who by this time had changed his political views (from a Marxist-Trotskyist he had become what might be equally well described as a left-wing Republican or a right-wing Anarchist), decided to start a series of lectures in the Village under the auspices of *Politics.* He himself gave the first of these lectures, and there were subsequent talks by Paul Goodman and Nicola Chiaromonte. At Dwight's suggestion I too gave a talk in the series, and mine was on the bomb.

By this time I had met and talked with Jean-Paul Sartre, Albert Camus and Simone de Beauvoir, who had visited New York City in turn. And by this time I had become acquainted with the new viewpoint which described itself as existentialist. But I must make one qualification here: Albert Camus insisted from the start that he did not hold to the philosophical positions Jean-Paul Sartre had advanced; in fact Camus did not call himself an existentialist, and did not want to be called that. On the other hand, he did insist that there was a heartbreaking absurdity in the human condition, and was not this fundamentally the revelation of existentialism, rather than any of the technical notions which Sartre had put forward?

In any case, what was important to me at that time, and what I would like to stress here, is that there seemed to be some interconnectedness between the kind of technology which had made the bomb possible and the kind of philosophy represented by Heidegger and by Sartre. Let me put the matter thus: existentialism, stressing nothingness, seemed a plausible philosophy for describing the kind of world in which a weapon like the bomb had been invented and been used. Other viewpoints put forward or held to during that period seemed irrelevant to, or unconnected with, our invention of the bomb.

Certainly the Marxist groups had not predicted or foreseen any such technological breakthrough in the science of war. (I am excluding, of course, the Russian scientists—not necessarily Marxists—who, under Stalin's orders, had been trying to make such a bomb even before our Manhattan Project was set up.) Some Marxists did not hesitate to assert that the bomb was only a problem for the bourgeois world: Communists had no reason to fear it. This is more or less what Stalin himself said in a famous speech in which he urged the Russian Communist party not to think of retreating in the coming struggle with American imperialism, and not to fear the United States' atomic bombs. Years later the same points were to be repeated by Chairman Mao when, during the Cuban missile crisis, Khrushchev withdrew the atom warheads which had been placed in Cuba. To the Chinese assertion that the United States was a "paper tiger," Khrushchev replied, "the so-called paper tiger has atomic teeth." This admission was a long time in coming, but we must rejoice that it finally came. Today, no group, party, class, or nation (including post-Maoist China) can claim political superiority on the ground that it will be more reckless about the consequences of atomic war. But it took more than a decade of confrontations for the Communist leaders in all countries where they held power to come over to the position now universally held. In 1947, all of this was still to come. There was the bomb. We alone possessed it, we alone had used it. Those who defended our use of the bomb said we had used it to end the war. It is to be noted that Bertrand Russell suggested at that time that the bomb be used just once more, against the Soviet Union, in fact, to prevent that country from developing a bomb of its own. Only in this way, by using the bomb against Russia or threatening to do so, could a new atomic war be avoided. Such was the view of the British philosopher, whose political judgment had never been exceptionally keen. As I remember at the time, the French philosopher Jean Wahl responded that one does not avoid war by acts of war or by the threat of war, and that, contrary to Bertrand Russell's thinking, peace would be much more likely if the Soviet Union developed its own bomb. As it turns out, it was the French philosopher who was right on this matter, for, as Winston Churchill indicated, peace has been maintained by the balance of terror.

But about the talk I gave: I came, in fact, not to exhort my audience to do this, that, or the other thing, but to express my own doubts about some of the ideas and values I had previously held, in view of the new fact of atomic weaponry. Trotsky had written: "All the great problems will be settled arms in hand." He had so written, of course, before the creation of nuclear weapons. Had he witnessed their creation, would he have reversed his prior judgments and said that the great problems would all have to be settled *without* using weapons of mass destruction? In any case, we would have to find the answer ourselves.

But here I want to say something about the feeling of catastrophe that was in the air in that period. There was a felt sense that there would probably be no way out of catastrophe except through ideas as drastic and as unprecedented as what had befallen Hiroshima and Nagasaki. Nothing less than that could express or dispel the sense of menace by which everyone felt beset, first of all because of the war itself, then by the discovery of the Nazi death camps, and finally by our own use of nuclear bombs against Japan. But perhaps the most striking expression of the "catastrophism" of the late forties and early fifties can be found in theoretical writings that have nothing to do with military matters or politics. I'm thinking of the writings of Immanuel Velikovsky.

In 1950 he was to issue his first book, *Worlds in Collision*. It was about possible disruptions of life on earth by cataclysms in the solar system. I read some of his manuscript during the war, having been recommended to him as an editor of his text. However, I did not find the project of revising his text to my liking. I mention Velikovsky here because his ideas, which could only be verified by the sciences, had, like the notions of the existentialists, some qualitative relation to our new nuclear weapon. The idea that this earth of ours had already been buffeted by the tail of Venus, a "protoplanet," that the earth's poles had been reversed, that the dragons of poetry and folklore were recollections of real facts—the facts of atomic and electrical discharges in the skies—all these ideas and others still more fantastic put forward by Velikovsky, seemed possibly true in the fifties because of the existence of the bomb. One of the objections to Velikovsky's revision of celestial mechanics and also of prehistory, was that his version of a cosmic catastrophe in the past might occasion despair about the future. Velakovsky, to be sure, was not motivated by any such emotional considerations; he believed he had discovered important facts about our history on earth and was determined to prove the correctness of his notions. But despair about society here on earth led others without his learning to think about cosmic catastrophes to come. What I have in mind is a conversation I had in the year 1947, three years before Velikovsky's first book appeared.

I ran into someone I had known in the Trotskyist movement. A member of the Writers Union, he had supported me in the ideological brushes we had regularly with the Stalinists. He had lived a large part of his adult life in the Trotskyist SWP, been educated by it, and worked for it; the parties he went to were for, to, and of the Party. He had tried to marry in the Party, and failing in that, had remained a bachelor. This true, tried, and deserving Trotskyist I met one day in a cafeteria (in those days one still met people in cafeterias), and I saw at once that he was disconsolate, almost morbid. "What's the matter, Morris?" I asked him.

Morris: I'm beginning to have doubts. I: About what? Morris: About the Party. I: *You* have doubts about the Party? Morris: Yes. I: It's not possible, I don't believe you. Morris: I'm the one

who doesn't believe . . . and as you know, I used to believe
. . . Can you help me? I: Maybe you think the Party can't lead
the workers. . . . Maybe you think the workers aren't really
revolutionary. . . . If these are your doubts, then I can't help you.
Morris: But those are not my doubts. I think we have the right
program. I think the working class is as Marx described it. My
doubts concern not what may happen on earth, but what may
happen up there.

With this, he pointed to the sky. Had he become religious?
Was he mad? He said, "What bothers me is that everything
might go according to rational Trotskyist plan: We might lead
the proletariat to power, take over the instruments of production, set up a new world market and a new economy, democra-
tize society, help the nations that are still backward, and institute world peace. We might do all this . . ."

"Then what's wrong?" I asked. " 'This' sounds good to me…"

"We might do all this," he repeated, "and then be destroyed
in a collision with some heavenly body. Can you promise me
that this is never going to happen?"

Of course I couldn't make him any such promise, but could
it be that so unlikely a prospect had so thoroughly upset and
discouraged him? Weren't his feelings of discouragement due to
events that had already occurred and were in fact fairly well
known? First of all, the bomb itself, then the organized mass
murders in eastern Europe, and, finally, a fact, this: the war had
ended without any manifestation of revolutionary will by the
class that was supposed to lead a worldwide action of revolt.
Wasn't it because of these matters that he had become discouraged? I think it *was* these matters and not the reason he gave
me. All the same, some years later when Velikovsky's book had
appeared and been denounced, I couldn't help thinking of Morris and his fears of cosmic catastrophe. But on that occasion in
1947 when he expressed his fears, I told him that I was going to
give a talk on the bomb, and asked him to come to it.

In fact Morris did come.

My audience was composed in the main of stragglers from
various radical groups. They were the kind of disoriented radicals looking for a new doctrine who regularly attended the

lecture series organized by Macdonald—*schwarmerei*, Philip Rahv called them. Who knows what they expected of me?

I've already indicated that I saw some qualitative relation between the typical emphases of the existentialists and the facts of atomic energy. There was something about Heidegger's and Sartre's ideas that jibed with the existence of the bomb. Since that time, Heidegger himself commented on atomic energy, and in fact privileged that kind of energy to describe this age, but he had not yet discussed the matter directly in 1947.

I was at that time much more familiar with the ideas of Jean-Paul Sartre, and I think I took my cue from him rather than from Heidegger. Sartre had stressed that everyone is in a situation and that our problem is for each of us to recognize the situation he is in. From such recognition comes a certain strength: the strength to take a dramatic posture, to take an attitude. Now I applied these notions to the situation humanity taken as a whole found itself in with respect to atomic energy. Insofar as atomic weapons were now capable, or could be made capable, of destroying the whole human race, humanity was objectively in a dramatic situation. This had never happened before. And never before had it been necessary for the whole race to take up a dramatic posture. But did it make any sense to think of the whole race taking a single dramatic attitude? And if not, where was humanity going to derive a strength proportionate to the weakness modern science had placed it in? Here was the whole question, and one to which there was hardly any possibility of a clearly optimistic response. Would it have been better, then, for the human race had it not been dramatized by the new scientific discovery? Then should there have been no splitting of the atom, no transformation of mass into energy? Should physical science have stopped at the point of what is certainly a very great achievement? But if science was to be curtailed, then was not our whole civilization in question? Its justification was and had been the possibility for a better life served by the forces our technology released. And if technology and science were not to develop further, what was the new thrust of civilization to be?

As I recall it now, this was more or less the substance of my talk, and a rather violent discussion followed, as was typical in those days. Those in my audience who were persuaded of Marxist views accused me of yielding to the arguments of reactionaries and to the spite of pessimists. Some said they were not afraid of a new war, even one waged with atomic weapons. Others maintained that such a war would never be fought, that one had to take the risk of such a war and yet go on with civilization as if the risk to it did not exist. And there were some who simply took a class view of the matter and said that atomic energy was itself innocent and would be no threat to humanity were it controlled by representatives of the working class. The danger to humanity came, not from science, but from the capitalists who determined its direction and scope. But these were the very people who controlled the bomb.

Someone in the audience suggested that the United Nations, which was then being organized under American leadership, was perhaps a positive sign that humanity as a whole could indeed take cognizance of its situation and act to insure its survival. But it was very soon clear that few in my audience had any faith in what the United Nations could or would do.

As I have indicated, the views I expressed that night had not been stated either by Sartre or by Heidegger, but they did represent an application of certain existentialist insights to the problem raised by atomic energy. All that Sartre himself wanted to say on the matter appeared in his editorial in the first issue of *Les Temps modernes,* in 1947 I believe, in which he noted that his generation was the very first generation which could envision itself as being the very last on earth. As for Heidegger, in a 1953 lecture he spoke of this era as the era of atomic energy, and he tried to give some justification for calling it that. Why had atomic energy been discovered? What was the condition of its possibility? Causal thinking. Because of "because" there was atomic energy. Yet was not Heidegger himself in these statements yielding to the very kind of thought he was attacking? If you ask "Why?" you are calling for an answer which calls for a "because." I mention these matters here to indicate that I do not myself think that anything has been said directly by Heidegger or Sartre on the subject of atomic energy which is of any

great importance. What I believed though, in '47, and still believe, is that some of their ideas have an application to, and some
qualitative connection with, the kind of questions atomic energy
has raised. Could humanity take up an attitude now that it could
be said to be in a dramatic situation? If not, then it could also
be said that, dramatically at least, humanity did not exist. And
if humanity was in fact dramatically nonexistent, was not this
something worth knowing, even at the cost to us all represented
by the invention of the bomb?

I do not want my readers to imagine, though, that all of the
ensuing discussion was on a serious level. Most of those who had
the habit of coming to meetings of this sort hardly ever came to
hear the speaker out; what interested them was the possibility
that he might let drop some remark to which they could object.
To be sure, there were in the audience Marxists who stated what
they took to be a Marxist view on the matter of the bomb. There
were anarchists for whom the very existence of such a weapon
indicated that there was no government which could be trusted.
And then of course there were any number of odd persons. One
of them, whom I had observed from the platform, was a young
man, Armand Levinger, whom I had become acquainted with
as a co-worker on a government project. He was of Hungarian
origin and of extraordinary intelligence. And he always had an
interesting line on almost any question. But, as he confided to
me, he had little hope of getting anywhere socially. Once he said
to me, "People don't like me for some reason which they do not
know and which I myself cannot find out, and because they do
not like me, they can't bear the fact that I'm so intelligent. What
shall I do?" But he didn't wait for me to suggest anything; he
told me his own plan, which was this: He would take his Ph.D.
at NYU (he was a graduate student there), after which he would
do postgraduate work at Oxford for an additional degree, and
with that achieved he would translate the philosophical writings
of Pierre Duhem, the French philosopher of science. This done,
he would go to the French embassy and ask to be awarded the
Legion of Honor. "Now," said Armand Levinger, "despite the
fact that so many people seem to hate me, with a Ph.D. from
NYU, maybe an Litt.D. from Oxford, and the Legion of Honor

for having translated Duhem, perhaps some obscure college would want me as an instructor. This is all I can look forward to." Well, there he was, in the audience, and after some others had spoken, he raised hand and I recognized him.

Armand Levinger did not disappoint me. He did have something to say, something interesting, and something no one else would say for several decades still, on the topic. He began with a quote from *Prometheus Bound*, some dialogue of Prometheus with the chorus in an early scene. (Levinger didn't say what texts he used. I am relying here on a recently issued translation of the play by James Scully and C.J. Herrington):

PROMETHEUS: Humans used to foresee their own deaths. I ended that.

CHORUS: What cure did you find . . . ?

PROMETHEUS: Blind hopes. I sent blind hopes to settle their hearts.

CHORUS: What a wonderful gift you helped mankind with!

PROMETHEUS: What's more, I gave them fire.

CHORUS: Flare-eyed fire?
Now! In the hands of these beings who live and die?

PROMETHEUS: Yes, and from it they'll learn many skills.

Armand Levinger then went on to connect the disclosure Prometheus made to men about the uses of fire with his having hid from them the certainty that they would die, and also from each one the likely time of his own death. The *revealing* power of science—and technology, too—went hand in hand, according to Aeschylus, with the *veiling* of human mortality (I must interpolate here that in 1975, Hans-Georg Godamer made a very similar point in his essay entitled "The Question of Death," published in *Sens et existense (en hommage à Paul Ricoeur)*. I quote from Godamer's essay: "The non-elucidated question is this: How are the two things linked, the unveiling of technics, the hiding of death . . . there would have to be an implicit connection between knowing and not knowing, a relationship between the thought of death and the thought of progress, a connection certainly dropped by Aeschylus if not explicitly made by him." These remarks by Godamer, the contemporary philosopher of the art of interpretation, are surely more masterfully expressed than the very similar idea Armand Levinger developed at the meeting. Even so, on that evening, Armand actually went further than the German philosopher was able to go almost twenty-five years later, for Armand directly connected the deliverance of Aeschylus on technics and death with the new fact of atomic energy. In this discovery, he said, we have a development, maybe the final development, of all that Prometheus taught us about fire, and probably the final lifting of the curtain hiding the death awaiting us. Ignorance has become knowledge now, but how are the scientists of the Manhattan Project going to convince us to hope blindly against the demonstrated facts? "I suggest to you," said Armand, "that the new discovery does not at all go with our human condition, as the discovery of fire and everything that developed from that discovery technologically until now did."

It was a very striking statement; recalling it I cannot but wonder what may have happened to Armand Levinger since. How had he been able to form those ideas? I suppose it was the sense of catastrophe which was in the air then, as it was probably his sense of the catastrophic which stimulated Velikovsky to see in a new light the ancient texts about fires and floods, which, as he scrutinized them, loomed larger and larger, until they finally occupied the skies. It has been suggested by Heidegger that it is our effort to penetrate the darkness of the future which opens up and illuminates the past . . .

The sense of catastrophe which was so present in the lecture hall that night is of course not always helpful to clear thought or to communicative speech. I had, in the course of my lecture, said something to the effect that the magic of physical science, as revealed by the new discovery, was a magic of disenchantment, which diminished rather than increased our sense of wonder. Because I had said this, one speaker accused me flatly of supporting magic *against* science. And then a bearded man took the floor and in a droning voice lectured us on the three kinds of magic, a discourse which even had a Communist twist to it: "There are three kinds of magic," he said, "red magic, black magic, and green magic, and three kinds of magicians, red magicians, black magicians, and green magicians, the most authoritative being the red, and after them the black. We shall have an orderly world when the green magicians obey the black magicians and the black magicians obey the red. When William Green [then president of the American Federation of Labor], who is obviously a green magician, obeys John L. Lewis [head of the Miners' Union], who is most certainly a black magician, and John L. Lewis in turn obeys the Communists, who are, of course, red magicians, then we will not have to worry about the atomic bomb." Dwight Macdonald, who was the chairman, had to call the house to order.

≺ Seven ≻
AS PARIS WAS
(1948–1951)

I THOUGHT I knew what I would think of Paris when, on December 24, 1948, I disembarked at Le Havre from the *de Grasse* —one still went to Europe by ship in those days. And on the boat train all the way to Paris, I was still able to construct— without constraints imposed by any real details—the city I had gone abroad to see. But once I was out of the Saint-Lazare station and had my first glimpse (from a cab window) of a Parisian street, my main feeling was one of astonishment: Paris, yes, but not as I had expected it to be. It told me then that it was different from other cities; it had yet to tell me what the difference was.

My friend the late Livio Stecchini, an authority on ancient weights and measures, claimed that when he first came from Europe to New York City, he knew exactly how to get from the Italian line to Times Square, and thus was able to correct an out-of-the-way route opted for by his taxi driver. How was Stecchini able to do this? He said that he had seen enough American films abroad to know how to get around New York City, or at least the Manhattan part of it. But of course, there was something else at work here, too. Our New York City streets run up and down, from left to right and from right to left, making hardly any circuits as they go. "O meandering curves," murmurs Paul Valéry, "you hold secrets of the liar." New York's straight-running streets do not hold such secrets, and the streets of European cities, of Paris especially, do. But it was not only the layout of Paris that surprised me in 1948. It was also the color and oddity of its shops and signs, its comfortably graying nineteenth-century architecture, and profound mixture of places for business and places to live in. (A blessed mixture, that which in our country the shopping malls are now threatening to rid us of forever!) All of this cannot of course convey the novelty Paris may have for one who has not already visited there. What, besides its beauty, makes Paris strange? Perhaps it retains the effects on it of those who lived there in times past. But other old cities, some of them beautiful, do not strike us as strange. Maybe Paris is strange in that it tries to inform you of itself (it did me) like the character in Jean Giraudoux's play who comes forward saying, "I am Irene; I adore the beautiful; I detest the ugly." What would Paris say finally?

It did not say much on December 24, 1948 (it was cold, then, and only half lighted), but I was determined to remain abroad until I had heard it out.

An American at that time enjoyed all kinds of advantages in France. Just by being an American you were entitled to a certain amount of gasoline, even if you did not drive, and you could sell this to the French, whose gas was rationed. Moreover, the dollar was very strong in 1948 and seldom exchanged itself into European currencies without some gain for you. And prices seemed to have some relation to what you were able to spend, rather than the other way around. I think I never paid more than a dollar a day for a room in any of the hotels I stayed in.

One thing that makes Paris different I did grasp, if not right away, yet fairly soon. Most cities let you know that unless you are already acquainted with persons there, you are going to spend a good deal of time alone. Visitors to London in the nineteenth century who were not acquainted there have testified to the coldness of the city and the distantness of its inhabitants, and visitors to New York City in our own century, most especially in recent times, have told of their sense of alienation and separateness from the life around them. Although of New York City one can certainly say this: One tends to become part of any crowd that one is in, but in this becoming part of something wider there is hardly room for a personal relationship, what you feel is merely the glow of some nameless union. But Paris tells everyone who enters it that he or she will meet other persons there. It is a city that must have been designed for meeting others; in Paris there will always be rendezvous. During the late forties not to know anyone was almost better than to have acquaintances on arriving. For you were going to get acquainted there no matter what, if not by your own efforts then by some chance, which in this particular city had taken on the power of design.

As it happens, in 1948 I was well acquainted with a few Parisians, some famous. I knew the painter, Jean Hélion; I had met Jean-Paul Sartre, Simone de Beauvior, the philosopher Jean Wahl, Albert Camus, and the composer, conductor, and enthusiast for Schönberg's twelve-tone music, René Liebowitz; I had met them all in New York City. Also in Paris there was André Breton, whom I had worked with in New York on *VVV*. But after his denunciation of Matta, I did not expect to have friendly relations with Breton. So I did not look him up though I had his address on the rue Fontaine. And in fact, I ran into him one day while I was walking with Matta, and when I noted that he was not going to greet Matta, I decided not to nod to him. So that was the end of our relations.

In addition to the French artists and writers I had met in America, there were then in Paris personal friends from New York City who had given America up, perhaps for good. For this was a possible option in 1948. Among those who had taken it up were my good friends Nicola and Miriam Chiaromonte, who then believed it was spiritually (politically?) necessary to leave New York City and go to live in Paris. By coming there myself I gave them an extra reason for liking me, and soon Nicola took me to see Andrea Caffi, of whom he had told me so much and some of whose articles I knew from Dwight Macdonald's *Politics*. About Caffi I'll have much more to say presently, but since I cannot speak at length of him here, let me repeat just one remark he made to me about Paris when I met him. "I've never been in New York City," he said (after humming—he thought this would please me—the tune of "Home, Sweet Home"), "but

161

I've lived in most of the great cities of Europe, and I don't think there's another city at whose heart there is anything like Saint-Germain-des-Prés." In fact, one felt in 1948 that Saint-Germain-des-Prés was the heart of Paris, though I doubt that anyone could have that feeling today.

A short time after I arrived, I had the luck to be invited by a French family to a New Year's Eve dinner. There I met a number of people who formed what my friend Joseph Frank (the literary critic and biographer of Dostoevsky) and his wife Marguerite call "the group," a circle they still rejoin whenever they visit Paris. Among "the group" were Pierre Andler, René Chenon, his sister Pauline, her husband Gaston Louis Roux, and the physicist, Georges Ambrosino.

Zeno—this is what Ambrosino was called in the "group"—was its natural leader and dictator. In fact he boasted of being the group's tyrant, and those he tyrannized over boasted of his acts of tyranny. A happy despotism, in which it was very hard, in the atmosphere of Paris at that time, to talk about principles of democracy.

I still remember that first New Year's Eve dinner. It was given by the Rouxs in their apartment, which amounted to two rooms, one quite large, on the *impasse* Ronsin, right across from Brancusi's studio. The Rouxs were by no means affluent. Gaston Louis, a painter, eked out a living by reading Racine, Corneille, and Hugo to the blind, which, however expertly done—and Gaston Louis's readings were admired by all his friends—was not especially well paid. Nevertheless there were some thirty persons to dinner that night, and I too was invited, if only for the reason that I had taken the trouble to cross the Atlantic to come to Paris. (I was told at dinner that the others would all like to cross the ocean in the opposite direction just to see the Bronx.) Anyway, there were some fifteen courses for that New Year's dinner, white and red wines, and then at least one glass of champagne for everyone.

Which reminds me that when in 1947 I took Simone de Beauvoir, whom I had just met, to a party in uptown Manhattan along with some other friends, one of them as we left said something against our host, and Simone remarked, "Now I know I'm in Manhattan." But can one judge the life of a city by what happens at a party there, or just after it? In any case, I shall describe two other parties I went to in Paris, striking enough to remain in memory.

Almost two years after that New Year's Eve affair, another dinner in that same apartment of the Rouxs. Once again, thirty or more persons at the table, some fifteen courses, white and red wines, and then some champagne for each of us. And now I must tell the occasion. One of the Rouxs' acquaintances had requested the dinner just to make public to his intimates that he was having a love affair with the wife of a friend—as it happens, his best and closest friend. The wife and her husband had both been invited. So the occasion was special. The one who had requested the dinner and was to introduce all of us to his new mistress arrived with his friend's wife, and the friend—that best and closest of friends—arrived right afterwards, dramatically alone, and immediately caught the attention of all the women present by his air of loneliness, melancholy, and selfmockery. I shall refer to the husband as M. and to the lover as P., no doubt influenced here by Peter Strawson's use of these letters to stand for mental and physical predicates. P., the lover, looked quite happy, though somewhat dulled by happiness. And he did not contribute much to the general talk. In this department, M., unhappy and alone, took charge. His wit was irrepressible. He flirted with the others' wives. He did imitations of France's political leaders and pundits: Mendès-France, de Gaulle, François Mauriac, Jean-Paul Sartre. He got up on the table and harangued us. He urged us not to be so solemn, also not to be too happy. Why didn't someone say something that would interest him? Was he going to exhaust himself just to keep us laughing? Alberto Giacometti, who was used to dominating such evenings by his conversation, tried once or twice to say something, but M. would not allow him to, interrupted him, mocked him, and took away the attention of the other guests. The married women at that table had eyes only for M. I think I've never watched a man publicly indicate so great an unhappiness, while giving so many people pleasure. As for P., the whole affair was a complete fiasco. M. had achieved this quite remarkable result: after a certain point, no one even knew that P. was there.

I have been at wonderful parties in Manhattan and in

Rome, but there is something quite special about Parisian affairs. Perhaps it is that when Parisians come together to enjoy themselves the matter is more serious. Their pleasure requirements are stricter and must be satisfied in a more absolute way. Members of the "group" held that a party was something to which one should go with the hope, and maybe even the expectation, of having a shattering experience of some sort. What did they mean by a "shattering" experience? This was the response: One could not, of course, invite sworn enemies to a party. This would be simply vulgar. You invited people to enjoy themselves, and not to fight. But on the other hand, a party at which life-long friends publicly broke off relations would always be remembered . . . In any case, the "group" made too many requirements of their own social affairs, which were often quite dull, and sometimes even painful. There is such a thing as wanting to enjoy oneself too much . . .

But there is another party I must describe, which as a matter of fact was an especially painful one. As it happens this was not put on by any member of the "group," but by a sort of fellow traveler of theirs, an enchanting Parisian blonde who owned a great apartment she had gained in the very best way, by personal heroism during the resistance. Madame Françoise, I shall call her. Short of stature, but sturdily built, blue-eyed and *ravissante*, vivid with energy and appetite, she was then living with a young Arab she had snatched from a street career in crime and drugs, a quite handsome boy of about eighteen whom I shall call Bébé. Two or three generations ago there was the famous Bébé of Montparnasse; the Bébé of my story belonged to Saint-Germain-des-Prés. We went to dinner, and at the table Madame Françoise flirted outrageously with all the males there, including a handsome and possibly overcivilized Englishman of some wealth, who was hoping to become a Labour party MP. Bébé at once became quite drunk and had evidently made up his mind to act with decision. He took up a bottle of scotch, smashed it against the wall, breaking it in half, and then turned towards the guest nearest him, extending the jagged end of the bottle close to the other's face, and said: "Now better be honest." "Do you mean I'm not?" the guest asked. Bébé nodded and began to circle the table with the bottle extended and instructions to all of us to better be honest. Each guest was threatened in turn with mutilation if he did not satisfy Bébé. Time went by, but slowly, our fears holding it back, and there seemed to be no way of dissuading Bébé from his intimidation of us. I tried to argue with him, but it was quite useless. Could he have been overpowered? He was a big strong kid and armed with a dangerous weapon. One had to risk mutilation to disarm him! I whispered to the hostess, Madame Françoise, "Shall I try to take him out?" "No," she said, "I'm afraid of what might happen." So we sat there, while he asked again and again of each of us, "Are you honest?" which nobody was or could be under the threat of his broken bottle. And then the Englishman said to Bébé rather sweetly, "I haven't been honest so far, but I want to be now," and whispered something in his ear. Bébé at once set the bottle down on the table, and the two left the apartment arm in arm. The Englishman had indeed been honest. He had wanted to take Bébé home, and told him so.

One of the persons I visited in Paris was the philosopher, Jean Wahl, whom I had met on Long Island during the summer of 1944, when Paris was being retaken by the Allied armies. I was ill that summer, suffering again from a collapsed lung, confined to bed, and Robert Motherwell one day dropped in with the philosopher, slight, dark, diminutive, with blue eyes that pierced and pierced. He came after that every morning for breakfast, and I had to marvel at his eating habits, for he loved cornflakes without milk or cream, gobbling them down like popcorn. We became close friends almost at once.

In Paris, Wahl introduced me to Lucien Goldmann, who was then writing *Le Dieu caché (The Hidden God)*. He became my landlord, renting me the first apartment I had in the city. It was a semi-apartment, a room and a half on the famous rue de la Montagne Saint-Geneviève, in a very old stone house up a winding staircase of crumbling stone. Lucien charged me something like four dollars a month for the place. He was the owner of several other apartments too, which he rented, and he watched over his tenants. One day he woke me up early in the morning and asked me to get dressed and hurry with him to help him break down the door of another one of his apartments, on the rue Bonaparte, where he was afraid his tenant might have committed suicide. "If we break in and she's still breathing," he said, "we may save her." Who was the tenant? An American girl, as a matter of fact, whom I had known in Greenwich Village, and whom Lucien described as "very interesting." Why did he think she might have committed suicide? "Why shouldn't she?" he said. "She's in love with me." He had been to her place, and she had not answered the bell. I got dressed, we collected Nicola Chiaromonte, and Nicola, showing his usual good sense, suggested that instead of breaking down the door we get a locksmith; this we did. The locksmith opened the door, and we found Lucien's tenant unconscious, got her to a hospital, and saved her for the further torments of continuing love for Lucien.

Wahl had told me about Goldmann: He's very nice, but whatever you talk about, the name Lukàcs is bound to come up, so I hope that won't put you off. Well the name Lukàcs did come up, of course, in most of the conversations I had with Lucien. He had made himself the personal representative in Paris of Lukàcs's type of Marxism, and he was very explicit as to one of the reasons for his having done this. "When one goes into the Café de Flore," he said, "one must stand for something. One can't just walk in, flash white teeth and say, 'I'm Herbert, the American.' "

In the two-and-a-half or three years I lived in Paris, I think I was able to explore every part of the city. From the rue de la Montagne Saint-Genéviève I went to the Hôtel de L'Academie on the rue des Saint-Pères, where Andrea Caffi lodged, and for almost a year I saw him almost every day at lunch and dinner. But then I moved to an apartment on the rue Ranlagh and then to another on the rue Saint-Jacques, and I also stayed for a time on the rue des Augustins, near the Bourse. And for one summer I occupied Harold Kaplan's fine apartment on the boulevard Montparnasse. So I did get to know Paris rather well.

DAILY life in Paris calls to mind the French attitude towards money, which most Americans I think misunderstand. One often hears it said of the French that they are miserly, whereas they themselves say, using an expression I find capital in its precision, that they are merely *regardant*, which is to say, "scruitinizing" or "aware" of what they spend. Here I am reminded of something Merleau-Ponty called to my attention. According to Hegel, no one can be normal about money, or take an utterly rational attitude towards it. Money is that, according to the German philosopher, which abnormalizes. According to Merleau, it was from this insight that Simmel deduced some of the most interesting observations in his great book *The Philosophy of Money*. But if we think merely of the persons we have known, do we not find that those who are careful about money are too careful, and those who are careless much too careless? It is very hard to find in relation to money that point between the extremes which, according to Aristotle, would express a rational attitude. Probably one cannot arrive at a mean point in a natural way, and it is only wisdom then to recognize the need for artifice. The French have cultivated the habit of being *regardant*, that is, spontaneously methodical in matters involving money. This is the attitude Americans often misunderstand.

I want to give one example. A French friend of mine, René Chenon, had offered me an apartment while I was living at the Hôtel de l'Academie. He was not then using this apartment himself, and the rent was practically nonexistent, amounting to little more than two dollars a month, and I was paying a dollar a day at my hotel. On the other hand, I wasn't quite ready to leave the hotel. I think I enjoyed Caffi's conversation at lunch and dinner too much, and also I had a rather large debt at the hotel, which I was not then able to make good. And then something else came up. A Spanish friend of mine, the painter, Juan F., had come to Paris from New York, and he was looking for a studio. His intention was to stay for a couple of months, and so I suggested the apartment which Chenon had offered me. Chenon agreed to this, and Juan took over the apartment. Gifted at carpentry, he built various bookshelves, alcoves, a table, and other furnishings, which made the whole place more attractive. Finally his two months were up and Juan was ready to go back to the United States. He thanked me for letting him have the place and told me he would regard the furniture he had made for it as a small repayment for my kindness to him. But things were not so simple. As Chenon explained the difficulty, if I moved into his place after someone else had occupied it for only two months' time, the landlord might suspect that Chenon was subletting it at a profit, and this might cost him the apartment. What could we do? "This is what I suggest," said Chenon, "If you have a girlfriend with an apartment, she can move into my place and you might take hers." And he explained that if a woman moved into his place the landlord would assume she was his mistress, and of course he had some right to sublet his place just as long as sex was involved. I told my friend D. of Chenon's proposition. She liked the apartment, and agreed to switch hers for mine, which we did, I taking her place on the rue Saint-Jacques. There remained the matter of the furnishings which Juan had offered me. For these, D. offered him twenty-five thousand francs, then about a hundred dollars. The painter would not hear of it. Had I not made the place available to him when he had despaired of finding a studio? D. was welcome to the furnishings. She should have them, and for nothing, they were his gift to me. I said to him, "What if you hear that D. and I have quarreled, and that the furniture you made is now benefitting some couple who never did you a favor?" I tossed off the remark as a pleasantry, and never thought twice about it, but before my Spanish friend left for the States, he called D., then comfortably installed in Chenon's apartment and demanded not twenty-five thousand, but fifty thousand francs for the furnishings he had left behind. D., a level-headed Frenchwoman, replied: "I offered you twenty-five thousand francs and that you shall have, but not one franc more." She had analyzed his work and determined that this was exactly what it was worth. So my Spanish friend had risen to generosity and then fallen into cheapness. I do not want to blame him for this, but merely to point out what his weakness was: He depended on his nature. In such matters D. did not depend on hers. She was French, she had a system.

WHAT Lucien Goldmann had indicated about the Café de Flore was true of Paris generally: You could not point to yourself and

say, "I'm so-and-so," and let things go at that. For others would
convert your name into some meaning they found characteristic
of you, or thought should be your raison d'être. They would say
so-and-so is a scholar or so-and-so is a fool. Thus you were forced
to intend certain things even if you hadn't quite meant to, and
this greatly facilitated criticism of you, for if you were trying to
express a definite attitude, any failure to do so could be immediately noted. In the small community of Saint-Germaine-des-
Prés, at the end of the forties and in the early fifties, one lived
in a kind of moral mirror in which one saw one's own actions
and also the manner in which others responded to these actions.
I must say all this made life much more strenuous but also much
more bracing. You were always on the stage, always in the front
of the footlights, and you never knew when the audience—and
there always was one—might not become hostile. Your life was
not just something to be lived; more precisely, it was something
to be performed, and you had all the anxieties about your performance that actors have in new roles. One of the first things
Jean Wahl asked me was: "When are you going to see people, at
night or during the day? Because you have to have some time for
work." He added that Malraux saw people at night *and* in the
daytime and nevertheless found time to work. Then he said,
"But maybe he doesn't sleep." In any case, he was suggesting
that I decide what audience I preferred to appear before, the
matinée audience, or the night crowd. With which group would
I be at my best? I chose the morning for solitary work, lunch and
after lunch to be with others.

Nowadays I find a moral disregard for others, which sets
the tone for social relations in American cities, somewhat stulti-
fying. One has a feeling that no one is looked at by anyone else.
In any case, hardly anyone is looked at *morally,* for I am sure that
some are looked at or over with sexual interest. In Buffalo,
Rochester, Syracuse, Newburgh, New Rochelle, Yonkers, as in
New York City, one closes one's eyes, morally speaking, when
one goes out in public. But Paris was a city in which one opened
them wide. When you were asked by a friend *"Qu'est ce que tu
deviens, mon cher,"* you had to account for what you had done
with yourself since the last time that friend had seen you. In

accounting you also judged, and had to judge what you were becoming.

One day the bookshops of Saint-Germaine-des-Prés highlighted a very expensive edition of *La Chasse spirituelle*, the poem by Rimbaud which until then everyone assumed had been destroyed by the wife of Paul Verlaine. Who would not want to read *La Chasse spirituelle*, which might very well have been Rimbaud's masterpiece? Now one could: There it was, in chi-chi type and on expensive paper, in all the bookshops. And soon the bookshops were crowded with buyers. But the very next day *Combat* featured a powerful article by André Breton which attacked the poem as an impudent forgery. Was it a forgery? This was the main topic of discussion around Saint-Germain-des-Prés. The young surrealist poet Henri Pichette, whose *Apoèmes (Nonpoems)* has just been released, wanted to discuss the matter at lunch with me and I told him to meet me at the Hôtel de l'Academie. Pichette considered himself an authority on Rimbaud and in fact he carried with him five fountain pens, each with a different colored ink, so that he could write his own poems in the colors Rimbaud had prescribed for the vowels: a, black; e, white; i, red; u, green; o, blue! Against this tactic of Pichette's it was pointed out that Rimbaud himself never possessed five pens, and had written his sonnet on the vowels in ink of just one color. Anyway, at lunch Pichette declared roundly that anyone who denied that the poem in the bookshops was by Rimbaud was also saying that poetry was *de la merde*. We argued but our conversation settled nothing. And that very evening, the Rimbaud experts gathered in a room provided by Lipp's, the Alsatian restaurant on boulevard Saint-Germain, and after much wrangling two persons first charged that the poem was forged and then confessed to having committed the forgery themselves, after which they were unmasked as liars! It turned out that the true author of the forgery, known for other such forgeries, was Pascal Pia, and after this even Pichette admitted that anyone with a sophisticated understanding of French verse could have composed the disputed version of *La Chasse spirituelle*, which soon disappeared from the *vitrines*. In any case, the event was one which could only have taken place in Paris, and something of this sort did take place in Paris of that period fairly often. It was as if the Parisians contrived these events out of the fear that whole weeks might go by without anything worth noticing.

Perhaps it was the thought of producing a notable event—notable in the conversation of Parisians if not in the history of France—which led a noblewoman of nineteenth-century Paris to offer herself to the poet who most pleased her with verses of his on shit, she being the judge. As it happens, three poets competed for her—and two were the greatest poets of the country, Charles Baudelaire and Victor Hugo. The third poet may well have been Théophile Gautier, but of this I'm not quite sure. Hugo was the winner, and from the poems I read I think he won deservedly. In the poem he composed—a sonnet, as I remember—he was able to make an attractive showpiece of the substance we regularly hide from others and from ourselves: He was able to lift it onto a plane that is somehow proper for it, but only, of course, in his rhetoric. An account of the contest, giving the name of the noblewoman and the text of the three poems may be found today in a slender volume at the Bibliotèque Nationale in Paris, and only there. For these poems do not appear in the "complete" Pléiade editions of Gautier, Baudelaire, or Hugo. Evidently the French government intervened, perhaps finding it unwise to celebrate this victory of the idealizing mind over the unfailing—and necessarily submitted to—offensiveness of matter . . .

Like its liveliness, the beauty of Paris is something you never feel to be just a subjective impression. It is something you sense is there for others to be aware of, even as you are. This characteristic of being "given" not just for you but also for others is very seldom true of those traits, in objects or in persons, which induce us to call them "beautiful," and to say this as if we were doing something more valid than expressing a personal taste. And when you have feelings of this order, it is very hard to feel proprietorship. Probably very beautiful women feel they cannot be possessed by any one man, and I have heard it said of Greta Garbo, for instance, that she often performed symbolic acts to indicate that she was not the possession of the one she was intimate with. I remember hearing the head of the Parisian section of UNESCO say of Henry Miller: "When I discovered Miller I had the choice of giving him to the world or keeping him for myself." No, Monsieur Maheu, I do not think you had that choice. You must yourself have felt when you read Henry Miller's writings that they could not possibly have been intended for your pleasure alone. . . . The beauty of Paris, then, not intended just for those who are aware of it today, or who were aware of it in the early fifties, or in past centuries, was and is a stabilizing, tranquilizing, and distancing aspect of the city's life, telling us that the city will continue to be beautiful, and for persons very different from ourselves.

In 1951, Lawrence Vail, the American expatriate, invited me to his place in Mégève. (Vail was a contemporary of Hemingway and Fitzgerald. His novel, *Piri and I*, now forgotten, was published in 1923, in the same decade which saw *The Sun Also Rises* and *The Great Gatsby* win world fame.) When Vail and I returned to Paris together, we passed through Geneva and spent the night there, and Vail took me to a Geneva night club. At midnight a number of naked women appeared, and the guests were expected to ask them to dance and then perhaps invite them out. We found two girls we thought we might like, danced with them, plied them with champagne, and then quite disappointed them by leaving the club. Now it was not that our intentions had been insufficiently uxurious. The fact was that the atmosphere in the club was so boring as to make an adventure of any kind unthinkable. There was little conversation, little applause when the girls came on, and no one showed enthusiasm for the orchestra, which played American jazz as if it were an ultra-dull Swiss invention. Had the guests taken aspirin before coming, like the Perseus of Jules Laforgue when he went to fight the Gorgon? That this might have occurred was suggested to Vail by the remark of one of the waiters that the maker of aspirin, Monsieur Bayer himself, was in the club then. Well, we had not taken aspirin, and we were as passive as everyone else, and just as reduced as they to expecting the expected. When, after mid-

night, one of the naked girls clapped over her head a grinning
death mask and did an absurd dance, we said goodnight to our
new acquaintances and took our departure. But six months
later, back in Paris, walking through Montmartre one night, I
stopped in front of a nightclub there, and saw in the window the
photograph of a body, and of a face, too, with which I was not
unacquainted. This was the very girl I had danced with that
night in Geneva! But now on this other night I was in Montmartre. A nightclub there is not at all like one in Geneva . . .

Thus it will be seen that a woman could have a certain effect
in Paris when aided only by her being there, and without such
help as the city was always able to provide in the way of clothes.
That help must have been considerable in the nineteenth century, when Baudelaire could maintain that a woman's dress is
an essential part of her. In one of his beautiful pieces on Constantine Guys, we read this of Woman: She ". . . is a total
harmony, not only in her postures and in the movements of her
limbs, but also by virtue of the laces, the muslins, the vast and
iridescent clouds of stuffs with which she envelops herself."
Thus accoutred, he writes, she could be for men "the source of
their liveliest and . . . of their most lasting joys." We now know
that women's dress was to change from what it was in the Paris
of 1950 and the attitudes of men towards women also changed
with the modernization of France, of which the book of Simone
de Beauvoir, *The Second Sex*, which ran monthly in *Les Temps
modernes* in 1950, can be seen to have played a fundamental part.

In Saint-Germain-des-Prés, these were the most respected individuals: Jean-Paul Sartre first of all, for his writings, his editorship of *Les Temps modernes*, and his continuing interest in
political and moral problems; Merleau-Ponty was respected just
as much as a mind, but perhaps less as a person; and there were
some who thought Alexander Koyré, the Russian savant, wiser
than either of the French philosophers. Koyré it was who was
referred to, and often, as a sage. And there was a very great
interest in and admiration for the Russian-born Hegelian, Alexander Kojève, whom Roger Caillois called "the cleverest man in

Paris," and whose *Introduction to the Reading of Hegel*, given originally as a course at the École des Hautes Études, was probably
the original impetus to the French existentialism of Merleau-
Ponty and Sartre, who had followed Kojève's lectures. When I
met Georges Bataille, he announced to me, so that there should
be no misunderstanding on this point: "I am a disciple of
Kojève." I was told by people personally acquainted with the
philosopher that he lied invariably and on principle. He never
told the truth, but his were not the lies of the weakling who has
something to hide, but those of a strong-minded man who wants
to replace that which is (and has no other attraction than that
it is) with that which is not. Such was the manner in which
admirers of Kojève interpreted his regular and habitual false-
hoods, but all agreed that it was very difficult to have relations
with him because of his lying. I notice in one of his footnotes
to his *Introduction to the Reading of Hegel* a remark to the effect
that the Soviet propaganda against the United States is very
likely to succeed *because* it is false, and, on the other hand,
American propaganda against the Soviet Union is very likely to
fail *for the very reason* that it is true to the main facts. And all this
seems to show a conviction in Kojève, certainly strange in a
philosopher, that there is a power in lying unmatched by any
force in truth. I might add here that I've been told by Professor
Stanley Rosen, the American philosopher who has written interestingly on Hegel, that Kojève, who became an adviser on
economic questions to the French government, and in fact conceived the very plan which Schuman carried out, and which
bears the latter's name, is the one who was most responsible for
General de Gaulle's determination, when president of France,
to keep England out of the Common Market. Apparently what
Kojève told de Gaulle was that the British would represent
American interests in the Common Market; but the actual motivation of Kojève, according to Professor Rosen, was something
quite different. His real animus was directed not at the British
politicians, nor at the Americans he claimed to de Gaulle they
represented; what he was really against was British philosophy,
especially as represented by those British theorists who had
taken their cue from Wittgenstein. These British writers on

philosophy, Ryle, Austin, and Strawson, were having an enormous influence on American philosophy students, who without
this influence might have been open to the ideas of Hegel. So
it was not the political influence of America on England that
Kojève was so much against; what bothered him was the philo-
sophic influence of England on America. And to get even with
the British philosophers, he managed to get de Gaulle to keep
the British out of the Common Market!

Then there was Jean Wahl, who kept intellectual matters
lively at the *Colloques philosophiques* he chaired regularly in Saint-
Germain-des-Prés. There was Albert Camus, whom everyone
admired for his style and temperament, and there were David
Rousset and Emanuel Levinas, who had spent the war years as
prisoners in Buchenwald. There was Alberto Giacometti, admired for his art, his intellectual honesty, and also for the way
he dramatized a style of simplicity in morals and manners; and
there was Nicola Chiaromonte, whose intelligence, personal
warmth, and the transcendental turn he was able to give almost
any kind of conversation made him sought after by almost everyone. And of course there were many others whom I haven't
mentioned who formed part of the international community
that held the stage in the postwar years in Saint-Germain-des-
Prés.

BUT to me the person who represented the city of Paris as it had
been over the centuries and as I found it at the end of 1948, was
a Russian-born Italian savant, the very learned and most interesting Andrea Caffi, whom Nicola Chiaromonte had brought me
to see when I first arrived. Caffi was then in his middle sixties,
fairly tall, slenderly built, with greying hair and features that
did not proclaim him the outstanding personality he was. For
one thing, Caffi had a slightly bulbous nose, which evidently did
not please him. But when he spoke, his features were often
transfigured by intellectual exultation, so that he might have
been thought beautiful; on the other hand, he could never be
taken to be good-looking. Now had Caffi been given the choice
between occasional beauty and regular good looks, he would no

175

doubt have chosen the latter, but when you got to know him well, as I did, you were glad that the choice had not been up to him. He was unfailingly courteous, though he could be cruel in argument. I was of course a partisan of Caffi, even before I met him, both from what Chiaromonte had told me of him and from pieces of his I had read in *Politics*. And I was very taken with him on our very first meeting. Jean Wahl, to whom I had shown a couple of Caffi's pieces, and to whose apartment I brought Caffi one day for lunch, said of him, in the style he had of saying something definite, yet leaving it to you to make up your own mind: "He's either a very wise man or a great sophist." There was of course something of the wise man and of the sophist in Caffi, and one could never be sure which it was whose voice one heard. Why should one have been sure? I remember talking about Nietszche with Caffi, and at one point he began to insist that there was much about the Greeks which Nietszche had not understood at all. "What Nietszche never understood about the Greeks," said Caffi, "was their *duplicity.*" And he meant this as praise for the Greeks and against the German thinker.

But here I myself do not want to be misunderstood. Caffi was a man of the most extreme sophistication, morally and intellectually, but he did have a moral position, one which he held to with a fair consistency. As a matter of fact a moral position was required of everyone in the Paris of the fifties, no doubt because of the war and the occupation. Few persons in the atmosphere of that time dared to justify themselves in purely aesthetic terms. Perhaps the only one who did was Jean Genet, who had actually committed as well as defended crimes. And even he was not exactly an aesthete. Certainly he was no Oscar Wilde, thinking that what one did was of less significance than the manner in which it could be described. Genet was *morally* in favor of crime, not just aesthetically, and in this way he too expressed the prejudice for the moral which describes the fifties atmosphere in Paris.

Caffi's moral position can be glimpsed rather than stated from the description I would give of his regular behavior, which was to try to create around him, among those persons who sought him out, the kind of social atmosphere he would have

176

liked to see prevalent throughout society. The creation of a
social nexus through personal friendliness, this was the moral
principle to which I think Caffi was committed and which, in
all my dealings with him, he seldom departed from or trans-
gressed. Of course, if one wanted to argue that this is not exactly
a moral position, one can: One might even argue that as a moral
stance it was probably derived from a political position. Caffi
was for a politics of civilization against anything which he regarded or could regard as a politics of barbarism. All the same,
when it came to action—even actions that involved self-sacrifice,
and Caffi could be very generous and self-sacrificing—the aim
was never the good of one's own soul or merely some good to
another person one liked, but in addition, a further advance of
sociability within the surrounding darkness. Of course aesthetic
feeling has a lot to do with this, but aesthetic feeling on the part
of a man with political perspectives and a vast knowledge of
history. To me, Caffi represented, and tried in his own way to
reestablish, the kind of atmosphere that may have prevailed in
the circles of atheists and libertines in the seventeenth century,
and the salons of the *philosophes* in the eighteenth. He stood for
all those places, some historically notable, where men came
together and enjoyed themselves, hiding their "hateful" egos
behind the mask of good manners and of "pure" ideas. Insofar
as these notions related to politics, he could write:

> Here politics clearly appears as a substitute for—often a
> parody of—the social, that is, of the spontaneous commu-
> nion among men conscious of their destiny; the reality of
> which such terms as "civilization," "dignity," "equality,"
> "fraternity," "politeness" can only indicate roughly. . . .
> Now one cannot deny that in the idea of "socialism," there
> is the idea of "society." Ever since its remote beginnings, in
> the conception of the great thinkers as well as in the feelings
> of oppressed communities, "socialism" has above all meant
> attaching a preeminent importance to the person who lives
> in a network of spontaneous, equalitarian, and "civil" social
> relations: Only for such a person, in fact, can the problems
> of justice and happiness have meaning. . . . [From *A Critique
> of Violence*]

Basic to Caffi's conception of society was the notion that it was the creation of the few—a view unusual in a man of socialist political convictions. Curiously enough, I find the expression of a similar conviction in the novels of Henry James, for whom, of course, society was something created not only by the few but *for* the few. In his novels, society is not something that has a tangible physical existence independent of the thoughts, feelings, and moral impulses of his characters. Similarly for Caffi, society was fundamentally what corresponded to the sociable intentions—worldly and spiritual, at the same time—of a few individuals. As against the historians, the economists, and also the sociologists, the American novelist and the European socialist, the first in his novels, the second in his journalism but also in his conversation, projected the notion that true society *exists only at moments*, and mainly at inspired moments; it is produced by our sensibilities, not by the actions of industrialists, bankers, and politicians.

But on the other hand one can find the very contrary assertions by Caffi in his writings, as for example in the following passage, in which he declares his willingness to give up the culture of the few for the well-being of the many:

> From my youth on, I think I have not been lacking in feeling for the "heights of metaphysics" or for the "sublime" that may be found in music, painting, and poetry. . . . I must confess that it was often with a feeling of liberation and even of purification that I would step from the circle of some brilliant, super-refined intellects . . . in order to meet with some rough, and at times even coarse comrades to organize a demonstration that may well have been naive, or to compose with them an appeal to strikers put together out of Marxist clichés. . . . I will go further: I've always thought that if this kind of solidarity required that I renounce all the masterworks of philosophy and art I would not have hesitated for a single moment.

From this quotation it will be seen that while Caffi did indeed have a moral position, it was certainly not without antinomies; of these he was completely aware; in fact his thought often consisted in making them explicit, in pointing them up.

Caffi's training had been in historical studies. Simmel had been his teacher in Berlin—and so most of his ideas were either about history or had reference to it. And his notion of history itself was a highly individual one. He thought history to be ". . . the memory of the past, in even its most futile aspects."

With such a view of history he allowed himself to make moral, or perhaps cultural judgments of whole centuries. For instance, one of his most deeply held views was that the nineteenth century had been wrong and the eighteenth century had been right. Now we shall have to look at this notion a little more closely, to see what it does and what it does not mean.

Certainly Caffi did not mean that if we were to take four outstanding intellectual figures of the eighteenth century, like Swift, Voltaire, Sam Johnson, and Goethe, they would outweigh, let us say, in intellectual grasp and cultural significance, Marx, Kierkegaard, Flaubert, and Tolstoy. No, this is not what he meant at all. He did not mean that there was more genius in the eighteenth century than in the nineteenth. In fact the opposite was probably the case. What he had in mind was rather the kind of observation made by the essayist E. M. Cioran, who remarked to me many years ago that the style (in the French language) of third-rate writers of the eighteenth century was superior to the style of nineteenth-century writers ranked one notch above them, and oftentimes to that of many of the writers of the nineteenth century we still consider first rate. But of course Caffi was aiming at something more than a judgment of comparative style. It was the spirit of the eighteenth century which he endorsed and the spirit of the nineteenth century he criticized. And what he approved of in the eighteenth century was the readiness to seek spontaneity in sociable relations with others. (The great exception here was Jean Jacques Rousseau, who sought spontaneity in isolation from others, and it was Rousseau whom Caffi disliked.) For Caffi, the nineteenth century had followed the lead of Rousseau in a flight from the sociable, which was finally a flight from spontaneity. (I must note here that D.H. Lawrence, in his remarkable *Studies of Classic American Literature*, has suggested that those Europeans who migrated to America were fleeing the society and spontaneity possible on the old continent. It is certainly interesting to think that men made the long, hazardous trip over the Atlantic to America partly in order not to be spontaneous. We are still living with the consequence of this fact.)

In what sense can one reasonably say that the eighteenth century was right and the nineteenth century wrong? In the sense that the eighteenth century was more rationalistic than the nineteenth? But in fact, the irrationalists of the nineteenth century, Schopenhauer and Nietszche and Kierkegaard, let us say, defeated the rationalists of that century in the arguments between them. So that any rationalism of the twentieth century has had to be modified so as to take account of the insights of precisely Nietzsche, Schopenhauer, and Kierkegaard. Or, to put the matter somewhat differently, the eighteenth century produced the enlightenment and the nineteenth the counterenlightenment. Does being for the eighteenth century against the nineteenth mean being for the enlightenment and against the counterenlightenment? Now Caffi was certainly for the enlightenment, and he tried to find enlightenment positions in all the nineteenth century writers he most admired, for example, in Tolstoy, and in Flaubert. But on the other hand he too recognized the inadmissibility of the kind of rationalism the eighteenth century had made its own, and as the counterenlightenment expressed itself in Tolstoy's commitment to religion, and in Flaubert's commitment to the religion of art, in Caffi this became a predilection for the mythological, of which he made a cult. So that he could even go so far as to assert that societies could be judged as civilized or barbarous in terms of the importance they accorded to myth—certainly a far cry from judging societies as civilized or barbarous in terms of the importance they accorded to reason! I remember hearing a French intellectual say that the myths of Plato were "for the imbeciles." Caffi had no patience with such a rationalism, classifying it with the "antimythological DDT" of Saint Thomas's thinking, and with the efforts of Hegel to encircle all past mythologies within "the barbed wire of his dialectic."

So the eighteenth century was right, but not for its rationalism, which Caffi distinguished from its enthusiasm for reason. Was it right then for its taste, its manners, its gentility? For there were many more gentlemen in the eighteenth century than in the nineteenth. Or perhaps it could be called right because of its democratic outlook—the democratic outlook of its aristocrats? And just what was an aristocrat? Here was Caffi's definition: "A man of excellent understanding, whom you have to know for a long time to realize that he understands anything."

What made the eighteenth century right as against the nineteenth century and our own, was the importance it recognized in the man of good manners who might also be talented. The nineteenth century had chosen to admire instead the man of talent, whatever his manners, however badly he had been brought up. Caffi's position on the eighteenth century as against the nineteenth came down to supporting the gentleman against the genius, though the gentleman could sometimes be a genius, as was the case with Voltaire. On that famous encounter of Beethoven and Goethe—it was like a meeting of the eighteenth and the nineteenth centuries—Beethoven playing for the German poet and Goethe in accordance with the conventions of the period respectfully wiping a tear from his eye, which did not please the musician in the least—Caffi sided completely with Goethe. Our century of course has chosen to side with Beethoven.

What made the gentleman so important was, for Caffi, his sociability; he it was who made society enjoyable, and a truly civilized life possible. The genius could be unsociable or even antisocial, and so, however desirable in his special sphere, he hardly provided a basis or outlook for any general thinking about values. The eighteenth century had understood this very well. Had not Swift said that the most undesirable of all persons were the poets, and the most uncivilized? For they would only talk about those matters of which they were the most, and the rest of the company the least, informed.

The eighteenth century, if not always right in its taste, was right in its insistence that taste was important, as was the perception of the limit which defined it. On this matter Caffi could

181

wax eloquent. I remember a discussion we had about Joyce, to whose *Finnegans Wake* Caffi took exception. Joyce was full of the hubris of modernism, he said. "I don't object to modernism, but I do to hubris, and this aspect of modernism is now being praised on every hand. The hubris possible to every novel idea or endeavor is urged on the young rather than warned against." I must say I thought Caffi was completely right about this. For it is one thing to admire the great skills of Joyce and Pound and quite another to approve the odd and often unsociable purposes to which these skills were addressed. To make his point against *Finnegan,* and also to show that he was not unaware of its often wonderful qualities, Caffi referred to the story in Herodotus about Cleisthenes, the despot of Sicyon, who had offered his daughter to the suitor who excelled in sporting events; he wanted "the best man he could find in Hellas." All the Greeks who were proud of themselves and their cities came to ask the lady's hand—and, Cleisthenes had them contend in running and wrestling. As it happened, Hippocleides of Athens was favored, both because of his lineage and his manly worth. And he outdid all the other suitors. But then he asked the flute players to play, and began to dance, and danced marvelously indeed, making the most unexpected movements, so unexpected in fact that he was finally disqualified, not for being lacking in talent, but for being too good. "You have danced yourself out of your marriage," said Cleisthenes. For Caffi, Joyce, with *Finnegan,* had disqualified himself not for lack of talent, but for being too good, for exhibiting talents nobody required him to have.

These, then, were Caffi's fundamental values or principles: sociability, manners, reason, and myth, arranged by him into a personal system as I have tried to describe it. Sometimes when we walked around Saint-Germain-des-Prés on summer evenings, and passed Diderot's statue at the corner of rue Odéon, he would say to me: "If we were living in the eighteenth century, do you know what I would suggest doing? I'd say let's drop in on Baron Holbach and maybe Diderot would be there." What conversation he would have had! Actually, Caffi's was conversation at its best. I remember bringing Giacometti to the hotel for lunch. I introduced him to Caffi, and talk began. We drank a good deal of wine at lunch, then had liqueurs, and Giacometti stayed through the afternoon. He also stayed through dinner, and did not leave the table before midnight, so fascinated was he by Caffi's talk, which mainly had to do with his own experiences in Russia, and his judgments of Stalin and of Stalin's policies. Many times after that Giacometti referred to the story Caffi told—I never found out what documents he based it on—of Marshal Tukashevsky's death: of how Stalin had had him sent for, accused him of treason, refused to hear anything the marshal had to say in his defense, ordered him shot on the spot, and then in a rage seized a pistol from one of the KGB men present, and dispatched Tukashevsky himself. Giacometti remarked, "It was wonderful to spend that much time at such fine talk without ever discussing art."

There were others who found Caffi's conversation wonderful: the Italian poet Ungaretti, who came to the Hôtel de l'Academie with the Italy's ambassador to France to ask Caffi's forgiveness for the poet's support of Mussolini under fascism, and Georgio Santillana, who wanted to ask Caffi's aid in translating a text of Heraclitus. Of the Americans who came to the hotel, there was Harold Kaplan, then working for European recovery under the Marshall Plan, and whom Caffi sometimes called *Ka-Plan Marshal*; Joel Carmichael, now the editor of *Midstream*, whom Caffi liked for his good looks and his knowledge of Arabic and Russian; Max Shachtman, Saul Steinberg, Otto Friedrich—then hoping to become a novelist, now the author of many first-rate books and a senior writer on *Time*—and Saul Bellow, who regularly brought Caffi sections of *Augie March*, on which he was then at work, and which Caffi regularly praised to me.

There are no faults as interesting to us as those of the persons we love best and most admire. Caffi had his faults of course, and a dark side, too, which one felt in his animus against women—at the very least, half of the human race! And note that Caffi was an avowed humanist! He was a teacher, and a great one, but his pupils had to be males. There was no woman whom he wanted to meet, though he was generally courteous to any person to whom he had been introduced, even against his will.

He had read Mary McCarthy's pieces in *Politics* and one of her books, and had spoken approvingly of her prose style. But when Nicola Chiaromonte remarked that she might visit Paris (I think this was in 1950), Caffi said immediately that he did not care to meet her. When asked why, he became angry and irritable. Why meet Miss McCarthy? He did not feel intellectually up to meeting a woman so mentally endowed. Nicola recalled to Caffi that he had been acquainted with Rosa Luxemburg; also with Simone Weil, whom Miss McCarthy herself admired, and whose essay on the *Iliad* she had translated. But Caffi responded, "Miss McCarthy is just too intelligent. It would be fatiguing." Now this was to wound Nicola, whom he saw regularly. For Caffi did not rate Nicola below Mary in intelligence. I know that he had the greatest regard for Nicola and even thought him to have a better mind than Camus. He had said as much to me.

And I recall that when I introduced Caffi to my Parisian friend, the physicist Ambrosino, Caffi found him most interesting, that is until the day Ambrosino arrived for lunch at the Hôtel de l'Academie with his wife. The lunch went off well enough, without any untoward incident or spiteful remarks, but afterwards, when Ambrosino and his wife had left, Caffi said to me, "I'm very disappointed in your friend. I thought he was a real intellectual. I didn't know he had a wife."

I took Caffi one evening to Wahl's *colloque philosophique* to hear a talk by Koyré on Isaac Newton. The talk was a very brilliant one, and afterwards I introduced Caffi to Koyré, whose scholarship Caffi had told me he admired. There was some conversation, and I think Koyré quickly grasped the quality of the man I had presented to him. At some point, Koyré asked Caffi: "What are you working on?" For he must have assumed that a man with Caffi's ready wit and vast knowledge must have been working on something. Caffi was almost demolished by the question. He bit his lip, and looked around him as if searching for the nearest exit; then he mumbled something about a study of Byzantine history, which he was *not* working on at that time; moreover Caffi knew that I knew this. We left Koyré and walked back to our hotel in a heavy silence, Caffi not saying a word about Koyré's talk, which I knew had interested him deeply. I mention this to introduce the fact that Caffi was then in a state of despair, and this had made him unable to properly handle a very large sum of money which had been entrusted to him.

What he did was to turn the money over to a young friend, who, according to Caffi, happened to be in dire need. Friends of Caffi have told me that he had hoped the young friend would spend or lose the money and that in Caffi's ensuing embarrassment, he would have a motive for committing suicide. And Chiaromonte told me that Caffi was quite put out of countenance when the young man to whom he had lent the money proved more reliable than he had been expected to be, and returned the whole sum intact. In fact when Caffi told me about the affair, he described his feelings thus: "I felt," he said, "as if I had been robbed."

I had my own problems then about getting what I never had any difficulty in spending. Prices in Paris were rising, odd jobs were becoming harder to get, and the help I had received from the U.S. for editing *Instead* was now insufficient. I could have had a position in Geneva, but if I was not going to live in Paris, what could keep me from returning to New York?

I saw Caffi on the last day of my stay in Paris, in the fall of '51. On my next trip to Europe, which was ten years later, Paris seemed to me much emptier. Caffi was gone; he had died during the late fifties. In fact, the city had changed. It was colder, richer, Americanized. People were better dressed, had more money to spend, and were much less friendly than between '48 and '52. I was invited to lunch and dinner by the Parisians I had known, and I found that they now had refrigerators, automobiles, and money in the bank. They worked harder, and their lunches and dinners were less elaborate and much less interesting.

What had happened to Paris? Jean Wahl had hoped that it would remain a center of spiritual interest, that it would be the cultural capital of this century, as, according to Walter Benjamin's phrase, it had been in the nineteenth. But by 1962, Paris could no longer fill that role. For one thing, the achievements of the New York school of painting had had a destructive effect on Parisian art, on the confidence previously felt by the French painters in their own ideas and in their taste. In the Parisian art galleries one now saw imitations of American painting as during the thirties in the galleries in New York City one saw so much imitation of Picasso, Léger, and Matisse. The streets were more crowded with cars, the smell of gas was everywhere, and in '62 there was fear of violence from a group of French military officers, which was resolved not to submit to General de Gaulle's decision, already evident, to abandon Algeria. I was told that Sartre's apartment had been bombed and that he was in hiding. But in any case, Saint-Germain-des-Prés was no longer the heart of the city.

Will Paris remain a center of spiritual interest? No doubt. But the life of a city is determined by the lives of those who inhabit it, and what Parisians concern themselves with in the next two decades will unquestionably alter the character of the city. At one time, with its beauty, vibrancy, pleasurableness and grace, it was one of the only places on earth where one seldom felt a need for the sacred. Baudelaire remarked, "Sometimes I need God, sometimes I don't." And it seems right to me that this statement of nineteenth century humanism was once made in the city of Paris—but would anyone make that remark as arrogantly in the Paris of today?

POSTSCRIPT

Here I want to take up Caffi's views on politics, from my earliest contact with them; to do this, I shall have to go back to the time in New York City when I first heard mention of him.

As I think I already noted, it was Nicola Chiaromonte who first talked to me about Caffi; this was sometime in 1942. Here is what Nicola said of his learned friend: "Caffi is the only man in the world who might come up with a new political line, one for intellectuals, who, after the war, may still want to be radical." What this new outlook was to be one could infer somewhat from the articles by Caffi, signed "European," which were beginning to appear in Dwight Macdonald's *Politics*; and I was also able to cull something from a lecture given by Nicola (who was in political agreement with Caffi), in 1945. It appeared in *Politics* in 1946 under the title "On the Kind of Socialism Called Scientific," and makes interesting reading even today.

Nicola's audience in '46 was made up of the leftist intellectual elite of New York City, of those, in any case, who were anti-Stalinist. Let me list some names: James T. Farrell, Mary McCarthy, Meyer Schapiro, Harold Rosenberg, William Phillips and Philip Rahv of *Partisan Review*, Mike Stille, now of the *Corriere della sera*, Niccolo Tucci, Hannah Arendt, William Barrett, Delmore Schwartz, Walter Goldwater, Nancy and Dwight Macdonald. In a quite crowded basement somewhere in the Village, Nicola developed what was to me a surprising thesis: Marx had been wrong in trying to develop a socialist position which could be termed "scientific." He had not succeeded in any case, but success in this effort would not have been desirable. What was to be desired was a position based on the views of his Socialist predecessors, those Marx had characterized—and criticized—as "utopians." What we needed was a position of "utopian" socialism, and not of a socialism which could satisfy the norms, supposing there to be such, of science.

The response that night to these views, which were by no means dogmatically offered, was violent in the extreme. Nicola's thesis was rejected by almost everyone in the audience, and those who most violently rejected what he said were among his closest friends. James T. Farrell declared, with the brutality of one who thinks he cannot possibly be wrong, "At least Marxism isn't boring and you are." Harold Rosenberg wondered, "Why make the point that Marxism isn't scientific if you don't want it to be that?" And then Meyer Schapiro, a very particular friend of Nicola's, intimidated almost everyone who might have wavered, or gone over to his side, with this ominous prediction: "If you follow Chiaromonte tonight you won't know what to do in a week, month or year; you won't even know what to do tomorrow morning."* It was then that Mary McCarthy intervened dramatically, beseeching the audience thus: "In the name of

---

*Schapiro also made the point that no science, no matter how exact, would meet the test for rigor which Nicola demanded of Marxism.

humanity, stop attacking Chiaromonte." For my part, I wanted
to defend Nicola, even though I did not fully understand what
was at issue, and I was asked by some friends of his to speak in
his behalf. Finally, late in the evening, when Schapiro had already left the room (but I did telephone him the next morning
to repeat what I said against him) I took the floor and spoke to
this effect: If one is going to reconsider his whole political outlook, something he might have to reflect on for years, why
should it matter if he didn't know exactly what to do on the very
next morning? I did not realize then that few who heard Chiaromonte that night knew what to do politically the next morning,
or on mornings after that. I also did not know—few did who
were in that basement almost forty years back—that the positions Nicola had taken—I assume with Caffi's support—were
not very different from those held by Adorno and Horkheimer
of the Frankfurt school, who, however, had taken the precaution
of making it quite clear that they were not thinking of *doing*
anything in politics on any foreseeable tomorrow; they were
interested in making a reflective critique of society, of Marxism
and of the problems of Marxism, but were not trying to seize
power or to keep any particular group out of power. It is interesting to note here that the Frankfurt school's Marxism is the
only version of the doctrine intellectuals respect today. I should
note, too, that in leftist intellectual circles today, the kind of
view Nicola took some forty years back, stressing moral and
utopian values, is now more or less taken for granted, and not
treated as paradoxical. Lucien Goldmann, for instance, whose
whole intellectual career was based on an application of Marxist
social psychology to literature, told me in 1968 that he had quite
renounced Marxism once and for all, and that his values from
then on would be libertarian and utopian. I could list a great
many other instances, for the exodus of intellectuals from Marxism during the last ten years has been quite general. To be sure,
there is a difference between stressing moral values and utopian
visions because this is the substance of your thought, and making these your chosen themes because a previously held commitment—to class interest and political cunning—had not been
crowned with success.

I COME back now to Caffi, in Paris. It is now 1950. I had noticed that in the discussions of day-to-day politics Caffi had with Nicola (who came regularly to the hotel to lunch with us), Caffi never had tried to sustain the views he had led Nicola to take up, and to make his own. In most of their talks, there was Caffi defending the pro-Communist line popular in Europe then, and stated regularly by Sartre and Merleau-Ponty in *Les Temps modernes*, and there was Nicola countering with the arguments generally given in *Figaro* by the conservative advisor of statesmen, Raymond Aron. Neither Caffi nor Nicola expressed in these arguments what I understood to be their most deeply held values. It was a demonstration to me of how difficult it is to refer to such values in a political argument. Was it then not possible to be serious about values when talking "serious" politics? And was there no exception to this rule? Perhaps this was the reason the leaders of the Frankfurt school decided to take themselves out of political action.

One day I taxed Caffi with talking like a Marxist, and of defending Marxist views against Nicola.

"I do," he admitted.

"But," I pointed out, "Nicola is now advancing the very views that you convinced him of, and argued for so interestingly in Dwight Macdonald's *Politics.*"

Caffi replied, "It is because I have reread those pieces in *Politics*—not just my own, but those you think I inspired, the articles of Nicola and also of Dwight Macdonald—that I have gone back to the views you designate, probably rightly, as Marxist." (It is to be noted that the moral-political position Caffi was objecting to in *Politics*, and which he had himself inspired, has been taken over in recent times by Irving Howe (who having been a Marxist now calls himself a "radical humanist" and guides the group around *Dissent.*))

But was this the whole truth of the matter? I think there was something else at issue: a felt need for action, to which Caffi's formerly held views, even as restated by Nicola, gave no real answer. But this was the very reason Schapiro some years before had rejected these views, predicting: They will lead to inaction. "Adopt such views and you won't know what to *do*

189

even tomorrow morning." He did not say, You will not know what to *think* tomorrow morning.

As his arguments with Nicola continued, Caffi's rhetoric became increasingly unpleasant. To complicate matters, Caffi showed more and more jealousy of Nicola's wife Miriam, of Nicola's concern for and dependence on her, and it was this I think which made Caffi all the more unpersuadable and cruel in discussion. As it happened, Miriam Chiaromonte was about to leave Paris for the States to see her mother, who was ill. She came with Nicola to the Hôtel de l'Academie to join me and Caffi at a goodbye luncheon, an effort I would have urged her not to make, for there was no way she could make up to a man like Caffi for the harm of her having married his friend. Well, the luncheon was not a happy one. At one point, Caffi, noticing a medallion Miriam wore on a necklace, asked her "Is that a medal from the Daughters of the American Revolution?" Miriam kept her poise, made some amiable reply, and soon after that excused herself.

We were joined then by a young Italian, Antonio Sabatelli, who was staying at the hotel, and whom we all liked and helped in whatever way we could, for he was a wonderful fellow with a bent for involving himself in the affairs of others, and an incredible verve in talking about whatever distressed him. He had a wife and a child in Genoa to whom he regularly sent off tiny sums of money, but Caffi had said to him, "I'll help you forget them," and was as good as his word. After a point in their acquaintance, Sabatelli began to call Caffi *"mon maître,"* and indeed Caffi could be a real mentor to any young man he liked.

After Miriam's departure, the argument between Nicola and Caffi became a kind of fight. And at some point Nicola asked, "Then what do you suggest we should do? For you seem to think something has to be done. But what?"

"Yes," Caffi replied, "I do think something should be done and you should not ask me what. For everyone knows what ought to be done."

"You say everyone knows. Well I don't," said Nicola.

I felt then that the conversation shouldn't go further but I didn't know how to stop it, and Caffi then asked, "What should be done?" and answered his question: "It is very simple, though it will take some doing."

"You still haven't said what," Nicola almost shouted.

Then Caffi told him: "We should hang the bourgeoisie, that is what we should do."

"And who are the bourgeoisie?" Nicola asked him.

"Those," Caffi answered, "who can afford to take trips to America to see their mothers."

Nicola went white, stood up and left the dining room without a word. I was so shaken that I did not trust myself to say anything. After a while I too left the table and tried to find Nicola, but I did not see him on the street and could not reach him by phone. So I went to the Bibliothèque Nationale to distract myself. Hours later I got back to the hotel and there was Sabatelli waiting for me outside my room. What, he wanted to know, did I think of Caffi's behavior? I said, "Unforgivable. Why had he been so insulting to Miriam and Nicola? There was no reason for it but jealousy. He was jealous of Nicola for having a wife, and having the means to pay for her trip to America." "That is what I think, too," said Sabatelli, "and that is what Nicola must have thought. And this all goes to show what a genius Caffi is. Do you know what happened?" And then he told me. Nicola had returned to the hotel with a present for Caffi, an expensive cashmere sweater. I felt the very worst thing about the whole affair might be its effect on Sabatelli's character.

In Sabatelli's bohemian mind, the meaning of the distressing event was this (and it is no doubt why he had called Caffi a "genius"): the way to exact the tribute—to him not untrivial—of an expensive gift, was to insult a friend. And this after all the other things Caffi had taught him!

I did not criticize Nicola. Yes, he had given Caffi an expensive gift and in return for the latter's insult to him and his wife. But this did not seem inconsistent with Nicola's principles. He believed in returning good for evil (so did Caffi); moreover his gift showed he thought Caffi had not been prompted at all by ideals or by ideas, but by a childish need to be looked after, and in some trivial way. Instead of leading a bloody revolt, and then demanding the execution of Miriam Chiaromonte, he would now don the expensive sweater she had probably assisted Nicola in selecting. And he could hardly put on that sweater without feeling somehow morally diminished. Surely that was all the revenge Nicola could have wished.

But there was something dismaying in the event at the time, which I feel even as I recall it now. There was the great, the learned, the good Andrea Caffi, who could think of holding his own in conversation with Denis Diderot, reduced to the moral stature of Diderot's bohemian figure, the rascally nephew of Rameau. If some one as courteous as Caffi, as large-minded and intent on being just could so misbehave, from whom could one expect good deeds to come?

Eight

LOST BLOOM IN GENEVA,
THE MAD GRASS IN NEW YORK

I CAME back from Paris in the fall of 1951, and found New York somewhat different from the city I had left, hoping for a better life, in 1948. But before describing those features of our city which undeniably were changing, I want to take another look back at Europe.

JEAN Wahl, then at the Sorbonne, and an honored guest for years at the *Rencontres Internationales*, asked me in the summer of 1951 if I would like to participate in the conference of intellectuals the *Rencontres* held yearly at Geneva. I was to go in August that year as the delegate from the United States, selected for this purpose not by any American or group of Americans but by one of the delegates from France, Jean Wahl, who happened to be a friend of mine! This is the way things were done in Europe then. Friends were more powerful than the rules of officialdom.

So I went with Jean Wahl to Geneva, and was put up there in a fine hotel by the lake, with expenses paid by the International Meetings; thus, I was able to spend a week of luxury in the city where there are statues of Calvin and of Rousseau. Each evening, a lecture was given by one of the writers chosen to address the general public, and then, on the following morning, a certain number of delegates were selected to question the speaker of the previous evening at a closed session. Among those who addressed the public were Jules Romains; Ortega y Gasset; a Jesuit historian, *le Père* Daniélou; and M. Griaulle, a professor of ethnology, from the Sorbonne. Thanks to Jean Wahl, I was one of those chosen to question Merleau-Ponty, and also Ortega y Gasset on the mornings following their public addresses, and it was thus that I became acquainted with Octavio Paz, the surrealist poet, a delegate from Mexico. He, too, was one of those selected for the sessions with Merleau-Ponty and Ortega y Gasset.

The meetings, held in the city where, as Jean Wahl remarked, "Amiel told us he never met anyone,"* were full of political groupings, if not of outright conspiracies. Almost everyone I got to know was a member of some group determined to wrest power from some other group closely related to it in belief or purpose. For instance, the Catholics, who were there in force, were divided into three parties, each hostile to the others. There was one especially interesting grouping, which looked forward to the Communist conquest of all Europe, and not because its members were pro-Communists—at least this is what they said. An entirely different, and according to them, more spiritual reason, had determined their hopes in this matter. They wanted the Church to have to go underground, so as to be purified in a struggle against Communist tyranny. Swinging counterweight, there were those who defended the hierarchy of that time, and the then-reigning pope. Their leader was the learned Jesuit, *le Père* Daniélou, who, however, tried to remain on good terms with the other two groups, until, that is, he gave his public address, which, as it turned out, was devoted to denouncing both of them! But I have not yet described the third group of Catholics. This was made up of persons who raised the banner of what they called Christian existentialism; they had been angered by a statement against existentialism, just delivered by the pope. Among them was one priest who managed to find a quota-

*H.F. Amiel, the famous solitary Geneva philosopher who left us his *Journal intime* (*personal diary*) widely read after his death. Amiel was much admired by, among others, Matthew Arnold and Tolstoy.

tion from Luther to fit the arguments he gave in every discussion he had with Protestants. Hearing him was like hearing a Stalinist quoting Trotsky in arguments with Trotskyists, and, towards the end, of justifying the positions taken by Stalin! As a matter of fact, I can well imagine a discussion of that sort, for I have known very clever Stalinists who claimed that the best possible defense attorney for Stalin in any arraignment of him would have been none other than Leon Davidowich. (According to a recent article in *Encounter*, the Austrian Socialist Otto Ruhle, in an argument with Trotsky in Mexico, called him "the best of Stalinists.") There were also the more usual political groups of pro- and anti-Communists, and among these groups there circulated a Spanish-born intellectual, who proclaimed himself stateless and prided himself on being that. He taught mathematics and also psychology at the University of London, had come to Geneva by way of Egypt, and was called by most of those who got to know him, by a name which he had given himself; this was *"La Conscience mondiale,"* "World Consciousness." Ernst Ansermet, the Swiss conductor, and Jean Wahl, both took an interest in *"La Conscience mondiale,"* (he is today an accomplished theorist of language instruction).

"World Consciousness" had a number of ideas I found interesting, which does not mean that I thought any of them true. For instance, he insisted that it was easy to learn foreign languages—he himself spoke thirteen—and he claimed the difficulties people found in learning foreign languages were purely psychological. Now this of course is true if one leaves undefined what is meant by the word *psychological;* obviously there are certain difficulties in learning a foreign language after a certain age, and these have to do with limitations of memory that are in some sense objective. Anyway, "World Consciousness" was quite eloquent about how he could teach anyone to overcome any difficulty in mastering not only any language, but any number of languages. He had, by the way, worked with Piaget, and had been involved in inventing a machine, with Piaget's help, which could record brainwaves of someone under questioning, and in such a way that the thoughts of the person questioned could be accurately determined. I suppose the mechanism is not unrelated to the lie detector machines now in use, but I was horrified at the idea that anyone would use his intellect to create a machine which could become a threat to the knowledge of things we want to remain secret. I was told that he had indeed created such a machine with Piaget's help. It had been tried out on a goat, and the machine had recorded absolutely nothing. The inventors had endeavored in all sorts of ways to make the goat think of something, but the results had invariably been an unmarked sheet of paper. The goat, it appears, had, like some true mystics, thought of nothing. I remember saying to a friend in Geneva that there was one possible use for such a machine: it could be tried out on mystics; and if the machine indicated they *had* thought of something, we would know they could be frauds. Unhappily no such machine is likely to be produced with only this kind of use in view.

I have one more story to tell about "World Consciousness." He claimed that one day, when he was five years old, he went for a walk in Madrid with his father, and at some point the latter urged him to go on home, saying "As for me, I'm going far away." When the boy of five got home and his mother asked where his father was, the boy replied, "He's gone far away," which apparently can also mean in Spanish, "He's gone to hell," or "He's dead." The father, in fact, did not return, and the five year old boy who later became "World Consciousness" began to think of himself as his father's killer. Accordingly, at the age of five, he tried to replace his father and take over the paternal role in the family. He never attended school, but occupied himself with earning a livelihood, enough in fact to send his two brothers and a sister, all older than himself, to school. He claimed to have put them through the secondary schools and even the university, while he himself supported them and studied on his own. "It would have been undignified," he said, "for the father of a family, no matter his age, to walk into a public school classroom, and to be taught to read and write, also to be disciplined by a schoolteacher." Whatever the truth about this may be, "World Consciousness," according to his story, without diplomas or degrees from any institution, had learned to read, write, and speak some thirteen languages; he had become a fine mathematician, and by his own efforts, acquired an indisputable mastery in a number of disciplines.

Quite unforgettable too was the public address given by the French ethnologist, M. Griaulle, and the event it precipitated. For what happened then in Geneva was in a way prophetic of so much that occurred in New York City, and in the United States generally during the sixties. M. Griaulle lectured on a Sudanese culture in North Africa, a tribe whose religion, rites and laws he had studied for some years. These Sudanese, he indicated, had taught him more about metaphysics than he could possibly learn from Plato or any other Western thinker. Their consciousness, he asserted, should be the model for that of western Europeans. Their beliefs were finer and more profound, their intuitions sounder and more reliable, than those of the European whites who were in his audience. At this point a young black (and very black he was) sitting close to the platform, interrupted the speaker, and, after telling the audience that he had been born into the very tribe M. Griaulle had studied, went on to declare, and in the most aggressive way, that there was no good to be gained in praising the tribe from which he came for its backwardness; what he personally desired and felt he needed was a good European education such as M. Griaulle himself had had. M. Griaulle pointed an accusing finger at the young black and shouted, "You are just not a black!" and in the uproar that followed was not able to go on with his address; the hall had to be cleared. Afterwards Jean Wahl suggested to me that I should not think the event proved anything other than that ". . . there is nothing very distinguished about M. Griaulle."

M. Jules Romains was, of course, distinguished, as a novelist, essayist, poet, theorist, playwright, and commentator on the problems of his time, and he was an engaging figure on the platform as he addressed us one night in the Geneva University hall. He was, by turns, witty, sarcastic, eloquent, and slightly portentous in his consideration of this theme: What would happen to the Christian faith if it were discovered finally that there were conscious beings like ourselves on other planets or on other heavenly bodies outside the solar system? How could the faith of Christians be maintained in that case? Assuming that

Jesus Christ was indeed the Son of God, would he not have had to contrive to be born on other heavenly bodies so as to be crucified on them and redeem the inhabitants of these other stars from the sins of which they were most certainly guilty? So we would have to assume that either Jesus Christ was only interested in those on earth, and in that sense was, from a cosmic point of view, a rather parochial figure, or that he had gone through the agony of Gethsemane, the stations of the cross, and the Crucifixion many times, in distant areas of the universe. Jules Romains took what the Catholic priests who heard him regarded as a complacently agnostic satisfaction in the dismay which the prospects of new astronomical knowledge would produce among believers. As a matter of fact, Romains did not seem to be aware that Arnold Toynbee, in one of his volumes devoted to the relations between the higher religions, had raised this very question and even tried to give a positive and Christian answer to it. But maybe instead of saying a Christian answer, I should say a _syncretist_ answer, taking Christian values into account. Toynbee made the interesting point that multiple appearances of Christ on various heavenly bodies and multiple crucifixions and resurrections might seem unbelievable to Western minds, but would be in no way strange to Easterners, especially to Hindus, who were accustomed to thinking in terms of many universes—and by this I mean many to the point of infinity. Hindus, if they could be converted to Christianity, would readily accept an infinite number of crucifixions and might even require these of a Christian God. Yet there was Jules Romains speaking from the platform as if no one had ever raised the possibility of recurring appearances of Christ, and as if the prospect that it had to be considered could be a mortal blow to Christianity! To the Catholics in the audience at Geneva, Romains seemed a heaven-sent agnostic provided by Providence so that they, the devout, could show their intellectual superiority. And besides, there were many things against Romains in view of his past political behavior. He had been a friend of Abetz before the war, of Abetz, Hitler's chief cultural propagandist in France; during the occupation, Abetz had controlled _La Nouvelle Revue française_, giving its editorship to Ramon Fernandez, who had been converted to fascism. Then Romains had written a poem, a kind of epic, entitled "The White Man," in which he had expressed a delighted view of white supremacy over the native populations in Africa and Asia; this was a French hedonist version of Rudyard Kipling's ascetic vision of "the white man's burden." In view of all this, the Catholics in Geneva saw Romains as fatuous, worldly, self-satisfied, not too well informed, and spiritually insignificant. One of the Jesuits there said to me after the Romains lecture, "If only he were our main antagonist. . . ."

Romains represented, in his manner, rhetoric, and general attitude, the European civilization which World War II had mortally wounded; he stood for a civilized order that for all its virtues had found it possible to accept a philistine accommodation to injustices and inequalities which could no longer be passed over or successfully hidden by even the most brilliant rhetoric. He represented the old Europe, and the night after his talk we heard another address, by Ortega y Gasset, who ended his speech with this remark, which he did not just let drop, but shouted: "Europe is dead!" Then, after explaining why it was dead, he again shouted: "Long live Europe!"

ORTEGA y Gasset, with his solid shoulders, did indeed look like a matador on the platform, and one expected a Spanish intellectual to introduce some reference to death in concluding an address, and so it was not so surprising that he ended his talk as he did. Now the next morning some of us were chosen to question him in a closed session, at which he would make more precise what he had said publicly. Merleau-Ponty, Jean Wahl, Octavio Paz, I, and some others were chosen for this go at Ortega.

I myself thought Ortega y Gasset gave interesting answers to many of the questions we put to him. But Jean Wahl was much less admiring. When Ortega remarked in reply to someone that Einstein was by no means the best of modern physicists, a remark which Paz and the delegate from Argentina greeted approvingly, Wahl leaned over to me and whispered, "I

199

think he is anti-Semitic." Then Merleau-Ponty asked Ortega why he was so opposed to the use of the term "being" in modern philosophy. Ortega replied that we cannot be certain what the Greeks meant by the term, and by continuing to use it we deprive ourselves of some new linguistic creation which might better serve our metaphysical needs. I thought this a fair answer and so apparently did Merleau-Ponty. But Jean Wahl was furious. "We *do* know what the Greeks meant by 'being,' " he declared, and leaning over towards me, whispered about Ortega: "I don't believe he thinks. He is a *fumist*" [someone who likes to mystify; a kibitzer] "like Matta." I had introduced Matta to Jean Wahl only a week before.

I cannot, at this date, recall the other questions which were put to Ortega or the answers he gave, but I did have the very definite impression that instead of superficializing such questions so as to be able to answer them more easily, he went out of his way to restate them in terms which made them more difficult to handle, and also more profound. So I could not accept Wahl's adverse judgment of Ortega's performance at the morning session, but I had not responded favorably to his address on the night before. When, in his final peroration he exclaimed, "Europe is dead!" adding directly after that, "and is beautiful in death," he seemed to be consciously imitating the remark of Napoleon in *War and Peace*, when, looking down at the body of Prince André on the field of Austerlitz, he remarks to his officers, "*Voilà, un bel mort.*" As Tolstoy has it, though, Prince André was not dead. Napoleon was mistaken about this. But he thought André beautiful in death, because he was facing the French army when he fell. I could not help thinking that evening, "Perhaps Ortega too is mistaken." Now what were the reasons Ortega gave for announcing the demise of the old continent, or, rather, of its culture? For by Europe I took him to mean the culture of Europe. And once again, why was Europe beautiful in death? It was beautiful, according to Ortega, because it had not failed to carry out all the projects it had required of itself in all of the arts and sciences. And he pointed to two cultural facts to indicate that Europe could not carry its projects further. First of all, he said, Goedel's Theorem had put a final period to

200

the hopes that European philosophy could be carried further, and, he added, citing Heisenberg, that European physics was also incapable of any further development and perhaps only the Chinese, with their peculiar concepts of yin and yang, could carry it any further. (On this point Ortega has already been proven wrong. European, or, rather, Western physics has made some significant theoretical progress since, and such progress has not been especially influenced by Eastern thought.) As for Goedel's Theorem, it has had a devastating effect on the hopes for the building of formal systems, but at this date it seems rather strange to think that because of the difficulties for formal system building demonstrated by Goedel, European philosophy has come to a close. Ortega seemed to recognize that it was strange to say that even in 1951, and trying to meet possible objections, he went on to assert that if one could not make advances in physics, in logic, or in metaphysics, the prospect for making advances in social theory, in aesthetics, economics, or political science would have to be regarded skeptically. He even seemed to imply that if one couldn't make progress in logic and in physics, it was actually wrong even to *hope* to make any progress in the social sciences. This judgment, even on the evening he made it, seemed to me quite unjustified.

I recall this whole matter first for its intrinsic interest, but beyond that, because the question of the life or death of cultural institutions and of culture generally has been so often and so widely raised of late. In the United States there had been talk during the war of the death of the novel, and in recent years we have heard of the death of history, the death of philosophy, of society, and even of the death of nature; this was announced by Mary McCarthy a few years back in her novel *The Birds of America*. (Miss McCarthy did not seem to realize that nature is the only reality of whose death one cannot speak, for it is the only reality in connection with which the term death, if properly used about it, would *not* be metaphorical. But of course, if we talk about the death of the novel or the death of culture, we are speaking metaphorically.)

Can one talk with any precision about the death of culture or of cultural movements? When I came back to New York from

Paris, I found people saying that European, and especially French painting was dead, and that the Paris school of painting had been outmatched by the artistic brilliance of the New York school. It was like hearing in New York the shout of Ortega y Gasset once again, "Europe is dead!"—only this time followed not by "Long live Europe," but by "Long live America!" Clement Greenberg said quite openly that we had won the Second World War and were going to dominate the postwar world in the field of painting. He was correct in this prophecy. We did dominate the art world, and the painters in Paris finally began to imitate the Americans in making the kinds of paintings at which only Americans could excel. When the French painter, Soulage, and the American Franz Kline were both shown in the same season in New York galleries, even the French connoisseurs of art in New York City said, *"C'est la même chose, mais Kline est le plus costaud."* ("They're doing the same thing, but Kline is the sturdier.") This was a time when the facts of the day were translated into expressions of self-congratulatory nationalism. Mary McCarthy wrote an essay in *Commentary* trying to show that Europeans were the materialists and Americans the idealists, and Harold Rosenberg actually asserted in a conversation with me that the Americans were the only ones who understood modern politics. And this was during the Korean War, the reason for our entry into which are still not entirely clear or commendable.

What is meant by saying that a culture is dead? After the First World War, Spengler made this kind of judgment fashionable by describing cultural movements and art forms in organic terms. Just as the organism has a certain period of development, blooms, then withers and dies, so do art forms and even civilizations, he said. He went even further, claiming that logical forms and mathematical notions are also organic; thus, according to him, geometry, an essential element of Greek or classical culture, died with it, and the question arises, How is it that we can use, and to our own purposes, the science of geometry? To use it we have to understand it. This is that about which we are mistaken, said Spengler, for though we use it, we do not understand it. And in this denial of his, we can see the weakness of

202

his whole system. Long before Spengler, in the nineteenth century, Antoine Augustin Cournot* had thought this matter out in a much more precise way, pointing out that there were both rational and organic elements in any cultural development, and that the rational elements in a cultural whole could survive even after the organic elements supporting it had died. For it is only the organic that can die. What is rational has an aptness for eternity which the organic simply cannot have.

Suppose we apply Cournot's notion to the phenomenon of tragedy which appeared in Greece in the fifth century, died with the conditions that favored its development, and did not reappear again in Europe until the Elizabethan theater of the sixteenth century in England and the French classical theater of the seventeenth century. One reason tragedy is particularly interesting in any consideration of cultural life and cultural death is that its appearances in culture have been so infrequent and so brief. Moreover, Nietzsche's essay on tragedy, *The Birth of Tragedy*, traces the beginnings of tragedy to certain organic conditions, and in contemporary theorizing on the subject, there is George Steiner's book *The Death of Tragedy*, which says something very different and even quite the opposite from Nietzsche, but bases itself on similar assumptions.

Had Cournot treated the matter of tragedy, he would very probably have said the following: There are two elements in tragedy, a rational form and an organic matrix which gives that form its relevance and appropriateness. Without an organic development of some kind requiring the employment of a definite form, the effort at producing tragedy will be artificial, insincere, and poetically worthless. It will be literary in the bad sense of that term. But if an organic basis for the form is present, the form can again have the same power and influence it exerted in Athens. No doubt André Malraux had something like this in mind when he said that in his novel *Sanctuary* William Faulkner had done nothing less than bring Greek tragedy into the detec-

*The first mathematical economist was also a philosopher of history, whose view of history has been said to be the only real alternative to that of Marx. I owe the comparison of his notions with Spengler's to Emanuel Friedman, the editor of *Collier's Encyclopedia* and a Cournot scholar.

tive story. To be sure, this is not a very precise comment, either on Faulkner's novel, on Greek tragedy, or on the detective story for that matter. For the detective story can indeed be regarded as a parodic form of Greek tragedy, of which it is certainly a debased version. Greek tragedy could hardly be *introduced* into it, for Greek tragedy is already in it, though in a debased way. But I cite Malraux's remark about Faulkner, because it showed his awareness that the form of tragedy can reappear under special conditions, and in fact, William Faulkner, and Malraux himself, did find ways of giving expression to the tragic in modern life, finding organic situations to which it was appropriate, Faulkner in treating the problem of race in the American South, and Malraux the struggle of the Chinese against imperialist oppression in the late twenties.

It seems to me that any proper approach to the elusiveness of tragedy in most historical periods would be to ask this question: "What in fact are the organic elements that were propitious to the appearance of tragedy in fifth-century Athens, in sixteenth century England and in seventeenth century France?" In asking, "Is tragedy possible today?" one is really asking, "Are there organic conditions which require that form today?"

And I think Cournot's separation of the organic and the rational has to be borne in mind whenever we talk about the life or death of any tendency. Shirley Chisholm, speaking at the 1980 Urban League convention, urged that this country, not just the blacks in it, return to the spirit of the sixties. What could it mean to return to the spirit of the sixties in 1980? Was there a rational political form in the sixties which Miss Chisholm wanted us to return to? Did she not in fact mean that there were in the sixties a set of organic conditions whose absence from the scene she regretted? But if that were the case, then we could not return to the spirit of the sixties, however admirable one may judge that spirit to have been. The spirit is not the form, which cannot die, as the spirit, alas, can and does.

IF people in Europe were speaking in 1951 about the imminent death of the old continent's culture, in New York City some-

thing very different was being proposed about American culture, American politics, and especially about American painting. Moreover, changes were taking place in the New York
theatre which would lead later on to the development of the
off-Broadway movement, in which I myself participated. But
first of all I want to say something about what had been happening in painting. An art club had been formed which had its
headquarters in a loft on East Eighth Street, to which some of
the best painters in the city, among them Franz Kline, Willem
de Kooning, Esteban Vicente and Philip Guston came regularly, as did any number of still-unknown young painters who,
because of the club, were able to come into contact with mature
artists already recognized for their skills. Thus it was that
Gandy Brody and Robert Rauschenberg found encouragement
for the developments they later were to introduce into the world
of the New York school. And at the painters' club, in the excitement over the new paintings being produced and the feeling
that finally the city had the kind of art that was quite worthy
of it, a meeting place for the already established and the scarcely
known, the already famous and those merely hoping to become
that, the skilled, the semiskilled, and the unskilled, who, however, had aspirations, produced an atmosphere like that around
a race track (I am deliberately using the metaphor Joyce used
about Paris in the late twenties and early thirties, which he said
because of the atmosphere there, was the only city in which he
could write). In fact, the painters who came to the club were
treated by most of the people there, who were not themselves
painters, but admirers of painting, like horses moving impa-
tiently, sometimes hysterically, to the starting gate at the first
of the three great racetracks from which sometimes triple win-
ners emerge. A kind of miracle had taken place in New York
City which had transformed the painters' club on Eighth Street
east of University Place into something like Louisville, Ken-
tucky on the eve of the Derby. And it's to be noted that the social
arrangements at that time for bringing young writers or aspir-
ants in writing into contact with their elders and those who had
assured positions in the literary world, had fallen off. There was
a generational conflict already in the literary world, such as

prior to that had not existed, and there was no such conflict among the painters. Moreover, the painters had remained bohemian in their lifestyles while the writers who had had some success strove for respectability and had moved to uptown apartments.

I suppose what I have described were the organic conditions that made possible the breakthrough in painting in the late forties and early fifties of Bill Baziotes (whom Matta had always singled out to me as a fine painter—though he always said his neckties showed there was something wrong with his color), also, of course, Pollock, de Kooning, Guston, Vicente, and all other painters who contributed to what Tom Hess called "abstract expressionism" and Harold Rosenberg called "action painting." Suppose one asked, though, were any forms produced or discovered by the painters, like the multiplaned surfaces which the cubists favored, like the dot or the splash of the impressionists, like the stain which Da Vinci had said five hundred years ago could have all the beauty necessary for a work of art? Was anything of that sort turned up by abstract expressionism? Those friends of mine who know art history tell me no, that what was new in the paintings produced during that period was the enthusiasm with which forms discovered in Europe from 1905 through the twenties had been rediscovered. In other words, New York City had provided a new, organic situation for forms of painting which Paris and the Parisian school could no longer nurture, and which had some of their richest, wildest, most fantastic developments in what ten years before would have seemed the unlikeliest place—New York City.

On some evening in some month of 1952, at some party in someone's apartment in the Village, Tom Hess, who was then at work on the book in which he described the new painters as "abstract expressionists," asked me to give a talk on whatever topic I chose, at the Eighth Street art club. And I agreed to give the talk. Let me recall that evening: I was walking down Eighth Street towards the club, and two persons I met on the way and whom I stopped to greet urged me not to go on to the club to give my talk. The first was Robert Motherwell, whom I had not seen during the years I'd been in France, and whom I was glad to run into for he always talked intelligently about painting. As a matter of fact, I think he was the first person to herald the importance of Jackson Pollock, at least to me. I told him I was going to the club to lecture, and I think I even suggested that he come too, if only to hear my remarks. It turned out that he was not only unwilling to be part of the audience, he also wanted me not to appear before it. I said to him, "I can't do that. I've given my word to Tom Hess." Said Motherwell, "You know what the club is, don't you?" I said I wasn't familiar with it, but understood it was a new institution in the city, and important to the artists. "I'll tell you what it is," said Motherwell. "It's Bill de Kooning's political machine." So according to Motherwell, whatever I thought I was doing in giving the talk, I was in fact serving the political purpose of a rival painter.

I left Motherwell on Eighth Street and Avenue of the Americas and went on towards the club. But on the corner of MacDougal Street and Eighth, I ran into another painter whom I had not seen for quite some time. This was Attilio Salemmi, whom I had known in the Trotskyist movement. Attilio was the brother of a commercially successful academic sculptor, Antonio Salemmi, whom I had known long before I met Attilio. Antonio Salemmi was bourgeois, conventional, and rich, and Attilio in all respects was just the opposite. Apparently he had for some years been painting seriously, and I was told, not by him, but by others, that the French ambassador to the UN, M. Laugier, had bought some of his pictures and singled him out as the most interesting of New York City's new painters. After my encounter with Attilio that evening, I did find occasion to see some of his paintings, and I was very struck by them. I think there is one in the Museum of Modern Art's permanent collection. What makes Salemmi's pictures interesting (this is a personal view, for I do not know what critics or connoisseurs have said about him), is their outstanding oddity. Little of the painter's craft is involved in drawing the columns of colors he sets alongside each other against a white background, so you do not admire his pictures for their craft or skill, or even for any kind of thought either about the art of painting or about any aspect of real life. Let me put it this way: With most paintings, one feels that if one had the skill, the artistic feeling, or the knowledge of art, one might oneself have made that particular still life, that landscape, that abstraction. Salemmi's pictures are pictures you know instantly you would never have made or wanted to make even if you had the skill to do so, and hardly any skill, it seems to me, could have been involved in their production. There is some element of this strangeness, this otherness, in a good deal of modern art, but in Salemmi's pictures one felt at once this strangeness as oddly genuine and genuinely odd; certainly it was not the result of any deliberate effort to be different on the painting's part. Let us remember that Georg Lukàcs had made *specialness* a main category of aesthetic value. In any case, that was what I thought of Salemmi's pictures when I saw them some months after I ran into him that evening.

I told him that I was going to the club to give a talk, adding, "I just ran into Bob Motherwell, and he urged me not to go." "He's quite right," said Attilio. And then I told him what Motherwell had said, that the club was Bill de Kooning's political machine. "I agree with him about that," said Attilio. To which I responded, looking at my watch, "If we go on discussing this, I'll be late."

So I went on to the art club and gave my talk.

Bill de Kooning was in the audience, and I think what I said in my talk disturbed him as it did several of the other painters there, though I had not intended to be especially provocative. I said, speaking as a layman, not as an art critic or connoisseur, that when I had first become aware of modern paintings, I was often thrilled by pictures which were modern simply because they were that, quite apart from any superior aesthetic quality they might be said to have. Now, I said, I feel differently. I get a special pleasure from looking at paintings that are *not* modern. And if I look at a painting that is modern, I ask it to prove its aesthetic worth. Well this was not the right thing to say to members of the Eighth Street art club in 1952. The painters there were involved in making modern paintings, but I think few of them thought the word "modern" the right qualifier of what they were doing. They knew that what they were doing was rather different from what had been done before them, so that to place their worth under the same rubric with the art which had gone before theirs, seemed to them a misunderstanding of their effort, their motivation, their values. John Meyers, an old friend who had been managing editor of *Instead* when I got it out, and whom I had known on the staff of *View*, was particularly upset. He was involved then in setting up the Tibor de Nagy Gallery, which exhibited some of the finest new American painters, notably Grace Hartigan, Larry Rivers, and Robert Goodenough, and it must have been very upsetting to him to hear that paintings were extended a certain emotional credit simply insofar as they were *not* modern. It was modern paintings that he was interested in showing.

Sonia Orwell, when she wanted to make sure that those around would listen carefully to what she had to say, would dramatically fling her waves of heavy blonde hair back over her shoulders and announce, "The thing is that. . . ." The procedure was always effective. I have heard her announce to Robert Lowell on the subject of contemporary American poetry, "The thing is that . . ."; and he listened with maximum attention. So I am going to borrow her phrase to tell what it was about the Cedar Bar that made it remarkable. The thing is that . . . in the Cedar Bar, ideas were in the air. How remarkable that is, one will perhaps realize in reflecting on this fact: ideas have not often been in the air in New York City. New York was hardly ever the place where original ideas were first formulated or expressed. It was the place ideas visited first, having been generated somewhere else. Also, it was the place where they were welcomed. In general, in the late nineteenth century, and the early part of our own, ideas relating to art or manners were originated in Paris, first of all, but perhaps also in London, or in Vienna, and only after that were taken up in New York, from where they continued years later to Chicago and to Los Angeles.

Philosophical ideas were in the air in the thirties in Freiburg, in Vienna, and in Oxford during the fifties. And all these ideas, of logical positivism, phenomenology, and the philosophy of language, finally made their way to this country, but not to

New York City in any direct sense. They came to the colleges and universities in New York City, but also, and simultaneously, to the colleges and universities over the rest of the country. So that the University of California at Berkeley is in no sense more philosophically backward than are Columbia, Harvard, or Yale. And the ideas of structuralism developed by Levi-Strauss, Roland Barthes, and others in Paris, have also crossed the Atlantic, but have made no direct connection with what is thought or felt in New York City except for what is felt or thought by its university students. The sad fact is that New York City, too, is today almost as bankrupt intellectually as are the provincial cities of the country, for ideas no longer hit the centers of city life, but go directly to the campuses, where they are academicized by the various faculties.

But in the late forties and fifties this had not yet occurred. The existentialist ideas of Sartre entered into the consciousness of city dwellers in Manhattan, and I think had some effect upon the painters too. However, the ideas that were in the air in the fifties, at the Eighth Street art club and the Cedar Bar, even if influenced to some degree by the existentialist notions, were fundamentally ideas about the art of painting. It was the ideas of the painters and not of critics, connoisseurs, or art historians, that were in the air, and you felt this as soon as you stepped into the Cedar Bar.

In a famous article written during the fifties, Harold Rosenberg said it was a scandal that American intellectuals had ignored the development of abstract expressionism, or, as he called it, action painting. In fact, he was one of the few writers (Frank O'Hara was another) who ventured into the Cedar Bar, though neither came there often.

For my own part, I must say that the experience of ideas in the air is a very exciting one, and I think I can say, too, that the only time since the thirties I have ever been aware of anything like this was during the fifties in the art club and at the Cedar Bar. Now while this was exciting and stimulating, it also had a negative side for one who was not himself a painter. For one was stimulated by ideas that had little relation to one's concerns, and if these ideas actually inspired one, the case was even worse, for the feeling of inspiration brought with it the conviction that it would result in nothing. Paul Valéry, in an essay on poetry and abstract thought, tells us an experience he had had of musical inspiration which should have resulted in a score; however he was too lacking in the knowledge of musical composition to produce one. Well, that's what it was like at the Cedar Bar: one not a painter was stimulated, but what was one who did not paint to do about it? So there was nothing scandalous about the fact that writers did not frequent the bar. The real question I had to ask myself was, "Why did I go there?"

I went because some of the painters had been friends of mine for years, and because the bar was the one indisputably bohemian center in Greenwich Village, probably in New York City. But since the ideas that were in the air were those of painting, and since these ideas had little relation to my own concerns, there were bound to be misunderstandings in all the discussions in which I participated.

But I want to insist on this point: There was something *living* in that bar which gave reality to the ideas expressed there. Once again, a set of organic relations can be separated from the formal structure to which they give vitality. Something had made the painters who came to the art club and the Cedar Bar at that time similarly enthusiastic about the employment in painting of nonfigurative forms. What caused their excitement for these forms to that degree at exactly that time I cannot say. This is something for the art historians. But it was the conjunction of the excitement with these forms that made for the life of the bar.

And so I think that by this time, one of our poets should certainly have written, in verses we would feel worth memorizing, of what things were like in that bar. "Arms and the man I sing," Virgil began his epic. What would the verses we are still waiting for about the Cedar Bar have taken as their theme? Brawls and the brush, perhaps, for the Cedar was famous both for the painters who frequented it, and the fights they engaged in there. Jackson Pollock seldom came, for he lived on Long Island; but when he did come to New York he was certain to drop in at the bar, and he gave it, I think, the atmosphere that stayed with it until the end, long after Jackson was dead and could no longer carry on as was his wont. An ordinary bar it seemed, the first time I was in it, a bar on University Place just off Eighth Street, only a block or so from the art club, and that, of course, is what made the place's fortune. An ordinary New York City bar of the fifties, grimy, smoke-filled, noisy, filled with the drunk, the foolish, and the famous—though even those who were already famous in the early fifties were not yet rich. Even Jackson Pollock was not yet rich, though everyone knew he would be, and Franz Kline and Willem de Kooning were not yet rich, but they were famous, which meant that they were already sought after by the rich and did not have to choose their friends from the poor alone. The bar was open late into the morning hours, and the painters were generally there, some of them, anyway. Literary people did not go to the Cedar Bar. I think I have already indicated why. Some writers and editors deliberately avoided the bar because it was full of painters and painter's talk. I remember asking Philip Rahv to go there with me for a drink, and he refused. He didn't want to mix with the painters. Why not? "They have a trade union consciousness," he said, "and I'm not a member of the union." In one sense he was quite right about this. The painters did form an elite circle which regarded those not of it as against it, and by the way, they weren't so friendly to one another. Ad Reinhardt expressed it this way to me once: "We go there to meet the very people we hate most, the other painters." Actually, I don't think Ad hated any of the painters, but some of them may have hated him, for Barnett Newman hauled him into court for having published a witticism about him, and the fights I saw taking place in the bar were often quite violent. I saw Franz Kline shoe-whipped by his girlfriend in a most savage fashion just a few years before his death, and Bill de Kooning told me that just before the place closed down he was involved in a fracas with Clem Greenberg. Clem, according to Bill, had come up to him as he sat at the bar and made the accusation, "Why do you tell people that I got my ideas from you?" Bill said that he realized Clem intended to hit him, and so he thought it best to get in the first blow. He hit Greenberg on the jaw and then the two were separated.

Probably the closest that we had to the Mermaid Tavern was the Algonquin Bar and Luchow's in the days of the *American Mercury*, and we certainly did not have cafés like the Flore or the Deux Magots or the grand cafes of Montparnasse frequented by writers and painters. But in the fifties there was the Cedar. It was drab, grimy, and chaotic, but beneath the noise and the hum of conversation, the talk about art and by the artists—by Philip Guston, Franz Kline, Bill de Kooning, Spaventa, and Mercedes Matter, herself a painter of quality, but who preferred to be known as one who hung out with painters—beneath all the talk and noise and often desperate remarks, there was an extraordinary optimism, quite American in fact, about painting, and most especially, American painting.

Incidentally, the Cedar Bar was not dominated by a television screen, as bars almost everywhere now are, and the absence of television made the presence of the painters more emphatic. What was significant about the bar and made it different from all others could hardly have been guessed by anyone who did not know those who frequented it. Should George Bellow's painting of a prize fight have hung on one of the walls? Not really. It would have been appropriate there in view of the many fights and the many painters, but the very idea of appropriateness was not one congenial to the painters themselves. They did not want to mix on their canvasses colors that would conform to any already established taste. At least this is what some of them said, notably Franz Kline. Often, when I recall the bar and its lack of saliency for my own descriptive purpose, I'm reminded of a painter I knew slightly in Paris, a remarkable painter, but one whom one would never single out from a crowd as in any way extraordinary. This was Wols, said to be the illegitimate son of Rathenau, the German statesman assassinated by a proto-Nazi under the Weimar Republic. Nicola Chiaromonte pointed Wols out to me one day as we passed the Café Flore, where he was sitting, a most unremarkable looking man. Wols's wife, who knew Chiaromonte, got up from her table, came up to Nicola and asked for money to buy Wols a drink. We both contributed something in support of what Chiaromonte told me was killing Wols, his drinking habit.

Chiaromonte added, "He is the best painter in Paris today, and everybody knows it." Everybody knew it, but no one did anything for him. No dealer wanted to show his work, no checks were flourished to get him to turn over any of his already finished works. But after Wols' death, in 1951, I believe, André Malraux announced that Wols was more original than Pollock, and in fact that Pollock had taken his whole manner of painting from the Parisian.

The charge is quite unjust and does not reflect well on Malraux's judgment or motives. It has, of course, boosted the prices of Wols's paintings, but I cannot help thinking as I recall him, that had he been living in New York in 1951, his wife would not have had to beg for money for liquor from passersby. Wols would have been in the Cedar Bar, sitting with Franz Kline, Pollock, de Kooning, Guston, Vicente, and Spaventa. People would have made much of him. They even would have urged him not to drink, and it was my impression that his excessive drinking in Paris, though this required money, was at least partly due to lack of money, that is, money obtained by his painting, not by his wife's appeals.

Had the unremarkable looking Wols been found in the fifties in the nondescript Cedar Bar favored by the painters, he would, I believe, have been one of the main centers of interest. Dealers would have sought him out, and they did not seek him out in Paris. Someone would have compared him to Pollock and this would have brought a comment from Jackson. And the episode would have provided matter for an article in *Art News* or some other journal. From which we can see something of what it means to have a really creative art movement. For certain artists the difference between a creative scene and its contrary may be the difference between life and death.

When ideas are in the air, people become more daring, sometimes to the point of rudeness. Without the ideas expressed by the dadaists, would anyone have dared paint a mustache on the Mona Lisa? And the Cedar Bar, as I've indicated, was a place where rude words were spoken and, in drunkenness, blows struck. Also, parties were arranged there with the expectation that rude words would be spoken and blows exchanged. I have

214

in mind one particular dinner party at the New Jersey farm of a German professor of philosophy named Henzler, who had become friendly with Bill de Kooning and was trying to get him to take up some of Heidegger's ideas.

Here are the persons Henzler invited to his dinner party: Bill and Elaine de Kooning, Mercedes Matter, Franz Kline, Philip Guston, George Spaventa, Milton Resnick, and several others. It was to be a big affair.

I don't know how we all got out to Henzler's farm, and I don't know who brought Elaine, who had broken a leg, which was in a cast, but I do remember some of the details of the dinner party once all the guests were assembled. I don't know what Henzler had in mind for that affair, an intellectual discussion of Heidegger's ideas? Perhaps, but this was not to be. He had a good dinner served us, too, and fine Moselle wine from Germany, which I don't think the painters appreciated. They had one thing in mind, though, which they very quickly achieved: it was to transform the rather peaceful atmosphere of Henzler's dinner table into something like the brawling, noisy atmosphere, charged with insults and epithets, of the Cedar Bar. They seemed to have gone all the way out to New Jersey just to prove that they had never left Eighth Street and University Place. They ate Henzler's roast lamb, poured his Moselle wine on the floor, drank his scotch and bourbon, broke his crockery, made love in his bedrooms, and left on foot at four in the morning. Elaine de Kooning, in fact, walked with one leg in a cast all the way back to New York, leaving Henzler's dining room, and his whole house, like a disaster area. I never saw him again at the Cedar Bar, and I don't think he made any further attempt to convert Bill de Kooning to Heidegger's ideas.

Why had the painters behaved like this? Most of them were gentlemanly enough, taken as individuals. Now I don't want to insist that any of them were particularly well brought up, but on the other hand, I do not want to blame their behavior on bad manners alone. Their behavior is, I feel, better explained by the kind of inspiration they felt, and which related to the advances they were making in nonfigurative painting. And I think the feeling of having to be inspired in a context where such inspiration is quite irrelevant, is not required, is likely to lead to destructiveness. What the painters did that night was to make a Jackson Pollock out of Henzler's dining table and living room, a purpose he never dreamed they might fulfill when he invited them to dinner.

So this was America in the fifties, in the early fifties, or at least a microcosm of it: energy, destructiveness, money—on the scene or coming on the scene—and an inspired movement in nonfigurative art. I've often wondered, would the painters have behaved as badly had they been as skilled in painting landscapes as the French impressionists in the nineteenth century, or interiors, or nudes like Bonnard? I do have the distinct impression that they might have treated Henzler's place better if their inspiration had led them to paint objects like it or in it. But in nonfigurative painting, especially painting like Pollock's who, as Bill de Kooning said, opened the door for all the others, the world is converted into a ruin of lines and colors, beautifully painted, to be sure.

◄ Nine ►
OFF-BROADWAY

IN the art movement of the early fifties there was a rediscovery of nonfigurative forms, and behind this rediscovery was a certain Dionysian feeling of renewal, which even today resists our explanations. Why, after all, should the painters of New York City in the forties have suddenly felt a new sense of freedom? Bill de Kooning did say this to me, and I set it down for whatever it may be worth: "I was painting in the same studio on Tenth Street with Léger and Hélion during the war; and one fine day it struck me that what I was doing was just as interesting as what they were doing." But was it really contact of an intimate kind with European artists which released the New York City painters from a certain thralldom to the past? Certainly the contact had something to do with what then took place, and was probably a necessary condition for the sudden burst of creation; but it was hardly a sufficient condition, so an element of mystery remains.

After the new developments in painting in 1950, there was a new development in the theatre, the beginnings of what was called "off-Broadway," and it seems quite appropriate, when one looks back, that John Meyers, who was an editor on *View* during the War, and was managing editor of *Instead* in the period when Matta and I got it out, and after that directed the Tibor de Nagy Gallery (which showed some of our best and most advanced painters) should have played a leading role in organizing play productions in the Village, for what he called

The Poets' New York Theater. John Meyers was involved in play productions with its director the late Herbert Machiz, and together they produced the plays published by Grove Press in the volume entitled *The New York Artists Theatre.* The plays included works by James Merrill, John Ashbery, Frank O'Hara, and by me. My play appearing in that volume, *Absalom,* was, in 1956, awarded the first Obie given by the *Village Voice.* It was also singled out by *Show Business* as the best off-Broadway play of that year.

An off-Broadway play in the fifties meant a play in a theatre with less than three hundred seats, for according to Equity rules, the costs of production went up and were likely to become prohibitive once the theatre was large enough for three hundred or more spectators.

It is hard, perhaps, for people nowadays to realize how adventurous it was to produce an off-Broadway play at that time. People were used to going uptown to see plays. The idea of having small scale productions in the Village was a new one, and not quite accepted. When a play of mine, the *Death of Odysseus* was done in the Amato Theatre, on Bleecker Street, Harold Clurman, who went with me to the opening and was enthusiastic about the play, apologized to me for not reviewing it in *The Nation.* He said he was not allowed to review off-Broadway plays there. But nowadays, the most famous critics will go anywhere to see a play. They will go out of New York, to Boston, to Washington, to New Haven, and to Milwaukee. They will go into New York City auditoriums which seat no more than twenty to thirty spectators. The costs of production are no longer taken into account in determining whether a play deserves attention. From which one might conclude that there is more life in the theatre now than there was in the fifties. But this is not true; in fact, the opposite is the case.

Jean-Paul Sartre is reported to have said at the time that off-Broadway in New York was for the egotists, with the corollary that Broadway was for those lacking in ego. There is certainly some truth in the remark, if indeed Sartre made it. For ego was involved rather than money in the publications in small reviews, which, during the twenties, attracted the best writers.

Was the same thing now finally happening in the theatre? That was the hope in the fifties, a hope that enabled people with organizing energy, such as John Meyers had, to bring people into the theatre who had talents that had not yet shown themselves in connection with play productions.

Is it possible to clearly identify the organic ground of the off-Broadway movement during the fifties? In the nature of the case, anything of that sort has to have something mysterious in it, and cannot be made completely intelligible. There were people around with energy and a hunger for some kind of fame. There was money, there were actors without roles, there were empty auditoriums, and there was also a desire to see something different from what the public was being offered on Broadway.

As with the painters, there was not, in the off-Broadway theatre, a creation of significant new forms. To be sure, the possibility of what is formally new in theater is, and has to be, severely limited. One can look at a painting for anywhere from five minutes to a quarter of an hour, I, for one, hardly longer than that. (It is said that André Malraux, when he went to the Louvre, passed by the paintings hanging there, like a commander reviewing his troops, giving no more than a momentary glance at any one masterpiece.) On the other hand, you have to spend your whole evening with a play, so it has to hold your interest. The attempt to hold the spectator's interest has limited theatrical form and what is possible to it, so that it is hard to show any significant difference, formally speaking, between a play of Sophocles, written in the fifth century B.C., and the most advanced plays written in the fifties, let us say, the plays of Ionesco and Samuel Beckett.

Actually, when a really new theatrical movement developed in New York City in the early fifties, it was most strongly influenced by the trend coming from Europe, first of all from France, and later from England, of what is known as theatre of the absurd. Thus, no new forms were developed, theatrically speaking, on the basis of the new organic relations found in theatrical groupings: the new audiences for theatre, the new kinds of acting and directing that had come on the scene. All these during the late fifties and throughout the sixties were devoted not to new formal ideas, but to attacks on the old forms. For theatre became dominated by the mood of antitheatre. Probably the most talented expression of such antitheatrical techniques and antitheatrical play forms are to be found in the plays of Sam Shepard, 1979's Pulitzer Prize winner. I recall that in the early fifties there were young actors and actresses at the art club who talked about the possibilities of an abstract expressionist theatre modeled on Jackson Pollock's paintings. What they might have meant by this is not at all clear to me. But it is to be noted that Sam Shepard claims to have been inspired precisely by Jackson Pollock, so that a comparison between Shepard's plays and Pollack's painting is perhaps worth investigating. But not at this point; I'm going ahead of myself. I want to get back to the early fifties.

THE biggest productions of the fifties were two major plays of O'Neill's, *The Iceman Cometh* and *Long Day's Journey into Night*, the first of which, and I think it is the greater play, had been done unsuccessfully during the thirties.

Mary McCarthy, reviewing *The Iceman Cometh* for *Partisan Review* in 1937 had dismissed the play as tedious and its author, O'Neill, as incapable of writing a single good sentence. She was quite wrong in this judgment, for *The Iceman* is a very good play, but its failure in the late thirties demonstrates one of the laws governing theatrical life, namely that audiences have to be emotionally and intellectually prepared to accept a certain revelation, or that revelation will not speak to them. This is much less true of other forms of writing. The novel, the short story, the essay, and the poem can single out sensitive individual responses from the mix that is the public, and thus have at least a limited effect. But a play has to speak to the public, with its mixture of the sensitive, the uncaring, and the square. It cannot speak just to the most sensitive souls in a crowd, even as an orator cannot, that is, if he wants to be heard. He has to talk directly to the whole throng before him, to a common denominator of intelligence and stupidity, backwardness and progressivism, knowledge and ignorance, and of course the skilled orator can do this.

The men of the theatre have always done this, but they can only do it under certain conditions, and in the late 1930s, with the depression around us and the war ahead of us, these conditions did not exist for a proper response to O'Neill's *Iceman*.

I think it was the painter Esteban Vicente who urged me to see *The Iceman Cometh* at Circle in the Square, where José Quintero had just staged it, and Harold Rosenberg had also praised the play in the most eloquent terms. "So much has been written about alienation. But there it is, not the word, but the reality, in O'Neill's play," he said. So I went to see it.

Actually I do not think *The Iceman* is about anything like alienation, and I cannot understand to this day why Rosenberg thought of it in that way, but it is a wonderful work, though artless and full of faults, wordy, and in many respects poorly written. All the same these are more than compensated for by the humor and power of the work and its "formidable erosion of contours," to use Nietzsche's great phrase about Greek tragedy. If there is a real fault in the play, it is not in the verboseness, which could be edited, the long speeches, which could be cut; it lies in the fact that O'Neill, needing a character in his play to fulfill a certain dramatic function, was not able to produce a believable one, as Ibsen, working in the very kind of theatre O'Neill had taken as a model, always could. Thus Ibsen in his play *The Wild Duck*, which has very much the same theme as the *Iceman*, namely that self-knowledge is not life-giving (most often it is the very contrary)—needed to show us an innocent young child who is the victim of a sudden access to knowledge by the protagonist, and he was able to come up with Hedvig, one of his most beautiful creations. O'Neill, needing a young man seeking permission from some fatherlike authority to take his life, was not able to produce a credible character, and the staginess in the young man he came up with is the weakness in his play.

I must say, though, right here, that people did not go to see the play because they understood its virtues; they went to see it and also the other O'Neill play produced at that time, *Long Day's Journey into Night*, because they, the members of the audience, were going to analysts, and both plays involved analysis and self-analysis of a spontaneous kind by all the characters. In the

221

late forties, T.S. Eliot had had a great success with his *Cocktail
Party*, and he rightly attributed its success to the fact that its
theme touched on what people then were most interested in:
drinking and psychoanalysis. This interest remained throughout the fifties, and I remember saying at the time that one of the
enjoyments people felt in these plays of O'Neill was the feeling
that they were justified in sacrificing whatever sums they were
spending on therapy. Art has always had as one of its functions
the justification of life, and the way of life of Americans in the
fifties was, by and large, a psychoanalytic one.

At a party in New York during the war, the actress Ruth Ford,
whom I had known for some years through her brother Charles
Henri Ford, the publisher and editor of *View*, a magazine for
which I wrote fairly regularly, came up to me and said, rather
imperiously, "Lionel, write me a play." Now, up to that point
I had not thought of writing plays, and I had no idea as to how
one went about constructing one. But I did think about the
request, and some years later, when in Paris, I began to do what
I had never done in New York, and that was to go regularly to
the theatre. I did not write a play for Ruth Ford; William
Faulkner did. But it was much more successful in Paris, in
Albert Camus' translation, than in New York, where Ruth Ford
starred in it with her husband, Zachary Scott. Here the play,
Requiem for a Nun, did not succeed, and I remember a conversation I had with Charles Henri Ford in Paris, in which I maintained that it was unlikely that Faulkner could write a good
play, though I had great admiration for his stories and novels.
I maintained that one had to live in the city to write plays, and
that one could not be a playwright in the real sense while living
in a small town in Mississippi. Of course there is no way of
proving such a proposition, and one should not try to legislate
against the possible. Maybe at some date someone living in a
small town or on a farm will write a dramatic masterpiece, but
we should not expect this to occur. The life of the theatre has
always been part of the life that articulates itself in the big cities:
London, Paris, Madrid, Rome, Athens, Moscow; and, in fact,

Faulkner's play is a very faulty one. And while there is marvelous rhetoric in it, as we would expect, it has none of the craft and deftness of design that we look for in a theatrical work.

One may still ask, though, why cannot someone living in the country write plays? Once again, I do not say it is impossible. I do say it is immensely difficult, for a playwright has to gauge the mood and temper of his audience, and this is not something one can do in a solitary contemplation of the characters whose destinies you are interested in setting forth. As I already indicated, the playwright has to be like an orator, who must sense the mood of the crowd before him in order to know just what themes he ought to highlight in his oration. The novelist, the poet, the essayist, are less dependent on the moods and passions of those to whom they want to appeal, and they can gain their effects slowly over the years, building up larger and larger audiences with successive works, whereas the playwright has to capture his audience on the first night that his work is offered.

I was thinking of Ruth Ford when I finally wrote a play in 1953, a one act play, *The Death of Odysseus*, which John Meyers produced at the Amato Theater under the direction of Herbert Machiz. But I was thinking of a great many other things, besides, and some of the ideas I had in mind were much more literary than was perhaps proper for real success on the stage at that time. I had drawn up a kind of literary program for possible plays. My idea was not to write my own plays, but those of other playwrights which had been lost to the world through accident. For instance, *The Death of Odysseus* was based on a lost play of Sophocles for which we have no script, and only one line of dialogue. We do know the ending of the play through references to it by other writers, but we have no text of it, and I felt this was a sufficient reason to justify taking up the story. As it turned out, the production of *The Death of Odysseus* was a very successful one, and it has not failed to interest audiences whenever it was done again. And it was done several times, on various college campuses, over a New York City radio station, WEVD; in Stockholm; and in Rome. This was only the first stage of a plan I had at the time and then abandoned. But it is interesting enough to describe what I did not in fact fulfill. There were two more plays I wanted to write for which we have no text; we know that among John Milton's papers there was the title page of a projected work, which goes like this:

THE TRAGEDY OF MACBETH

by
John Milton

So John Milton had been contemplating writing his own *Macbeth*, as Greek playwrights had written about the same characters as the dramatists who preceded them. And what would John Milton's *Macbeth* have been like? What could Milton have added to what is perhaps Shakespeare's finest tragedy? How would he have altered the plot in his treatment of it? My idea, then, was to write, not my own *Macbeth*, or, as Charles Marowitz has done recently with both *Macbeth* and *Hamlet*, to revise the play in terms of modern tastes, modern expectations, but to do the very opposite: to try and discover the play which Milton planned, but did not write, to create it from nothing but the knowledge that he had planned it, to use of course his blank verse, which is imitable, and to shape the story in terms of what we know of his taste. It's still a worthy project, though not one I any longer care to address.

And there is another play that has been lost which interested me; this was Buechner's play, *Aretino*, about the Renaissance rhetorician, an artist and a blackmailer, who had tried unsuccessfully to blackmail Michelangelo, but did succeed in extorting money from other eminent figures of the time who were less strongwilled than the artist, who it is said died laughing and of a laughter which apparently caused heart attack, when a friend confided that the friend's mistress had been unfaithful. We know that Buechner, just before he died, had written a full-length play about Aretino, that his mistress had found it after Buechner's death, and, horrified by the scandalous language of the work, destroyed the manuscript. This play, too, it seemed to me then, was more worth doing than any dramatic theme or plot I was then able to think up.

I still believe there's a career open to some playwright who will make himself the servant of an inspiration that has been lost, and "restore" the masterpieces time and accident have taken from us, for a kind of archaeologist's interest is involved here, as well as a literary one. I must say I gave up the project of being someone other than I am, with much regret.

I pause here to speculate, or to state what was in my mind when I formed the project of "restoring" John Milton's *Macbeth*. What conceivably could the theme of that tragedy have been? Could it have been centered on the divine right of kings, which is certainly in the background of Shakespeare's play, but which Milton, with his political experience in the revolt against English monarchy, might have made explicit? What if Milton put on the stage some character, an advisor of *Macbeth*, let us say, or of Lady Macbeth, who argued that the personal decency and good moral character of Duncan in no way entitled him to power? The king had to be divinely appointed, and that Duncan had not been so appointed was evident from the insurrection, in which the greatly respected Cawdor was playing such an important part. And suppose that after this there came the revelation, possibly through an encounter with the witches (but of course they would have to have been conceived quite differently by Milton) that Macbeth himself was the one divinely appointed to be king. The whole play, then, could follow pretty much the pattern of Shakespeare's except that it would have to be dominated by a political idea carried to a tragic consummation, the idea being that the institution of monarchy is justified only by the notion of divine right, and that this notion is a false one. It leads men to perform violent acts, to prefer the morally vicious to the morally good, all on the grounds that the ethical norms which guide ordinary conduct do not apply to the institution of kingship. According to this version, Macbeth would not have been the victim of the witches, or of his wife's overweening ambition, but of an idea, an idea widely held in Elizabethan England, and an idea which justified Queen Elizabeth's father, Henry VIII, in his brutal execution of his wives and so many of his subjects, including his intimate friend and counselor, Sir

Thomas More. Come to think of it, there are very good reasons for somebody to undertake to restore Milton's *Macbeth*.

Such a project is of course a purely literary, and not a fundamentally theatrical, one. I must make this distinction here in order to make clear another point which I think important and about what theatre is. In any real theatrical project, society has to be involved along with the playwright, and society does not have to be involved, at least to the same degree, in the execution of a purely literary work. A novelist can be read, as Stendhal predicted he would be read, sixty years after his death. A playwright has to have his work performed during his life. Of course there have been exceptions to the rule; Kleist, for example, comes to mind, who had only one play produced during his lifetime. But no doubt this had something to do with his suicide at the age of thirty-four. Whitman has said that great poets need great audiences. As it happens, great poets have produced without such audiences. But outstanding theatrical works cannot be produced without the support of society. And, in revenge, a great theatrical work is a better indicator of social health than any equally great work in some other form. The novel and the lyric poem are less important indications of the quality of social life than is a theatrical work which requires cooperation between actors, director, stage manager, the playwright, the public, and the critics.

So once again, about Milton's *Macbeth*: Society could hardly be expected to be a partner in any playwright's effort to create it. That is why the project is a purely literary one.

In the late fifties, during the sixties, and on into the seventies, we witnessed the co-operation of society in promoting and sustaining the theatrical development known as theatre of the absurd, to which I have already referred. And society also, I should say, withdrew its support from any alternative or rival effort. To be sure, theatre of the absurd implies very negative judgments both of theatre and of society. It was a kind of suicidal development, in which society collaborated, but its very extremity made it interesting, and it called forth some of the best efforts of the best talents of that period. Fortunately the vogue is over. The theater now wants to do something else, and society wants something else of the theatre.

As already noted, I had heard actors say during the early fifties that what they would have liked would have been a theatrical movement comparable to the abstract expressionist movement in painting. Quite frankly, I was not hoping for anything like that. My hope was rather quite the contrary: That the need to keep audiences interested in what was happening on the stage would preserve theatrical form from the disintegration that had apparently become part of modern poetry and the modern novel. However, I was mistaken in this expectation.

The theatre of the absurd, happily, by now has run its course. Even one of the most skilled and famous of its dramatists, Harold Pinter, has by now addressed himself to writing a different kind of theatrical work. But for at least a decade it held the stage and prevented plays of any other type from winning recognition. It prevented many other things, too—real characters, real situations—and certain kinds of acting disappeared altogether, since they were quite unnecessary for the kind of roles offered actors in these works. There were masterpieces, yes, Ionesco's *The Chairs*, Beckett's *Krapp's Last Tape*, and more recently Pinter's *Old Times*. And it was good to have these plays presented, which perhaps would not have happened had there not been a movement supporting them.

The Irish dramatist and film writer Michael Sayers, who saw the first production of *Waiting for Godot* in Paris, I think in 1952, says that during the first weeks and months of its performance, the play was jeered by its spectators until a point was reached when the jeers and catcalls were expected and counted on and finally became part of the show. So here we had a contribution to theatre of the absurd on the part of audiences which were not originally in agreement with the playwright's style or view.

As for *Waiting for Godot*, it went on to London and played to an almost empty theatre for months. Fortunately, at that time, at least in London, it was possible to keep a play going even without real audiences. *Waiting for Godot* survived and finally caught on and became popular.

There is something singular, though, about the success of

theatre of the absurd. Its success was furthered, I believe, by a discontent with social practices and policies which was very widely felt. Thus, the energies that went into the critique of society, and of theatre, too, in these works seem to me to have been generated politically as well as aesthetically. I will make bold to suggest that the whole range of plays which we can now place under the rubric of theatre of the absurd represented a kind of propaganda for policies not yet clear to anyone, not yet precisely formulated. Thus it was that society collaborated with the absurdist playwrights by providing enthusiastic audiences for works in the main part without positive social direction or clear social meaning.

And here is another curious fact. The works of the absurdist playwrights have deeply influenced, in England at least, those playwrights determined to express social ideas, and not satisfied to denounce the world as illogical. So we have now today a whole group of talented English playwrights who have tried to combine a forthright critique of society, or, more explicitly, of class society, with the techniques of the absurdist stage. What may be accomplished in this way is not yet clear, but this much may be said now: the plays of Poliakoff, Brenton, and Stoppard are, at the very least, interesting.

What we had during the sixties was, on the one hand, a very widespread belief that it was important and valuable to disorganize and disrupt society, to weaken and destroy its institutions, to praise those it had calumniated and to calumniate those it had praised; and concurrently, in the theatre, there was an impulse felt at first by a few, but very soon afterwards by almost everyone, to break up the structure of the play form, to dispute the relevance or value of character construction and of a storyline, to convey neither message nor meaning other than the absurdity of an event directly described, to present fragments of a play to an audience determined or in any case willing to accept a fragmented society. Despite the masterpieces, one must give thanks that this effort in the theater is over.

One thing we may learn from all this: that an art form often makes better propaganda for some political purpose when it does not know what that purpose is and assumes it is serving its own ends, even when it is addressed to politically felt goals.

What we had in the theatrical movement known as theatre of the absurd was, first of all, a widespread discontent with political leaders, social institutions, the manners and morals of the time. And, secondly, resting on this reaction to events, policies, and purposes put forward in society, there was the development, not of a new logical form, but of a new feeling for the negation of logic—for illogic, for the absurd, as if it were a different or new logic. I should say here too that in a way this was not too different from what was happening in the art world at the time, for actually the abstract expressionist painters did not attract the widespread support in the early fifties which they received later. What I'm suggesting here is that the same discontent with society which provided support for theater of the absurd had already given support to the painters' discoveries in abstract expressionism. And these discoveries were not any more positive with respect to form than were the discoveries of the absurdist playwrights with respect to logic. Antiform and antilogic won the aesthetic confidence of a society generally discontented with itself.

About the matter of the life and death of movements and of tendencies, let me point out yet again that it is only the organic which can die. Forms or ideas—rational or irrational—do not die and cannot, and can always again be revivified by some new set of organic relations providing them with some real basis in life. Let us take as an example something said by the journalist Tom Wolfe interviewed on television by Ben Wattenberg: "The most important fact about this period," said Tom Wolfe, with the glibness and imprecision typical of some journalists, "is the death of Marxism." So according to Mr. Wolfe, then, Marxism is dead. But before asking whether or not this is the case, let us ask what the phrase means. Does it mean that ideas important or integral to the Marxist view of things, which were once thought true, have now been shown to be false? Or does it mean that certain organic conditions which made social groups believe in these Marxist ideas, true or false, have disappeared? Perhaps this is what Mr. Wolfe meant, but if this is what he meant, then his remark is still not clear. For supposing the

Marxist ideas were true and rational, unquestionably organic conditions would again arise which would again make them believable. But let's suppose their truth is uncertain, unsettled. In that case we cannot have certain settled convictions about their unbelievability, or that Marxism is dead. Let us go one bit further. There is one idea held by Marxists which, if true, would guarantee that the whole Marxist system simply cannot die, and while it may lose popular support at some particular moment, is certain to have a further life at some other point in time. This notion is the notion that the proletariat is a revolutionary class. What is so interesting about this notion is that its truth, if it is true, would guarantee that together with the other important ideas of Karl Marx, it would be assured of organic life. It is an idea that not only asserts itself to be true, but asserts also that an organic basis will inevitably appear guaranteeing its truth and believability. Now if this idea were false—and it seems to be the case that it is false—then it could be maintained with some degree of clarity that Marxism is dead. And this would be true no matter how many people could be found who still believe in it. But I very much doubt that Mr. Wolfe had anything like that in mind when he announced the death of Marxism.

In any case, we see what it means for there to be social support for a set of political ideas, of theatrical or pictorial forms. I must recall here that Eric Bentley, in his various criticisms of Eugene O'Neill's work as a playwright, always harped on the fact that the great American playwright gave the Theatre Guild audiences who went to see his works the philosophical fare they wanted. They wanted pessimism, said Bentley, and O'Neill gave it to them. And Bentley's implication clearly is that O'Neill was yielding to an imperative which he should somehow have resisted. Now it seems to me that what is typical of the theatre and has to be typical, is that the playwright gives his audience what it wants, plus something else. No one can doubt that there was something else besides what his audiences wanted in O'Neill's plays. Properly speaking, society can be criticized for what it wants of a playwright, but the criticism of a playwright should deal with whether that is *all* he gives society. If what society wants is something very great, and the playwright gives what it wants, and in addition something more, as in the Elizabethan theatre and the French theatre of the seventeenth century, then we have the kind of theatre that exerts immense force into the future.

In the sixties, society wanted playwrights to give it something negative, and the playwrights responded, the best of them adding something extra of beauty or precision of language, as in the best works of Beckett or Pinter. But here I must again make a distinction between what is possible in the theater and in other forms of writing, such as the novel and the lyric poem. As far back as 1850, Flaubert had expressed the idea that it was desirable for an artist not to give his readers or the public what they wanted, and to concentrate entirely on giving them only that extra element which the artist's skill made him capable of giving. So Flaubert conceived the notion of writing a novel about nothing, and of giving his public nothing but the language with which this nothing was set down. In fact he did no such thing. And the French structuralist critics are quite wrong who have said that *Madame Bovary* is a novel about nothing and nothingness. Flaubert in his novel did give his audiences what they wanted and much, much besides. And he did not succeed in separating this much, much besides, from the narratives he continued to produce. In lyric poetry, the idea of much, much besides the sentiments readers of poetry were accustomed to expect from verse, had more of a future than in the novel. After all, in a short poem one can bring words closer to nonsaying than one can bring them in a novel. So I should say that Mallarmé and poets after him were more successful than Flaubert in the project the novelist had outlined. But in the theatre, this very project is quite impossible. You cannot give a theatre audience anything at all if you do not give it what it wants and expects. You can give it more besides, but you cannot only give them this more besides. Beckett, let me repeat once again, gave audiences the negations they wanted to hear and a beauty of language and feeling they did not expect, a plus in addition to the minus they had come to the theatre to get.

Abstract painting could do what the novel and the play could not. It could give the spectator none of the figures—

landscape, the human body, interiors, objects of the external world—represented in past paintings, but only something more than these, the painter's manner of situating lines, planes, colors. Of course a situation developed in the art world where it may be said that this something more than what spectators had always wanted became precisely what they wanted. I recall that the French abstractionist, Jean Hélion, after he had escaped from a German prison camp during World War II and resumed painting in the United States, decided to employ the abstract forms of painting he had mastered, following Mondrian, to the end of representing real figures, real objects, real scenes from life. But his new paintings did not meet with approval, for the art world had by that time convinced the general audience for paintings that the important thing in painting was the something-more-than-the-objects-painted, and the objects could be left out entirely. Thus, Ad Reinhardt quipped, in a remark that has become famous: "I put everything in by leaving everything out." But by everything he must surely have meant his own manner of painting and not the things which his way of painting made no effort to describe.

WHAT we have in the theatre today, I think, is the absence of any dominant trend. We have an anarchy of taste, a proliferation of dramatic works which do not make the claim for priority of attention made by the absurdists of almost a decade ago. So probably anything can be done now on the stage for which an audience is available. However, I am inclined to think that this situation is not exactly positive, though I have no desire to see an intolerant rejection by audiences, of certain kinds of works. The contemporary tolerance, though, is not of a good kind. It represents, not the hope of variety, but a certain despair about the quality of whatever can get onto the stage. It also seems that audiences don't want anything in particular from playwrights, and this wanting or hungering for something definite by audiences is as invaluable for the production of good theatrical works as the talent of the playwright for giving such audiences both what they want and something in addition.

It was quite different in the late fifties and the early sixties. When the politically activist youth of the late fifties and early sixties threw themselves into the civil rights movement, and began their series of sit-downs in eating places in the South, a climate of political opinion was formed in the metropolitan centers of this country which anyone involved in producing a play had to take into account. In 1959, I wrote a play, *The Pretender*, which in manuscript excited many of those who read it, and when *Partisan Review* published the first act, I had several requests for stage productions. John Meyers, who was most enthusiastic about the play, even said to me, "This has to be done while the sit-downs are going on!" He thought, evidently, the same feeling of sympathy for the blacks denied their civil rights at that time, and determined to obtain them, would make audiences more receptive to the story line of *The Pretender*. Others who saw more deeply were less sanguine on this point. Jacques Traube, an associate to Jed Harris in many of his productions, wrote me enthusiastically about *The Pretender*, the first act of which he and Jed Harris had read in *Partisan Review*, but when I showed him the whole script he felt much less certain about what the response to it would be in New York. I remember his saying to me: "I'm not sure this is a play blacks will want to see, though it is about blacks. I think it's a play for a sophisticated Parisian audience. Here, there will certainly be problems." Now of course there are always problems in the production of any show, and most particularly an off-Broadway show, but the problems of *The Pretender* were quite special. After some period of indecision, I finally gave the play to Frank Perry and John Meyers, who produced it with James Earl Jones and Roscoe Brown in the leading roles, at the Cherry Lane Theatre, under the direction of Herbert Machiz.

The Pretender dealt with the reaction of a rather snobbish and well-educated black intellectual to the rape of his young wife by a Southern redneck. My protagonist wanted to punish the rape with a lynching, the lynching of a white man by blacks, and he was opposed in his effort to carry out this revenge by the very blacks he called on to help him obtain it. His position was that if whites merely stopped lynching blacks, no real equality had been achieved; such equality could only come when blacks also stopped lynching whites. But how were they going to stop what they had not yet begun to do? "I want to make a start," he said, but nobody in the play agrees with my protagonist.

And many who saw the play also disagreed with him. Brooks Atkinson, who gave *The Pretender* a quite good review in the *Times,* and judged it always interesting, had this caveat, however: He thought the protagonist selfish, where I myself thought of him as trying to live by a code borrowed from past aristocracies and which did not exist for blacks. But many saw the whole matter as Brooks Atkinson did. I recall that when I read the play at a backer's party for it arranged by John Meyers at his apartment, one of my audience, someone unknown to me, when I had finished reading, got to his feet and attacked me and the play rather abusively, and his point was precisely that the protagonist was unconscionably selfish and that no audience would stand for the way he carried on. As I remember, I lost my temper when the play was attacked. I said I had not come there to hear this kind of nonsense, and walked out. The next morning, I was told by John Meyers that the man who had attacked me had, after I left, contributed ten thousand dollars for the play's production. But I was not done with him, for when the play was produced, and had been reviewed by Brooks Atkinson, I had another confrontation with this backer, again at Meyers' apartment. He shouted at me, waving the *New York Times* review: "Didn't I tell you that your hero was much too selfish! Obnoxious in fact! I know now that I'm going to lose every cent I put into the play! In fact, I want to lose it! For I want you to suffer, too! And I've gotten this much for my money: I've been able to read my own judgments stated better than I could by the critic of the *New York Times.*" Whatever I thought of the man then, and it was not much, I have to admit now that he, too, was part of off-Broadway. For without men of such views and interested in such satisfactions, few off-Broadway plays would have been produced.

Not all the reviews of *The Pretender* were critical of it; the reviewer for *The Villager,* for instance, suggested that the audiences at the first performances must have felt like the audiences of Shaw's early plays, hearing cherished opinions turned upside down. Jerry Tallmer in the *Village Voice*, in a review that was not at all unfriendly, did, however, suggest that the actors, who were black, were not up to their roles. In fact, though, three of the actors in the cast are among the most famous black actors known in this country today: James Earl Jones, Roscoe Brown, and Brooks Alexander. Of the three, James Earl Jones is by far the best known, especially since his performances in *The Great White Hope*. I heard his first reading for the main part in *The Pretender* when he came down to try for it, and it was the most brilliant reading for a part I have ever heard at an audition; however, he never developed his understanding of his role or of his lines during the weeks of rehearsal. Roscoe Brown, on the other hand, cast in a minor part, was, during rehearsals, given the most important part after the lead, and his performance was outstanding. His acting I believe gained for it whatever plaudits the play won. As for Brooks Alexander, he was both excellent in and discontented with his part, which he wanted me to lengthen. I could hardly blame him for that. He was too fine an actor to be satisfied with a very minor part.

I think the play could not have succeeded at the time, for reasons which are also interesting in view of the light they throw on general problems of theatre. The moment when a play is most alive is when it is most controversial; but when it is most controversial, it is most likely to either fail or not even be produced, for producers will not risk large sums to put on the stage a work which may very well not succeed. Take Genet's play, for instance, *The Blacks*, which went on the same season as *The Pretender*, and which had a five-year run off Broadway. This play drew audiences from those interested in the civil rights movement, which was then getting the fullest support; audiences in New York City found in the play an instigation to continue the black movement of revolt. I was told that Gene Frankel, who directed it, conceived of presenting the work in such a way that it would appear to whites and blacks in the audience as an "acting out" of their fears, hatreds, and fantasies: a therapeutic session for members of both races. Whatever one thinks of Gene Frankel's interpretation of the play—and there were many

Europeans who did not favor it—the result in terms of audience appeal was a complete success. *The Blacks,* which could not hold the stage for any length of time in any other city, ran for five years off-Broadway in New York City.

But if one tried to redo *The Blacks* today, I think it would have no chance of even a short run on the stage. It is not that powerful a play, and its rhetorical virtues are not sufficient to make up for its monotonously slow pace and lack of plot. It probably cannot be done at all today, but when it was done, successfully, it required very special directorial treatment to succeed, and the success it enjoyed was greater than that of any of the much better plays Genet has written. One might even say that a play lives by succeeding at a moment when there is some real likelihood that it will fail. A play is much less alive when it is certain that the play will succeed, and it goes without saying a play can gain nothing from the certainty that it will fail. The life of a play is more like life than that of any other kind of art.

I WOULD like to take up again now in a more detailed way just what it means to say that society is a collaborator to a greater degree in the success of a dramatic work than in the success of any other kind of literary work, and hence deserves some of the credit for whatever plays we judge favorably. The idea seems clear enough when so stated, but there are difficulties in understanding when we turn to some examples.

Let's start with an unambiguous case, one in which society is clearly involved in the support of a controversial work, contradicting that society's major project at the time, i.e., the Peloponnesian War by fourth-century Athens. With his city engaged in a war with Sparta in which its continued existence was at stake, Aristophanes put on his most famous pacifist play, *Lysistrata,* and Athenians supported the play and were not interfered with in so doing by the government or by propaganda from the government. It has been said that toleration of the play's production during wartime was the highest expression of political liberalism in the arts known to this date. For an analogy, we would have to think of an antiwar play produced in

New York at a time when the American expeditionary force was engaged in fighting the German army in the Argonne forest. Anything like that would have been inconceivable in the atmosphere of New York. Nor were pacifist plays for mass audiences conceivable in the London which jailed Bertrand Russell for pacifism, nor in Paris, Berlin, Vienna, or Moscow. So the facts about *Lysistrata's* production are quite remarkable. It should be remembered, though, that a like liberalism of spirit was also present in Athens two generations before Aristophanes, when Aeschylus, only seven years after Xerxes' effort to invade Athens by sea, put on his tragedy, *The Persians*, the protagonist of which is precisely the Persian invader. This would have been like the French putting on a tragedy in which the protagonist was the German kaiser, only seven years after the Versailles treaty. No doubt, though, if the French had been capable at that time of so generous a spirit to a defeated enemy, they very likely would have eliminated the reactionary clauses of the Versailles treaty to which John Maynard Keynes objected, and which he warned would lead to another war. In any case it does seem quite clear to me that the people of Athens are deserving, in a very direct way, of the honor we accord to Aeschylus's tragedy and to Aristophanes' comedy.

But there are other examples where the point I am making is not yet clear, where it is in fact, at the very least, blurred. Modern nations are much more complicated than the Greek city-states, and there are different and multiple power centers, where in a city like Athens there was only one. So it might be the case, for instance, that a city like New York could be accorded some responsibility for the success of a dramatic work (on or off Broadway) which could not survive the cultural atmosphere in any other city. Let's take a very successful play produced in New York just after the Second World War, Arthur Miller's *Death of a Salesman*. The play as then written and presented to the public under the direction of Elia Kazan was nothing short of an attack on the American spirit of private enterprise, which was described in the most unflattering terms in the defeat and suicide of Willie Loman because he could no longer make good as a salesman, or even be hired at that kind of work by anyone any more. Did the success of this play by Miller in 1949 indicate that the people of the United States were in a self-critical mood, that the failings of the American economic system and the failings also of the spiritual values associated with it were very much in people's minds at that time? No, I do not think that is the case; I think Miller was speaking for an advanced segment of the population, situated in New York City and critical of the country as a whole, and it was only that segment of the population that deserves any social credit for the favorable reception of his play. More than thirty years after the first production of *Salesman,* it was done again by George Scott, and most successfully, but this time the actor, who also directed the production, gave it an entirely different meaning. In Willie Loman, as portrayed by George Scott, the values of American enterprise were not attacked; in fact, Willie Loman seemed an almost tragic figure, towering over his wife, his sons and acquaintances. It was quite a different play under George Scott's handling of it, and it was received enthusiastically, but it no longer brought the offense to self-satisfied feeling which had made the first production of the play so dramatic. One might say even, it no longer needed the support of society. If I may rephrase a line of Saint-John Perse's poem, "Exile": It could now inhabit its name.

It might even be said that when a play is not a response to some serious judgement made of or by society, or when it does not express some demand made on it by others, then, to all interests and purposes, it is dateless. It becomes, however well made, like those classical works done repeatedly, not because they repond to our troubles or fashions or goals in some way, but because in some magnificent sense they once responded to the interests of others, now dead. The purely aesthetic play, governed only by aesthetic values, carries with it very little of the quality of the *time* in which it appears, from which I conclude that the requirements of society on the playwright, when he meets them, confer on the work achieved its relation not only to society but also to a particular time.

I want to give one more example to make my point clearer. In 1980 the State University of New York at Buffalo theatre department produced a new and quite good play by Eric Bentley entitled *Lord Alfred's Lover*, excellently done and with a fine actor in the role of Oscar Wilde. The play has many virtues, but it is topical, it seems to me, in a way that is not exciting. The theme of the play, its message, is that gays should come out of the closet. But gays have come out of the closet, and so Bentley's play would only be really exciting if given in some quarter where gays had not yet asserted themselves or been prohibited from doing so. In Castro's Cuba, Bentley's play would be thoroughly theatrical. Unhappily, it cannot be done there, and from this we see the paradox that makes theater so difficult and so different from other forms of literary expression. The ideal moment for a play's production is that moment when its theme is most controversial, and that is the very moment when it is least likely to be done. No other form of writing is dependent to that degree on any condition of this kind. *Madame Bovary* was, it is true, involved in controversy when it appeared, but its effectiveness has not been lessened by the fact that what was controversial in the middle of the nineteenth century is universally acceptable today. Novels and poems do not have to agitate us. They do not have to turn the world we see upside down, attack our most deeply held convictions; but a theatre which does not challenge us in ways that are serious is not worthy of general support.

I must confess here that when the plays described as absurdist began to occupy the stage, I was inclined to see the danger to theatre which they represented rather than the positive aspects of their novelty. And when Martin Esslin's book, *Theatre of the Absurd* first appeared, I reviewed it critically in *Partisan Review,* and I even objected to the term which he, I believe, brought into our theatrical glossary. He has been proved right on this point; the term "theatre of the absurd" is here to stay, for there is no better term than that to describe works by Beckett, Pinter, and Ionesco produced during the sixties, and also the works of any number of other playwrights who followed their lead. But I still think Esslin was wrong to apply the term "theatre of the absurd" to plays created and produced in past periods: plays by Shakespeare, Molière, Aristophanes. When one does that one loses the value of the specificity in such a term as *theatre of the absurd:* it should only be used to cover a particular moment of theatre and a particular demand on theatre by audiences.

With the sixties and seventies behind us, surely it is possible to see with a little more detachment what that moment was like, what audiences wanted of theatre. I think there was a generally felt mood of exhilaration connected with the judgment that nothing was valid, that everything positively supported was in fact ridiculous. The state was absurd and so were its representatives, most particularly the military. The schools were absurd and so were those who served it. Teachers were objects of fun. Even the structure of the play, as it had been observed by past playwrights, was essentially a joke played on audiences. To take it seriously, one would have to start laughing at oneself. And if everything was absurd, then there could be no *raisonneur* in a comedy, and the presence of the *raisonneur* in the play had been essential to the structure of comedy. The mood of theatre of the absurd was an apocalyptic one, an apocalypse of the laughable; and I've often thought that probably the most perfect protagonist for this mood would have been the Greek materialist, Democritus, hailed by Santayana as the laughing philosopher, and who is said to have died in the following way: Looking down at Athens from the Acropolis, Democritus is said to have been so struck by the absurd actions of his fellow Athenians that he literally laughed himself to death.

That mood, of course, was bound to pass, but I think those audiences of the sixties who were interested in theatre of the absurd and demanded it, were the last audiences which demanded anything. We now have the suggestion that without any emotional demands or ideological demands on theatre by any part of the public, playwrights can still do something new, progressive, creative, if you will, by modifying certain purely formal arrangements in theatrical presentation. Thus, Mr. Robert Wilson has been greatly praised for productions which everyone admits to be dramatically boring and without content, but which are said to bemuse the spectator with scenic arrangements that are beautiful in the way mass scenes of Tintoretto or

Rubens are. The pleasure found in going to see a play of Mr. Wilson is, it is said, like the pleasure in seeing an old master. But can we call someone a new master in theatre who is simply trying to recall the effect of an old master in painting?

And even in the pictorial arts, a need is being expressed today to do something more than rearrange the planes of color, the shapes without figurative meaning which have become the sole concern of most of our best painters. Stamos and Vicente continue to produce beautifully colored forms on canvas, and introduce the novel and unexpected within limits expressly set within the resolve to be nonfigurative. But the late Philip Guston, a few years ago, began to set down on canvas the unsightly, which is visible now everywhere in our big cities. He began to paint scabs, broken objects, litter, urban insects, dirt, the other side of city life, which most of those who can afford to buy fine paintings can also manage to avoid seeing. He brought the scandalousness of our street life—regularly presented in a vulgar way on television—into fine art. Guston's work during his last years is a sign of the times, prophetic, I believe, of developments that are likely to take place in other forms of art.

≺ Ten ≻
BREAKUP

THERE are intellectuals, any number of them, in New York City today, but is there any one group of them able to speak for the others? I have had reasons for seriously doubting that there is, ever since one evening in 1958.

An evening in the Big Town that was indeed a Big Town evening in its animation and futility! But let me first sketch the political background to it: Boris Pasternak, awarded the Nobel Prize in Stockholm, had been denied permission by the Soviet authorities to go to Sweden and be honored for his work. Moreover, his novel *Dr. Zhivago*, for which he had been given the Nobel award, was denied publication by the Soviet government. Under these circumstances it seemed perfectly proper for politically interested intellectuals in New York City to send the Soviet government a letter of protest. (This our own press would have published, whatever the Russian response.) Surely, I thought, there was no great problem here. One had only to bring together a sampling of the New York City writers who had expressed political views over the years and had in the past been critical of Soviet policies. At least that was how it seemed to me. I consulted Meyer Schapiro on this, and obtained his agreement to suggest to some of the writers of our acquaintance that a meeting be held at which we might discuss the kind of protest which would be appropriate.

Here are some of the writers we invited: Dwight Macdonald, Mary McCarthy (she was then living in New York

City), Harold Rosenberg, William Phillips of *Partisan Review* (Philip Rahv was then in Boston), Norman Podhoretz, Paul Goodman, Hannah Arendt, Eric Bentley, Stanley Plastrik of *Dissent*, (Irving Howe was in the Midwest). To be sure we did not invite every single writer or scholar whom we knew to be living in New York City. But the ones we did invite were certainly representative; moreover, they were persons who had seen each other with some regularity over the years and had participated, on other occasions, in common actions. These were not the only intellectuals in New York City, but without them, could one say there was an intelligentsia?

We did not invite those intellectuals in the Committee for Cultural Freedom who had taken what I considered to be a cold war position towards the Soviet Union. The position I took, with Schapiro's support, and which I presented at the meeting was this: The Republic of Letters was indeed a reality, if not an actually existing entity. This republic, of which Pasternak was as especially honored member, was not itself a signatory of either the NATO agreements or of the Warsaw Pact. We were making our appeal as citizens of this republic on behalf of a fellow citizen.

Joseph Buttinger had offered us a whole floor of his townhouse on East Eighty-seventh Street, and he had agreed to chair our meeting. Just a word about Mr. Buttinger, who is, by the way, quite well known in left-wing intellectual circles. An Austrian worker with Socialist convictions, he had married a cultivated American woman of great wealth; she was sympathetic to left-wing causes, which the couple often backed. I am told they were very generous to Ortega y Gasset when he was in exile, and I know that Mr. Buttinger has been helpful to *Dissent*. I had visited the Buttingers once before, at their apartment on Central Park West, where they had hosted a party for *Dissent*, and I remember being struck by their library, which was just extraordinary, and also at the availability of the books, which Mr. Buttinger generously offered to lend to anyone at the *Dissent* party. By 1958, though, the Buttingers had left their apartment for the more grandiose townhouse on Eighty-seventh Street. Mr. Buttinger, needless to say, did not abandon his books. These now occupied the whole ground floor of the new townhouse, and if you wanted to borrow one of them, you had to discuss the matter with a librarian. In fact, if you wanted a book you had to first of all apply for a card, just as in the public libraries. And the date of your borrowing would be duly stamped, the book taken noted, and you could be asked, if need be, not to keep it beyond a certain date. There were many more books on the shelves, as I remember, and every single one of these was less available. Such was the march of progress in the Buttinger household, hardly differing in this respect from the movement of things in the world outside.

To be sure, there were reasons for controlling the coming and going of the Buttinger books. People who are not forced to sign on the dotted line when they borrow a book tend, the Buttingers had found, not to return it, thus depriving others who would also like the pleasure of not signing up for a book, of just this privilege. So what is one to do in such a case? The Buttingers had in fact done the sensible thing. They indexed the books, hired a librarian, gave their prospective book borrowers cards, and quite broke my heart when I arrived that evening in 1958 and saw what had occurred. Mr. Buttinger had of course also limited his own freedom. He could no longer say to a friend who wanted some book: "Take it; it's downstairs." Yes, of course the book was downstairs, or might be there. But wherever it was, it wasn't Buttinger's; it now belonged to his library.

The new order of the Buttinger library gave me my first shock in an evening full of crossed purposes. Here I want to briefly describe the main actors in the drama which was to follow. I shall begin with Paul Goodman who was, I think, the only one we invited who represented a generally dissenting policy with regard to the Pasternak affair. Others raised difficulties about what Schapiro and I proposed, but I think Paul had come *politically* prepared to make trouble for any such proposal. Here is my speculation as to why:

Goodman was at that moment in his career just on the point of becoming famous, but without the knowledge that this was about to happen. Lack of adequate fame, which is to say, a fame extending beyond small circles of admirers, had made him irri-

table for years, and especially irritable in those small groups
where he was well known. I believe he was aware at that time
that a consistently anti-Communist, or—what was almost the
same—a pro-American government attitude, would prevent any
writer from being taken up by the youth. Maybe Paul was even
more intuitive than I am suggesting, and, looking into the future, was able to read there that to successfully combat American military policy in Southeast Asia one would have to make
some kind of alliance with the pro-Communists among the
young. Let's grant Paul the best of motives. In any case, he had
come prepared to sabotage any kind of action on behalf of Pasternak. As he took his seat among us he announced for all to hear
that he had not read *Dr. Zhivago* and had no intention of reading
it. Then he said: "Pasternak can read me." When the first suggestion was put forward that we draft a letter of protest to the
Soviet government, Paul indicated that he would sign no such
letter. Why not? This was the reason he gave: Coming from us,
such a protest would be in bad faith, for we had not protested
the refusal of a moving picture house in Hicksville, Long Island
to show a recent Charlie Chaplin film which made fun of American anti-Communism. "Where were we when this film was denied a showing?" Paul wanted to know. "Where were we?"
Mary McCarthy countered, "We were certainly not in Hicksville." She had never been there, had no intention of going
there, and just because she hadn't gone to Hicksville did not
mean that Pasternak should not be allowed to go to Stockholm.
But, as I found on other occasions, a witticism was not going to
stop Paul when he felt himself deeply committed. He had two
other objections to our projected protests: First of all, we had
done nothing for James Joyce during the twenties when *Ulysses*
was banned, and secondly, he thought that in banning the publication of certain books, the Soviet leaders showed a respect for
literature which American politicians lacked. Miss McCarthy
responded: "Then hadn't a certain respect been shown for literature in the banning of *Ulysses*?" And returning to the matter
of the Charlie Chaplin film, she added that in her opinion anyone who had respect for Chaplin would not want to live in
Hicksville; so why should the film have been shown there? This

remark of hers was interpreted by Dwight Macdonald, who was sitting next to me, as an indication that from now on Paul Goodman was fair game, and after that whatever Paul said, Dwight attacked.

In fact, Dwight did have something against Paul, an article in *Dissent* in which Goodman had described Dwight as a man who thought with his typewriter. To complicate matters, Dwight that evening was also involved in a running battle with Harold Rosenberg, who had called him a Philistine in *Dissent* for his views on contemporary art. I think Dwight must have felt that night that Harold was politically allied with Paul and that he would have to do battle with both. But I must say that on this particular evening Rosenberg said little—this was most unusual —and made no really signal contribution to the chaos of our meeting.

In addition to the Macdonald-Goodman conflict, there was Mary McCarthy's feud with me. We had always had friendly relations, and I did admire most of her writings, though not her ventures in dramatic criticism. When she attacked Eugene O'Neill's reputation, remarking that not only was he incapable of writing an entire play, but incapable of composing one single good sentence, I did a piece against her in *The New Leader* in which I indicated that O'Neill was certainly the best of our playwrights and Miss McCarthy was just as certainly not our best dramatic critic. When she swept into the Buttinger living room, Miss McCarthy told me in the roundest terms that she had come, not merely to pay tribute to Pasternak, but also to tell me I should have informed her I was breaking off relations with her *before* I published a piece critical of her views. I replied, as I poured a drink for her from Mr. Buttinger's excellent stock, that I believed in the manners observed in Parliament, where one attacks one's opponent roundly and then exchanges compliments with him or her over drinks. Mary, though, thought this was not a matter of manners, but of morals, and let me know she would do her best to cross me all evening.

As for Hannah Arendt, she was not opposed, of course, to helping Pasternak, but she was doubtful that our intervention would help him. This was a serious consideration, and it is something everyone must think of now who is concerned to help the Russian dissidents. They do insist, and have insisted all along, that American intervention helps them, but of course such intervention has to be properly timed, properly stated, and as we have seen from the fate of Shcharansky, may well be counterproductive. In any case, Miss Arendt urged caution upon us and had nothing more positive to suggest. As for Pasternak, she was doubtful that any statement by us could help him, and quite sure that any but the most perfectly stated protest would actually hurt him, and she gave us the feeling that it was not possible for us to come up with a statement she would feel obliged to sign. At this point practically everyone present helped himself to a drink, and Dwight, by now quite drunk, indicated that he wanted to take the floor. Mr. Buttinger, who was chairing the meeting, denied it to him. I cannot remember what his reason was, but I do remember that at the time I did not think it arbitrary. But Dwight thought it was. "Let's get another chairman," he shouted, as if another could be supplied as easily as an additional drink. He had also forgotten that Mr. Buttinger was not only our chairman, but our host. As I recall, Mr. Buttinger gracefully relinquished his chair, leaving us to our own devices for contriving chaos.

And chaotic it was after he left.

Meyer Schapiro pleaded with us to try and find some measure of real agreement so that we could at the very least express our feeling that Pasternak deserved support. He spoke with the clarity and eloquence which had so often, in past meetings, thrilled most of those in the room. This time, though, his eloquence was unavailing.

Paul once again asserted his unwillingness to sign any statement which implied any approval of the policy of our government, most especially its policy on literary questions. Any attack on Soviet policy, he said, was an endorsement of that of its opposite number. To this I objected that the United States was without any policy on literary matters, at which point William Phillips, who had so far not intervened in the argument, took moderate issue with me and gave support to Paul's position.

I have observed William Phillips's behavior at general meet-

247

ings and have noticed a certain political line he always seems to follow. During the sixties, at a meeting called by *Commentary* to discuss the civil rights movement in this country, a meeting at which James Baldwin, Nat Glazer, Sidney Hook, and Gunnar Myrdal were the panelists, William Phillips, when he took the floor, announced: "I'm probably the only intellectual here who agrees with Jimmy Baldwin." In fact this was not the case. There were others in the audience who did not agree with what had been said by Sidney Hook, by Gunnar Myrdal, by Nat Glazer, and who did agree with Baldwin's comments. At Buttinger's in 1955, William took what amounted to the same line, though he did not say: "I'm probably the only one here who agrees with Paul." What he said was this: "I'm trying to understand what Paul has said because I would like to agree with him." Now I'm quite sure that this was a correct description of his desire; he did want to agree with Paul. For Paul was clearly the one taking a line that could be interpreted as *left*. But William did not say, "I want to agree with Paul because he is taking a *left* line on this." William has a certain gift for subtlety, and so he put his proposition differently. He said: "I think Paul wants us to respond as writers to the Soviet treatment of Pasternak, rather than as persons committed to a certain political line." According to William, Paul was the one who had talked like a writer, though William did not go so far as to say that he had talked on behalf of literature. What Paul had in fact said was that he did not want to defend Pasternak and that he would not criticize the Soviet government. Somehow, as William saw it, those of us who wanted to defend Pasternak, and who, by the way, unlike Paul, had actually read his novel, were not thinking as *writers* hoping to defend a fellow writer.

It was precisely to rule out this sort of argument that I had suggested at the outset of our meeting that we had come together as citizens of the Republic of Letters, and that it was in the name of this imaginary institution, and not of any actually existing state, that we were determined to protest the Soviets' treatment of Boris Pasternak. What Paul Goodman had done, and what William Phillips supported him in doing, amounted to denying that there was any such thing as a Republic of Letters. There were only states like the Soviet Union and the

United States, hostile to each other, and we could not attack one of these states without giving comfort and support to its opposite number. To cap the confusion, we were now being told by William Phillips that Paul wanted us to think of ourselves as writers in what amounted to nothing less than a round denial that there was any purely literary institution to which we could say we belonged. I replied that Paul was trying to say that we were just United Staters or Soviet Staters, and that the so-called Republic of Letters was just a literary dream.

At this point somebody noticed that our host Mr. Buttinger had left his chair (in fact he had left it in some dudgeon) and suggested that it was only proper to invite him back. Not, however, to resume the function of chairman, Dwight insisted. Somebody said to Dwight, "You won't ask him to leave if he comes back and sits down quietly?" Somebody went to fetch Mr. Buttinger, but when asked to return, he indicated that he had had enough of our drunken shenanigans, and declined.

Just two more details about the meeting. I, too, had helped myself to Mr. Buttinger's bourbon, and no doubt this had been duly noted. When at one point I suggested that we propose to the leading Soviet literary journal that it publish Edmund Wilson's favorable review of *Dr. Zhivago* (which had appeared in the *New Yorker*) and, in return for this concession to American literary opinion, would try to obtain publication in some leading American publication, preferably the *New Yorker*, for any critique of *Dr. Zhivago* by a Russian critic chosen by the Soviet authorities, Miss Arendt airily dismissed my suggestion. She said: "Schnapps's ideas."

When it was finally apparent that no statement would be agreed upon, the meeting broke up. It had been suggested that Harold Rosenberg write a provisional statement which would then be sent to Irving Howe for revision, but as we left the Buttinger drawing room, Eric Bentley, whom I had brought to the meeting, whispered to me, "I'll never sign a political statement edited by Irving Howe." Nor did he. And Harold Rosenberg wrote no statement, and none was presented for Irving Howe to revise. None of those present at that meeting were able to sign a statement on behalf of Pasternak. It was evident that the New York intellectuals could no longer act as a group.

What broke up our meeting? Personal rivalries? Drunkenness? Lack of seriousness? Political differences? All these, of
course, played a part. But if I am to single out any one cause that
was more than merely contributory to the general disorder,
then this cause was none of the ones I have already mentioned,
but something quite different; in fact it was fear of a very particular kind which in recent times I have seen dominate many
meetings, many movements, much action and inaction. What
fear? The fear that what one did or said might be regarded as
contrary, and even harmful, to the Left.

One must in no case do anything that might be harmful to
the Left. What if the projected action seems a good one? Then
one must be all the more careful. One must consider every
possible consequence, even the most remote. Many actions that
at first sight might seem beneficent, when looked at more closely
turn out to involve a possible damage to the Left. What Left?
Which Left? Never mind. And do not ask. Indeed there is need
not to ask, for the very fact that we don't know what the Left
is today means that whatever it be, its situation is precarious. We
don't even know what the Left is? Then we must be all the more
careful of it. We must do nothing that by any stretch of imagination may be regarded as against whatever it is that remains of
this Left, which we can no longer identify. And it was on this
fear that Paul Goodman had played when he assailed us for not
having done battle for Chaplin's film in Hicksville during the
early fifties, or even for Joyce's novel during the twenties, when
most of those in the room had been too young to know of Joyce.
And it was this fear which William Phillips tried to make us feel
when he said that Paul had wanted us to respond to the Pasternak affair like writers. But nobody had been invited to the Buttinger townhouse who could be described as antileftist, and
almost everyone there wanted to be thought of as a leftist or as
a supporter of the Left. Also, there was not one person in the
room who then knew with any degree of clarity just what it was
still possible to mean by the term "Left." I have observed that
it is in such moments of political confusion—that is, when we
don't know what the Left is—that our fear of being thought
against the Left, or anti-Left, is greatest.

But there is reason, I believe, behind this fear of damaging the Left even when one is not sure what the Left stands for or is at any particular moment. For fear of damaging the Left may represent fear of dissolving intellectual unity, the intelligentsia, in fact, which in America in recent times has only been brought together, shaped into some kind of unity, by leftist interests. So for any of my readers who may judge William Phillips's behavior as I described it at the Pasternak meeting as devious or personally motivated, I want to make this clearly contrary judgment: I think William was motivated by a desire to keep the intellectuals together, and this he may have very well believed could only be done by steering clear of any action which could be interpreted as anti-Left. And the fact is that the New York intelligentsia came apart simply because it could not agree that it was in the interest of anything that could be called the Left to protest Pasternak's treatment by the Russians. In Europe, of course, there have been right-wing intelligentsias. I'm thinking of, for instance, *L'Action française*; and even in this country we had for a time at least the grouping of Southern writers led by Donald Davidson and Allen Tate. But this grouping was of only very short duration, and one of its most gifted writers, Robert Penn Warren, threw in his lot finally with more moderate intellectuals in the North. Today of course there are some right-wing writers grouped around the National Review. But generally speaking, whenever there has been any significant coherent activity by intellectuals, involving more than just a few persons, this activity has been leftist in character and motivated by left-wing interests. In a period where it is said that there is a conservative tide sweeping the country, and at a time too, when leftism is in intellectual difficulty and cannot define itself clearly, it is still hard to find any clearly articulated right-wing intelligentsia in this country or in fact in any country in western Europe. If there is going to be an intelligentsia of any sort, it apparently has to be left-wing.*

*Some may say: What about the group of right-wing or neoconservative intellectuals who came together to back the Republican candidate in 1980? Now the reason they backed the Republican candidate was because he promised *changes* of the kind many thought needed for our economy, and the Democratic party to the left, together with

Now why should this be the case? About twenty years back, M. Mascolo, one of the editors at Gallimard and the author of a book on communism, which he called the only interesting thing to talk about, wrote an article on the Left in *Les Temps modernes* in which he tried to make what might be called a poetic analysis of leftism and its appeal. He brought up the term *gaucheur*, the French word for southpaw, and he associated with the word *gaucheur* the other meaning of the French word *gauche*, that is to say, awkward or erratic. Now southpaw pitchers in American baseball are not always awkward or erratic, nor are such tennis stars as Jimmy Connors and Rod Laver. Yet, all southpaws are expected to be erratic. It is a great surprise to us when they are not. What Mascolo suggests in his essay is that the Left is composed of *gaucheurs* or southpaws in political or social life: Jews or members of racial minorities, people who are expected to be deviant or erratic in their behavior, who do not represent the steady, sobering outlook of the center, or the robust simplicities that are presented by the Right. Mascolo almost suggests that the Left is composed of individuals "sicklied over with the pale cast of thought" in counterposition to the Laerteses of this world who are on the Right.

M. Mascolo's idea of the Left as composed of *gaucheurs* may explain this surprising fact which appeared in the press of September 4, 1978: Samuel Beckett, Jean-Paul Sartre, and Eugene Ionesco sent the following telegram to Victor Korchnoi, then engaged in a chess match for the world championship with the Soviet champion, Anatoly Karpov: "We are one hundred percent for you." No doubt, for these three writers Karpov represented the Soviet political establishment, which Jean Paul-Sartre for a long time had supported, but to which he was finally opposed. In any case, let's assume the challenger was not, like Korchnoi, simply a defector from the Soviet state (which was also punishing his wife and children, whom they have prevented from joining him abroad), but an openly declared right-

---

the intellectuals who supported it, was *against* change. It is clear to me that intellectuals come together to bring about change, and in most instances change has come from the Left.

winger in politics (whatever political position that might mean); could one expect a comparable telegram from leading literary figures on the Right? In fact it's hard to think of any. In any case, right-wingers representing traditional ways of doing things operate with society rather than in opposition to it. When they enter into radical conflict with society, they tend to become out and out reactionaries. *Gaucheurs*, to use Mascolo's term, or southpaws, on the Right, are most generally Fascists.

In any case, M. Mascolo's ideas do not explain at all the importance of leftist ideas for any intelligentsia to maintain itself. I suppose the reason for this is historical. Change has come basically from left-wing actions, and historical change requires the effort of organized groups. Society is not changed by the behavior of even great individuals in isolation: Solzhenitsyn cannot himself change the character of Soviet life. And he recognizes this in the financial and political support he is now giving to the groups of Soviet dissidents.

The name Solzhenitsyn suggests all that has happened in the last two decades when we think of the relation the great Russian writer and dissident has to intellectuals of the West, as compared with that between them and Pasternak. First of all, let us consider the way their work has been judged. Pasternak's *Doctor Zhivago* was, I think, greatly overrated. On the other hand, Solzhenitsyn's remarkable study of Lenin, a single volume excerpted from his vast novel on the First World War, has been miserably treated in the press. I think it's the greatest fictional work about an historical figure I know of. And when I made this point to one of the intellectuals who had been present at the Pasternak meeting to which Paul Goodman had announced that he had not read and would not read *Doctor Zhivago*, I met with this comment: "It didn't even occur to me to read it, seeing that the reviews were so bad."

Why were the reviews of *Lenin in Zurich* so bad? The reason is very simply this: Alexander Solzhenitsyn asked for a different kind of support from that which Pasternak received. One could support Pasternak as a writer who was not really opposed to the policies of his country, but only to a certain harshness in the application of those policies. And as one who stood not for a different society or a different politics, but for the right to express oneself in literature. Alexander Solzhenitsyn stands for a frontal direct assault on Soviet policies and on all those in the West who want to get along with the Soviet Union and do not want to engage in ideological warfare with it. Alexander Solzhenitsyn stands for, and in fact calls for, a return to the cold war attitudes which prevailed in the United States until our adventure in Vietnam ended in disaster. He has called on the intelligentsia of the West to take a stand which it cannot identify as "Left." And as a result, Solzhenitsyn is isolated.

Three young French philosophers, *les nouveaux philosophes*, have tried to organize a new intellectual grouping in France, taking inspiration from Solzhenitsyn's writings. Are they trying to form a right-wing intelligentsia? They have been charged with that, and one can see the reasons why. But on the other hand, if one looks a little more closely at the intellectual situation in France and their response to it, one realizes that matters are not so simple: these *nouveaux philosophes* charge that the French Left has become identical with the French establishment. They are the heterodox and not the representatives of orthodoxy. They are the southpaws, rather than the leftists in France who are entrenched in the universities and the publishing houses. In any case, M. Levi and company will not succeed. The problem of making a leftist criticism of the Soviet Union, a problem which Leon Trotsky and Koestler and many other radicals over the past forty years could not handle satisfactorily, is not going to be resolved by shouting a few anti-Soviet slogans and calling this a new philosophy.

Behind these follies there is of course a real problem, and a problem felt with especial keenness by intellectuals: the problem of the Soviet Union. This state is, as Pasternak rightly said of it, unprecedented. It came into existence as a result of historical forces, but also unquestionably as a result of a specifically intellectual interpretation of those forces: i.e., the interpretation made of them by Lenin and his followers. And in this sense it was correct of Trotsky to say in his *History of the Russian Revolution* that without Lenin the revolution would never have taken place. So intellectuals everywhere have always felt a responsibil-

ity for the Soviet Union, and they have not spared themselves
in the effort to defend, justify and protect it, often from slander,
sometimes from perfectly just accusations. In a way the Soviet
Union is their product, the product of their intelligence, born
of their speculative historical thinking as Athena was from the
brain of Zeus. And that is why André Salmon's image of the
Russian revolutionary as a man at the controls of the locomotive
who is at the same time reading a book, is a poetically exact one.
But responsibility for an existing and powerful state is not easily
borne. Responsibility for the Soviet Union, as it turns out, also
means and has meant responsibility for the secret police, and for
their empire of slaves, for the Gulag Archipelago, revealed to
the world in all its horror by Alexander Solzhenitsyn. And since
that revelation, admiration and affection for the Soviet state felt
by so many intellectuals has turned into a kind of hate. Jean-Paul
Sartre, who more than anyone represented the idea that it was
impermissible to criticize the Soviet Union, for to do so would
mean to take the side of capitalism and imperialism against it,
finally expressed his hatred of the Russian Communist party.
Solzhenitsyn, for his part, evidently wants to exonerate the Russians for the creation of the Soviet state and its empire of slaves,
and to fix the whole guilt for this securely on those intellectuals
of whatever nationality who played leading parts in the October
Revolution. Thus he would have it that there was not a single
great Russian on the central committee of Lenin's Communist
party. What about Vladimir Ilyich himself? Here Solzhenitsyn
availed himself of recently turned-up evidence that Lenin's
grandmother may have been of Jewish origin. I think his emphasis on this point unworthy of the great Russian novelist, and it
was quite rightly condemned by Boris Souvarin. But undeniably the Soviet state was born of an interpretation of historical
forces in which intellectuals, many of them Jews, played a leading part.

On the matter of southpaws, that is to say, of leftist support
for southpaws: surely the term has included under it certain
national states which were regarded as privileged—the Soviet Union; the People's Republic of China, especially during
the so-called "cultural revolution;" Israel; and, most recently,

Khomeini's Islamic Iran. Probably the illusion that national states can be southpaws began with the Bolshevik propaganda for the Soviet state. It took Jean-Paul Sartre some forty years of reflection to decide that the Soviet Union, and China too, were right-handed. I am not sure, though, that he was convinced that they had to be that. Now in my judgment, all nations, including Israel, are right-handed and have to be that, so I think that the support of intellectuals for any particular state on the ground that it is *not* right-handed is one of the worst and most tenacious of modern political mistakes. And it is a mistake, too, to demand of any state that it be a southpaw state or try to become such a state. The support of intellectuals for any kind or type of state, let it be the best and most humanly serviceable of welfare states, while certainly in no sense intellectually objectionable, cannot be said to flow from intellectual principles held at any depth. For even the best of welfare states cannot but develop problems of unjust preferment to which intellectuals may on occasion take exception. We may find a model of intellectual integrity, I think, in the attitude taken towards Israel by Gershom Scholem, who told us in the clearest terms that while he insisted on calling himself a Zionist, he did not admit to being a Jewish nationalist. On the other hand, Scholem never assailed the state of Israel for carrying out nationalist rather than strictly Zionist policies.

But to come back to that evening in 1958 when our inability to judge the Soviet behavior toward Pasternak led to the breakup of our meeting. If any one person was responsible for breaking up that meeting, that person unquestionably was Paul. And his reason for breaking it up was basically that he did not want to make publicly an unfavorable judgment of Soviet literary policy. Yet Paul, however much he may have wanted to get along with leftist youth, was in no sense a Stalinist. And I think he may have felt some regret for his own actions as we left the Buttinger townhouse that night. For as Meyer Schapiro and I were getting into a cab, Paul, who had come up behind us, called to me. What did he want? As I remember, he shook his fist at me, and I interpreted the gesture as hostile, and especially hostile to me. On the other hand, he called out, "Lionel, wait!" But I thought, "Why should we wait? So that he can shake his fist in my face?" And I told the driver to drive off. He did, and we left Paul on the curb calling after us, "But I wanted to come with you!" All the ambiguities and contradictions of the evening were somehow present in that last upsetting scene.

≺ Eleven ≻
JEWS WITHOUT "THE JEWS"

I OFTEN missed the point when I was young—and even when I was not so young. Until recent years I rarely gave enough serious thought to facts which should have been of the first importance to me; how, without having brought them clearly into view, could I have hoped to understand my situation, my story, my essence, my whatever? And in truth, for a very large part of my life some of its main items have meant little to me. Here are some of the facts in question, whose reality I contrived just to note: I was born of Jewish parents; moreover, my father was a rabbi (of the Reform variety), and I was instructed by him at an early age in the traits—mysterious, intriguing, and intimidating—of the Old Testament God, also in the principles, rational and arbitrary, the customs, and the practices which sustain Jews in their faith. And this faith I chose to abandon (also at an early age), and not for some alternative faith, but for no faith at all.

Why did I make such a choice, one calling for a seriousness beyond my years and quite beyond any character I might at the time have had? One reason, no doubt, was that in the public schools I attended (generally in small towns) I did not want to stand out too conspicuously from the rest of the boys who in the main were not Jewish. Then, too, I had been reading with enjoyment the atheists and the agnostics, and I had reacted negatively to my father's propaganda for Judaism, and, in fact, for all things Jewish.

I use the term "propaganda" advisedly, for my father's fervor for "Jewishness" was, I thought, and still think, political through and through. Being a rabbi, his enthusiasm for things Jewish served his interests—this I knew. But how, I wanted to know, could a like enthusiasm serve mine? Once, when already in high school, I asked him:

"Isn't it just a matter of chance that you were born a Jew?"

"There is no way," he answered, "that I could have been anything else."

"Supposing your parents had been Buddhists?"

"Then I would have had to become a convert to Judaism," he replied, adding, "Buddhists are very tolerant and see a certain truth in all religions. So this wouldn't have been too difficult."

"Jews," I came back at him, "particularly religious Jews, are not famous for their tolerance. Once you became converted to Judaism, wouldn't you have denounced your parents for remaining Buddhists?"

"Yes," he said, "I would have denounced them if they had been unable to see the great spiritual advantages in being of the Jewish faith, just as I denounce you, my son, for the same blindness."

I, of course, thought that he was the one who was blind. He still did not know himself as I had come to know him. (And this thought made me feel the elder of the two of us.) What didn't he know? That the pride he felt in being Jewish was merely one component of the very much greater pride he took in being the person he was. For he was egotistical about being Jewish, as he was egotistical about every one of his personal traits and even his oddest personal habits, some of which were no end strange. I knew that he would have taken pride in whatever creed had been foisted on him from birth. He was one hundred per cent for whatever he was, and I, as it fell out, was not for him.

He hoped, I suppose, that in the matter of religion, at least, I would not totally disregard his wishes. And knowing me to have a certain weakness for literature, he may have thought that I would be more open to some idea of his if it were well expressed. One day he said to me:

"Your mother and I at one time had many gentile friends."

"I hope you don't expect me to fault you for that," I said.

"My point is," he explained, "that some of them were quite clever, and tried to influence your mother. I suppose they thought that they could *shicksa* her a bit with witty remarks against Jews. They were mistaken, of course. But thinking of this has given me an idea. Maybe I should try to do for you the opposite of what they were trying to do to her . . ."

"The opposite?"

"If I could come up with a phrase, a catchword if you like, but one well put—this might protect you like a talisman; it might keep you from becoming a complete *shegetz*. You might recall it when contemplating a step in that direction—and hesitate."

"You have found such a phrase?"

"I've come up with something."

"It had better be good," I warned him.

"You may not think anything of it now," he said, "but some day you might recall it . . . and it might help you . . ."

"Well, let's have it."

"To prosper spiritually," he said, "Jews need the Jews."

"Is that all?" I asked, exaggerating my disappointment, for I had not expected him to say anything unusual.

"Bear this in mind, though," he said. "I am making a distinction between Jews and *the Jews*. The former are comprised by all those persons you come in contact with who happen to be Jewish. *The Jews*, on the other hand, are made up of your ancestors and your descendants. That is, if you have any descendants."

"I'll think about it," I said, but this was just to humor him. I don't believe I recalled this phrase of his until many years later, and then it was as if I heard it for the first time.

DURING the thirties I was in my twenties, and it was only then that I became aware—at least in part—of the *political* significance Jewishness had, whatever one thought the other meanings of being Jewish were or should have been. In 1931 and 1932, when Hitler's tirades against the Jews for the part they had played in

Germany and in world politics were coming over the radio, I began to see that if I was not particularly interested in my religious background, there were powerful groups in the world which were. I remember visiting a good friend in 1931, a man who since then has become identified with the Marxist line of political theory and with many left-wing causes. In fact, he has been called the most perspicacious of all the left-wing intellectuals in New York. He and his wife had been listening to a harangue of Hitler's on an overseas broadcast, and they were both tremendously impressed by the Fuehrer's oratory. The wife said to me, "Lionel, if you had heard that speech you would have thought of joining the Nazi movement." Her husband was as outspoken, but at least he did not try to put on me the guilt of having been strongly tempted. He said, "I am glad that I am Jewish, for if I were not, I think I might be drawn to Hitler's movement." This avowal is, I think, interesting; it helps us to see the attractiveness to intellectuals of totalitarian movements, something liberals never seem to take sufficiently into account.

And in the left-wing movement, too, the fact of being Jewish was important, and in ways one might not have foreseen. If one was Jewish, one was expected, almost automatically, to join up with some group on the Left, and accorded very little credit for having done so when one did. It was assumed that if you were Jewish you had *no right not to be in a left-wing group*, whereas non-Jews had such a right, and so gave greater evidence of seriousness and judgment in becoming left-wingers. Also it was assumed that Anglo-Saxon left-wingers of Christian background would have more success in spreading the true doctrine among workers. Was it likely that Jewish intellectuals could convert the miners, the toughest and hence the most respected members of the organized working class, to a radical political stance? Few believed this possible. In point of fact, though, it was a Communist group that formed the first CIO unions, and fought to a standstill the detectives hired by the big steel companies. Among these organizers, and prominent among them, were Jewish members of the American Communist party. And Jews were involved in the great Minneapolis strike of the late thirties. But on the Left it was thought best for Jewish strike leaders to play down their Jewishness. For Jews in the left-wing movement were supposed to give up, or at least forget about, their Jewishness for the sake of the universalist (not truly universalist, by the way) principles they were supposed to serve. We were all told in the Trotskyist movement that after the Revolution, when Lenin asked Trotsky to serve as foreign minister, Trotsky had demurred, saying in effect that it was not a good idea for him to represent Soviet Russia internationally, seeing that he was Jewish. Lenin was said to have replied that it was a very good idea for him, seeing he was Jewish, to represent Russia internationally. But when this story was repeated in the Trotskyist movement, and it was often repeated, its point generally depended on the teller. Sometimes the story was told as if Lenin had been in error, as if *it had indeed been wrong for Trotsky in view of his Jewishness, to become foreign minister.* Sometimes it was told as if Trotsky had been wrong in remonstrating with his leader. Didn't Lenin know better than he? Now, the Trotskyist group of the thirties was a most extraordinary one, considering the number of talented individuals in it at that time who since have made real contributions in many fields of thought. But even in this elite circle, composed almost entirely of Jews, one felt at a certain disadvantage in being Jewish. So on the Left as well as on the Right, Jewishness was given a negative meaning.

AND something of this sort had been going on in intellectual circles, among artists and writers not particularly concerned with politics. I have the following story from Jules Karlin, a *bel esprit* if ever there was one, to whom I was introduced by Harold Rosenberg on some summer night during the thirties—I can't remember the year—and with whom Harold and I spent several hilarious evenings. On one of them, when we were quite drunk, Harold asked Jules, "What should we do now?" Jules responded: "We'll go to a delicatessen . . ." (there was a good one then, on Eighth Street between Sixth and Fifth Avenues) ". . . and get some little roasted chickens, and tear them in the street." This we did. Afterwards Jules recounted his adventures with the

Hound and Horn, at that time the best literary magazine in the country. Jules, who had a sophisticated knowledge of philosophy, literature, and of the social sciences (he taught sociology in a small college in Chicago), had been offered the editorship of the *Hound and Horn,* which was then going through a crisis. Finally the offer was withdrawn, for reasons Jules did not reveal, but in any case he had spent some evenings of intellectual discussion with Bernard Bandler and Lincoln Kirstein, editors of the review. At this time there was great interest in the writings of Saint Thomas, due in part to the writings of T.S. Eliot and of Jacques Maritain. It seems that a whole group of young writers, mainly Jews, had decided to meet regularly in Bernard Bandler's Manhattan apartment to discuss the works of Saint Thomas over champagne, brandy, and the finest cigars. Some of the young Jewish writers in the group had begun to show an interest in converting to Catholicism, and Bernard Bandler's friend, Rabbi Louis Finkelstein of the Jewish Theological Seminary, who had been asked to take part in the group's discussions, became alarmed. He suggested that the group also read some relevant texts of Maimonides—surely his *Guide to the Perplexed* was in order—and this the group members did. But the result from Rabbi Finkelstein's viewpoint was not a good one, and his alarm increased, for it soon appeared to many members of the group, though not to the Rabbi, that of the two medieval philosophers, the Catholic was by far the more profound. Thus the Jewish members of the group were even closer to conversion as a result of having made passing acquaintance with Maimonides. Deeply disturbed, Rabbi Finkelstein had still another card to play. He arranged for a meeting of the group at which Professor Harry Wolfson, the renowned scholar who held the chair of Semitics at Harvard, would reply to any question put to him by a group member. When Jules Karlin, stirred by anticipation of a great occasion, entered Bernard Bandler's magnificent penthouse apartment, he saw standing by the bookshelves the slender figure of a man, short of stature, engaged in reading a book. This was Professor Wolfson, and he apparently had no intention of wasting any time during which he might increase his knowledge before the questioning began. So, Jules told us, he immediately asked a pointed question. It was: "What about the *active intellect*, which Aristotle tells us makes all things what they are?"

Professor Wolfson snapped shut his book and spun around to face his questioner. "On this matter of the active intellect," he said, "Aristotle is most obscure . . . I know that for the Arab commentators on Aristotle there is supposed to be only one active intellect, but when I think of the many interpretations of the concept, I begin to imagine there are some sixteen distinctly different ones. Which one did you have in mind?"

Now Jules did not know which of the sixteen distinctly different active intellects he had been asking about, and when this became apparent, Professor Wolfson turned his back on the group and resumed reading. After a long pause, full of scholarly ignominy for everyone but Professor Wolfson, the latter closed his book once more and faced the group again. "My students," he informed them, "make two different kinds of errors in thinking of Aristotle. Some fall into the error of thinking God Himself is an Aristotelian. . . . The better students, though, think Aristotle himself is God. . . ." Then he asked Karlin directly: "Which type of error are you closest to?"

Jules responded that he was inclined to rate Aristotle only just below God, but he didn't see why this should lead him into intellectual error. "There is always intellectual error," said Professor Wolfson, "in thinking that highly of anyone." All the while, Jules told us, he kept looking down at his knees, to make sure he was not still in short pants. After another long pause, again endured as painful, another member of the group asked about another scholastic concept. Apparently of this there were some thirty-two versions, and of which of the thirty-two was the questioner speaking? When he did not know, Professor Wolfson resumed reading again. Three or four more questions were put to Professor Wolfson with similarly unsatisfactory results, and the dismay of the Jewish members of the group who were thinking of converting to Catholicism mounted steadily while Rabbi Finkelstein practically purred with pleasure. There was no discussion of any philosophical issue; here was an instance of the victory of learning over any kind of thought.

But the matter of note was the interest Jewish intellectuals were taking at the time in any doctrine that might relieve them of their Jewishness, which was felt then as a burden. This was the period in which it was bandied about that Jewish intellectuals of the highest eminence, like the philosopher Edmund Husserl and his secretary Edith Stein (who was executed by the Nazis during the War), had become converts to Catholicism. Then there were those intellectual Jews who, as Hannah Arendt remarked to me (at a time when we were still friendly), went over to Catholicism simply in order to make themselves interesting. She added that there were certain non-Jewish intellectuals who had taken up Jewish causes for the very same reason. I think she was quite right in both judgments, and I know of one Jewish intellectual, the French writer Maurice Sachs, whom it is proper to cite in this connection. Almost everything Maurice Sachs did, as he himself either admitted or came close to admitting in his extraordinary memoirs, even the final incredible action he took after France's defeat in World War II which cost him his life, was done for the purpose of making himself interesting, and did make him that.

Of Maurice Sachs, Jean Cocteau wrote to Max Jacob: "Don't trust Maurice. He's a charmer. He would try to charm God Himself." By *charm*, Cocteau no doubt meant *seduce*, so we may think of Sachs as someone ready to seduce God Himself even as Lia, in Giraudoux's play *Sodom and Gomorrah*, is prepared to seduce the angel sent by God. At the moment just before Apocalypse, Lia does not take flight into virtue; she refuses to repent and even propositions the angel on whose judgment her fate and that of the two sinful cities depend. Similarly Maurice, when France fell, did not take flight to America, as other French Jews did. He chose instead to proposition the conquerors of France, leaving Paris for Hamburg, in Nazi Germany, where he lived until 1943, when the Nazis found him out and killed him. Had he really counted on seducing the German victors? In any case, the letters he sent back to Paris from Hamburg are full of praise for the Germans among whom he had chosen to live. Moreover, we know this about Maurice. His career had been a failure. Cocteau had said to him, "You can succeed in anything except in being a writer." Now Maurice Sachs wanted to succeed as a writer, and in France. He was one of those Frenchmen for whom literature in its truest sense can only exist in the French language. So it was in France that he had to succeed. He failed, and then France failed in the great test of war with Germany. My suggestion is that in going into Nazi Germany voluntarily after June of 1940, Maurice Sachs hoped— relying on his charm—to conquer the enemies of, and victors over, his countrymen, in which case he would have turned the tables both on France and on its literary representative, Jean Cocteau.

Now in going into Nazi Germany, Maurice Sachs never seems to have taken into account or reflected on the fact that he was a Jew. We have recently heard of another Jewish writer, the American journalist and philosopher Walter Lippmann, who in all his writings constantly skirted the fact of his Jewish origins, notably in never having written, after the war, a single line about the Holocaust. His biographer, Ronald Steel, has seen in this attitude something to reproach, as if there were some clear reason for thinking that Lippmann's Jewish origin was some-thing that should have been accepted by him. Now in order to defend Mr. Lippmann against Mr. Steel's charge, I shall have to change my focus for a moment and even appear to have dropped what was, and what I promise shall again be, my theme. Instead of treating what Jews have thought or failed to think about their heritage, I now want to consider what Jews have thought or perhaps should have thought about Shakespeare's play, *Hamlet*.

It is my belief that Jews, of all people, should be the least inclined to accept the psychoanalytic interpretation of Shakes-peare's *Hamlet*. In fact, they are in the vanguard of those who have taken Freud's views of the play seriously. First of all there were the Jewish psychoanalysts who followed Freud, and then the Jewish literary critics and Jewish English professors who have chosen to explain the difficulties in Shakespeare's play in Freudian terms.

Here is the reason why, to my thinking, Jews especially should reject a Freudian view of the play: Whatever light might be thrown by any of Freud's theories on some aspect of family psychology, insofar as this may relate to the motives of the main characters in *Hamlet*, the interpretation resulting would only serve to obscure what is probably the most important meaning of the play, and a meaning that points up the problem Jews have felt about their past and the past of Jews before them. When we look at *Hamlet* dramatically, in terms of what actually occurs in it, we cannot help but see that it deals with the transmission of a heritage: Hamlet is called upon to avenge an evil and perfidious action of which his father was the victim, and in which his mother was involved (though the degree of her involvement is never made quite clear). The cause of the prince's distress, and of his inability to respond with the confidence which action of a resolute kind requires, lies in the very revelation which is supposed to make him act: the family past, contaminated by his uncle and his mother, which the prince is commanded by his father's ghost to take into his being and make his own. This Hamlet is only able to do at the end of the fifth act, after trying in one way or another to outwit his fate with all sorts of ruses and rationalizations. To reduce this extraordinary story to the banality of a Freudian theme always seemed to me absurd. And Jews, I think, should be especially sensitive to what is absurd in such a banalization, since the true and complex meaning of *Hamlet* is so related to their own experience. Anyone born of Jewish parents has had to decide whether to take up or break with the Jewish past of exile, alienation, and persecution.

According to Michael L. Marrus, writing in *Commentary*, August 1982, Walter Lippmann, as a young journalist, made the following judgment of the Jewish past in drafting a statement on Jewish representation at Harvard:

> I do not regard the Jews as innocent victims. They hand on unconsciously and uncritically from one generation to another many distressing personal and social habits which were selected by bitter history and intensified by a pharasaical theology.

Lippmann is saying here that the Jewish heritage is contaminated. That is why he has rejected it. But would he have continued to reject it after the facts of the Holocaust became more widely and intently discussed among Gentiles as well as Jews? Who can say? As the matter stands, one may either conclude that Lippmann was an anti-Semite, or—and this is what I prefer to think—that he was a Hamlet who happened to die before the fifth act.

There is little to indicate that had he lived longer—I believe his end came when he was in his seventies—Lippmann would have responded to the demands silently voiced by the six million Jewish victims of Nazism. But very few Jews or non-Jews responded, either, until very recently. Lippmann, of course, drew the logical consequences of an assimilationist position. He was a Jew assimilated into a non-Jewish America. I would like to suggest here that this in no way implies a cowardly act of self-forgetfulness, of self-negation. When Sartre published his quite remarkable essay, *Anti-Semite and Jew,* and exhorted Jews, in this essay, to insist upon and even proclaim their Jewishness, arguing that in not doing so they were guilty of cowardice, of an act of flight from some fact they lacked the courage to confront— I argued against him, in Dwight Macdonald's *Politics,* that every individual Jew had the right to determine for himself what attitude he wanted to take toward the fact of being Jewish. And I quoted Kenneth Burke's remark against the Freudians, that what is often described as "flight" is by no means objectively that. "One can describe the very same behavior," said Burke, "as running from or running to something." But of course there are other arguments than Sartre's for the position that Jews are obliged in some fundamental sense to recognize and even make more explicit their Jewishness. One of the most interesting is in Gershom Scholem's essay in a recent book, *The Jews and Judaism,* in which this outstanding scholar discussed the relation of the German Jews to Germany and to German culture.

As Scholem saw the matter, and as he saw it when quite a young man, during the First World War, when he resolved to become a Zionist, Germany was the country in which the Jews of Europe had made the greatest effort to be assimilated, and

German culture was the culture of the gentile world best loved by them. They wanted to be Germans more strongly than they could want to be Frenchmen, Americans, Englishmen, Italians, after which came the terrible response of Hitlerism. The tragedy of the German Jews, says Scholem, is that they were destroyed by the nationalist political movement in the nation they loved best.

I personally am so taken by Scholem's way of writing, and his thought generally, that I should like not to disagree with him, and particularly on a matter so important to him, on which he has written movingly. All the same, it seems to me not quite correct to insist that Jews in Germany loved that country better, for example, than Jews in the United States love the nation in which they have prospered. It is true that German Jews in the United States during the First World War continued to love Germany. Yet even with them there was another factor present. The love of Germany by America's German Jews was no doubt strengthened by hatred of the Russian czar and the "black hundreds" of Czarist anti-Semitism. But something deeper is involved when one compares the relation of Jews to the culture of the United States and to that of any western European country. I believe that German Jews, the most distinguished of them, gave up many Jewish characteristics to become cultivated Germans. So did the French and English Jews I have met. In the United States something else was possible. One could retain, in some cases even accentuate, one's Jewish traits and yet remain American. One could contribute something of one's Jewishness to the not yet completely formulated American spirit, to the not yet completely fixed American psyche. A French, an English, a German, an Italian Groucho Marx is just inconceivable. The German, French, English, and Italian Jews who desired to love themselves as Frenchmen, Englishmen, Germans, or Italians, were required, in the situations they found themselves, *not to love themselves as Jews*. A similar requirement, not absent from the American life scene, was simply not as powerful here. So for all these reasons, I do not think it correct to say that of all the countries in which they were assimilated, the Jews loved Germany best.

THE facts of the Holocaust were not generally known in the United States during the war. Alfred Kazin has declared that he knew about the mass murders, and wrote something about them at the time in the *New Republic*. I myself never saw his piece, and it was certainly not discussed. Walter Laqueur, who has made a documented study of how information about the Holocaust first became known, reports that when a Polish refugee in 1941 told the American Supreme Court Justice, Felix Frankfurter, of having witnessed mass executions of Jews, Frankfurter replied, "I don't say you're lying, but I don't believe you." In Trotskyist circles, it was generally assumed that stories of mass executions were Allied propaganda, for the Trotskyist did not rate Allied political aims higher morally than those of Hitler. When Arthur Koestler, who had been a Communist but supported the war effort of England, wrote in a *New York Times Magazine* article that the war with Hitler could be described as a conflict between a half-truth and a total lie, this was taken by Trotskyists as propaganda for the Allied cause, and unacceptable.

For their position was that there was equal lying on both sides, and this naturally created on the left an additional difficulty in assessing the truth of stories of Nazi mass murder, and when the war was over there were other embarrassments for the Left. How was it that the Polish Socialists had not generously provided arms to the Jews fighting the Nazis in the Warsaw ghetto? How was it that the Russian Red Army had remained on the other side of the Vistula—thus giving the Nazi army time in which to put down the Polish resistance movement and execute its leaders—before advancing into Poland? On the Trotskyist response to the stories of Nazi terror, I must cite the remark of a very good friend in the movement: "If someone had told me about the German murder camps during the war, I would have dismissed it as Allied propaganda."

During the war, I met many Jewish refugees from Europe, and I heard stories of Nazi terror. And I did hear some talk about the possibility that the Germans had instituted extermination camps in eastern Europe. But I had no real revelation of what had occurred until sometime in 1946, more than a year after the German surrender, when I took my mother to a motion picture and we saw in a newsreel some details of the entrance of the American army into the concentration camp at Buchenwald. We witnessed the discovery of the mounds of dead bodies, the emaciated, wasted, but still living prisoners who were now being liberated, and of the various means of extermination in the camp, the various gallows, and also the buildings where gas was employed to kill the Nazis' victims en masse. It was an unforgettable sight on the screen, but as remarkable was what my mother said to me when we left the theatre: She said, "I don't think the Jews can ever get over the disgrace of this." She said nothing about the moral disgrace to the German nation or to the Nazi cause, only about the disgrace more serious than one incurred by moral culpability, a more than moral disgrace, and one incurred by the Jews. How did they ever get over it? *By succeeding in emigrating to Palestine and setting up the state of Israel.*

Certainly, the Holocaust was a *tragedy*. It is not wrong to invoke that term in connection with it, and when we think of tragedy we must remember that the best critics of tragedy considered as an art have told us that at the end of tragedy there must be a moment of reconciliation. The human spirit, offended by the excesses of the pitiable and the terrible, has to be reconciled to the reality of things. Some good must come of so much evil; and for the Jews, this good was found only in the setting-up of the state of Israel. What came out of the Holocaust was the success of Zionism.

And this success was essential to the self-respect of all Jews in all parts of the world, whether Zionist or not, whether they supported Israel or not. But in fact most Jews did support Israel, even the Jews of the Soviet Union, who shocked Stalin by staging the first spontaneous demonstrations seen in the Soviet Union in more than two decades by coming out in throngs in 1947 to greet Golda Meir, then Golda Meyerson, on her first visit from the state of Israel to the Soviet Union.

It was generally thought that the Germans had a special problem when the facts of the Holocaust were revealed. The problem was how to erase the moral stain on the nation as the Nazi exterminations became known. Apparently the Germans chose not to confront the terrible facts but rather to disregard them, though they did contribute very large sums of money to victims of Nazi atrocities, in Germany, in America, and in the new state of Israel. But they have been very much criticized for not dwelling regularly on the history of Nazi activities. The Jews, on the other hand, regularly made public all the facts, even to the most horrible details, and, as citizens of the new state of Israel, redeemed their honor with successful feats of arms in the several wars the Arabs imposed upon them, including the remarkable victory of the Six Day War, in 1967.

But early in the sixties something else came up which raised the question once again as to whether the Jews remaining in Israel and elsewhere could recover from the humiliation of the Nazi Holocaust. In their newfound pride as leaders of a modern state —which had defended itself successfully against the attacks of several hostile Arab nations, supported in turn by the many Moslems and Moslem states outside the Middle East—the Jewish leaders of Israel determined to lay their hands, legally or illegally—the means here did not count—on one of the main architects of their ignominy during the war: Adolph Eichmann, the Nazi organizer of the mass deportations and executions of Jews. Eichmann was then in hiding in Argentina. Simon Wiesenthal, with a group of fellow commandos, discovered his whereabouts, kidnapped him, and transported him to Israel where he was placed on trial to answer for his part in the extermination of millions of Jews. The trial was attended by journalists from all parts of the world; conspicuous among them was Hannah Arendt, commissioned to write a series of articles on the trial for *The New Yorker*. In fact, she wrote a volume on the trial, which appeared under the title *Eichmann in Jerusalem*.

The sensational effect of Hannah Arendt's commentaries on the Eichmann trial were felt even before her book appeared, as her articles on the trial ran regularly in *The New Yorker*. The actions of the Zionists in setting up the state of Israel, the struggle of the concentration camp survivors to defeat the British blockade of Haifa and other Mediterranean ports, the successful military struggle against the Arabs, all this apparently had been unavailing in the way of redemption for the humiliation of the Holocaust. According to Miss Arendt, Jews themselves had much to answer for with respect to the Holocaust, for without the cooperation of the Jewish leaders, the organizations known as the Jewish Councils, the Holocaust could not even have taken place! The darkest chapter in the whole story, she wrote, lay in the actions of the Jewish leaders themselves.

There were other details in her report which made it equally sensational. She denied that Eichmann was ideologically committed to Nazism, interpreting his behavior as following entirely from the commands of his superiors. And she never took into account significant facts which alone justified the Israeli court in sentencing him to death. For to so sentence him, it was necessary to show that he had done something on his own initiative, not commanded by a superior, towards the liquidation of the Jews. And this was shown by the Israeli court. Hitler had ordered the deportation of some four hundred thousand Hungarian Jews, and Admiral Horthy, dictator of Hungary, had agreed to their deportation; but at this juncture, President Roosevelt, who had so far scarcely recognized officially the plight of European Jewry during the war, sent the following communication to Admiral Horthy: If you permit these deportations, the American government will not treat Hungary as a civilized nation once the war is over. As a result of President Roosevelt's threat, Horthy urged Hitler to withdraw an already-given order for the deportation of some seventy-five hundred Hungarian Jews. Hitler complied with this request, but Eichmann proceeded with the deportations as originally planned. This was an important part of the evidence on the basis of which the court of Israel found Eichmann guilty as charged of the mass murder of Jews.

Miss Arendt did not consider these facts at all. On the contrary, she turned her attention to the language and the arguments of the Israel prosecutor, which to her seemed—and in this she might have been right—overblown. She interpreted Eichmann as a mere cog in the Nazi machine. He was an ordinary family man, a mediocrity, a banal figure, though an important instrument in the carrying out of mass murder. Eichmann had said: "I'll jump into my grave laughing because I have killed six million Jews," hardly, by any stretch of the imagination, the kind of statement one can expect from an ordinary man. Yet no statement of this kind gave sufficient motivation to Hannah Arendt to suspect her judgment of bias or to concede that it was perfectly possible to judge Eichmann differently. No doubt she was carried away by a theoretical notion which she herself insisted was the one original point she wanted to make about the mass murders and Eichmann's role in them. Her theoretical point was summed up in the phrase, "The banality of evil," and what she meant by this was that the conditions of modern bureaucracy convert into banal factual matters, actions which in human meaning and numerical amplitude are simply horrible. Her theory was that modern life has banalized the most evil actions, and that the Nazis with Eichmann at their head were dramatic evidences of a kind of spiritual catastrophe which enveloped the whole world: Evil was no longer just evil; it was now also banal.

I WAS drawn into controversy over Eichmann in the following way. I had written a review for *New Politics* of a group of essays of Miss Arendt, *Between the Past and the Future*; the review was a harsh one, it is true, and I probably would not review that same book quite as harshly if I were to write on it today. On the other hand, it is not a very good book, even as read today, and I would still make some very serious criticism of it. On one point, Arendt perhaps was right, or at least partly right. She stressed the antimetaphysical tendency in Heidegger's thought, and at the time I countered by stressing the defense he had made for metaphysics in his famous lecture, "What is Metaphysics?" But the truth probably lies somewhere between, Heidegger being a thinker who renders most of the concepts he handles thoroughly ambiguous. In any case, my review of Arendt's book was a very critical one, and I mention the fact simply because when the *Partisan Review* editors asked me to review Miss Arendt's *Eichmann in Jerusalem*, they must have been *expecting* a

piece that would be very critical of Arendt. I had already criticized her in print, and very sharply, and had defended that
criticism against Irving Kristol's challenge in an exchange of
letters in *New Politics*.

So when I picked up *Eichmann in Jerusalem*, I was prepared
to be critical of it. But I had no notion of the passion to which
I would be stirred by what I read in that work. I remembered
how, in Arendt's book on totalitarianism, she had argued that
no one under Nazi domination could possibly act in morally
clear terms. For instance, if you knew that members of your
family—your children let's say—were in the hands of the SS,
and that if you did not cooperate with the Nazis your loved ones
would be tortured or killed, how could you refuse to cooperate?
Whatever you did would make you guilty; and how is it possible
to act resolutely in such circumstances? Under Hitler, Arendt
claimed, there were great difficulties in even being a martyr.
You could die, but probably not with any feeling of guiltless-
ness. This analysis of what the Nazis had done in the countries
they occupied, to the souls of those they dominated militarily
and politically, was of course one of the great things in Arendt's
The Burden of Our Time and I think justifies even now the fame
that work brought her. In that work, she had applied this notion
to European peoples with national states—with armies, navies,
governments, all of which had not availed the Dutch, the Bel-
gians, the French. The individual person in these nations could
die in an action of resistance to the Nazis—he could wreck a
train, blow up a bridge—but he could not be sure in dying, even
heroically, that his very heroism had not entailed the deaths or
torture of many of his fellows. Nazism, Arendt said, destroyed
the very possibility of morally justified action, even in opposition to nazism. Such was the burden of totalitarianism on
humankind.

But now, in *Eichmann in Jerusalem*, she was berating the
members of the Jewish Councils, the leaders of the Jewish com-
munities in Europe, but most especially in eastern Europe, for
not having been able to break through the moral impasse which
she recognized to be beyond the strength of other Europeans so
much better circumstanced than the Jews. I read *Eichmann in*

Jerusalem with a kind of horror. It seemed to me that this book took back the very insights into totalitarianism which had made *The Burden of Our Time* an important and probably enduring work. I was, as I said, quite horrified by the very pages which stimulated and enthralled so many of the intellectuals who sprang to Arendt's defense when I criticized *Eichmann in Jerusalem* in *Partisan Review*. Why were some so thrilled to read that many Jews had been unable to find a way to act with dignity or honor under Nazi tyranny? Why were the weakest people in Europe to be criticized in a manner not addressed to peoples so much better equipped to resist? On my first reading of *Eichmann in Jerusalem* (for I was not then aware of the numerous errors of fact—on every single page, according to Jacob Robinson) I was stirred to anger by the clear bias of her judgment. And I recalled the remark my mother had made when we saw that first film of Buchenwald, when she had said, "The Jews will never get over the disgrace of this." I thought they had gotten over the disgrace with the establishment of Israel, but here was Hannah Arendt's *Eichmann in Jerusalem* saying that they had not. And thus it came about that I wrote for *Partisan Review* the article on Miss Arendt which set going a controversy splitting the intellectual community in New York City, often dividing former friends. I was sharply criticized for my essay by Dwight Macdonald and Mary McCarthy, with whom I had so often sided in the past on politically divisive matters.

What was most shocking to me, though, at that time, was the behavior of many members of the intellectual community who supported Miss Arendt in the *Eichmann in Jerusalem* controversy. For some reason or other, they wanted her to be right, and whatever evidence was advanced—and there were mountains of it—to show that she was wrong, simply infuriated them. Why did she have to be right on this matter? Her position was at best controversial, which means that something could be said on the other side. Why was what amounted to a moral indictment of the leaders of the Jewish Councils—many of whom died in the camps—why was this indictment necessary, and why did it have to be justified? Even conceding Arendt's superiority as a social theorist, couldn't she have made a mistake, an error, in

276

this single instance? She had made errors before, as she herself admitted. In 1954, she had written an essay opposing the decision of the Warren Court to desegregate the schools, an essay which nobody wanted to publish, and which finally appeared in *Dissent* accompanied by powerful rejoinders to it by David Spitz and Sidney Hook. But none of the individuals who defended Arendt's *Eichmann in Jerusalem* had defended her attack on the Warren Court's decision to desegregate the schools, not one. Her friends had left her isolated with her argument against desegregation, and she finally admitted that she was wrong. Why, then, did they feel that it was their clear duty to defend her far more mistaken judgment of Zionist policy in general, and of the Jewish Councils' actions in particular. Why did Arendt have to be right when her criticism was directed against the Jews?

ALL this is in the past—but not altogether, not entirely. Elisabeth Young-Bruehl's biography of Hannah Arendt, *For Love of the World*, calls forth new judgments of Arendt's work and of *Eichmann in Jerusalem*. Now that the dust of controversy has settled, it should be easier to see the main facts more clearly, but such unfortunately has not been the case. Most of the remarks made by critics about the controversy are quite false, as are the judgments of Miss Young-Bruehl. It is not true that the defenders of Arendt were more distinguished than those who criticized her. Meyer Schapiro and Gershom Scholem are, as a matter of fact, more respected for their judgment than Mary McCarthy and Dwight Macdonald. It is not at all true that arguments of her critics were demolished by Arendt's defenders. In fact, their main arguments were never met, or met superficially. Perhaps Arendt was within her rights when she called Jacob Robinson's *And the Crooked Shall Be Straight* a nonbook. Robinson was not a skilled polemist and his work has many faults of style, but the factual material in it is devastating to all of Arendt's main contentions in *Eichmann In Jerusalem*. And Gertrude Ezorsky's masterly arrangement of Jacob Robinson's research was never answered by Arendt nor by any of her supporters. It is simply untrue that the case for Arendt's Eichmann book has been made. The arguments given to defend its thesis were often poor, and the selective character of the evidence Arendt adduced for her theories—a charge made again and again—was never answered. But I do not wish to dwell on this matter. What concerns me here is the note of anti-Semitism that was introduced into the controversy by Arendt's defenders and which arose naturally when it was assumed that disagreements with Arendt's theses sprang from a decision made by what is called the Jewish Establishment, as if such controversial theses as Arendt's could not be objected to on purely intellectual grounds, as her theses on the American and French Revolutions, on the Hungarian revolt of 1956, her theses on human labor, human work, and the nature of totalitarianism—all of them controversial—have been objected to by certain critics, all without an order from any "establishment." And that note of anti-Semitism still creeps into references to the controversy, even in very minor ways.

Young-Bruehl's biography of Arendt has brought forth much critical comment, some of which is very unfair to Arendt. I am not interested in defending Arendt, but I am not going to make common cause with quite unfair attacks on her—anymore than I could support her own unfair attacks on European Jewry. So I must point out that the meanings Ernest Gellner in the *Times Literary Supplement* has seen in the revelation that Arendt had had a love affair with Heidegger when his student, seem to me quite farfetched. Gellner actually says that she was attracted to Heidegger, *not* despite his being a Nazi, but *by* that in him which drew him to the Nazi movement. Now how can Ernest Gellner know just what draws one person to another? He claims that Arendt was drawn toward Heidegger because she sought a German *Gemeinshaft,* and at a time when restoration of German *Gemeinshaft* meant Auschwitz for the Jews. This charge against the author of *The Burden of our Time* seems to me outrageous.

Certainly Ernest Gellner did not make his point against Arendt on behalf of the Jewish Establishment. For he charged Arendt with having rejoiced too much in the military victory of Israel in 1967. He even suggested that victory may have really tragic consequences, quite forgetting how clearly tragic the consequences would have been had Israel been defeated.

SOME criticism of Arendt—once again, it is not a criticism I have made or would make—may have been prompted by her clearly stated wish to separate herself from those Jews who have felt their Jewishness as a *fatality*, connecting them with *the Jews*, comprised, as my father put it to me when I was a boy, of one's Jewish ancestors and descendants. Gershom Scholem, writing to Arendt in 1963, characterized her book *Eichmann In Jerusalem* as heartless, flippant, and almost sneering on the tragedy of the Holocaust. And then, in what I took to be something more than a gesture of friendship, he wrote: "*I still regard you as a daughter of our people.*" To this Arendt replied: "*I come only from the tradition of German philosophy.*"

It is my fancy to conclude by bringing up Prince Hamlet once again: What if the ghost had found Hamlet after the prince's great soliloquy on being and nonbeing, and had accused him of being too interested in philosophy. Perhaps this was why he had delayed acting against Claudius! And what if the prince had replied, "I think I come only from philosophy." I imagine the ghost would have lost patience and shouted (we know from Shakespeare that ghosts can lose patience and shout): "*That is quite false. You come from me, from your father.*" And I can imagine voices shouting across time to those of this decade who happen to be Jews: "You do not come from philosophy, or from politics, of the Right or of the Left. You come from us, from your fathers." Blood was spilled in the Mideast, also in Goldenberg's kosher restaurant in Paris. The right-wing Senator Helms urged the U.S. to break off relations with Israel, and the Italian leftists have shouted, "To the ovens with the Jews." So we ourselves must make an effort to hear our ancestors once more, those my father distinguished for me as not just Jews, but as *the Jews*.

‹ Twelve ›
A LETTER FROM—
AND FOR—NEW YORK

Dear Michael,

I am sorry you have decided to live in California, even for
a little while. When I was about your age I decided differently:
I left Niagara Falls, a town my parents thought it wonderful to
live in, and urged me to like and admire and I came to New York
City, which for many years I could not even imagine leaving,
except during the summer's hottest months. So now I have to
ask you this: how much do you like Santa Monica, and what
would have to happen on the coast to make you think it wonderful to live there?

You write that you are very happy, and I am tempted to
reply coldly, "Why mention that?" But I do want to say something about happiness, which, Rimbaud was perhaps wrong but
not without honor in saying "none escape." Of course I do not
want you to think I mean to be critical of happiness, or given
to what would be a foolish disdain for it. What can one have
against happiness? Only this, perhaps: when someone says "I'm
so happy!" we cannot help but wonder if he or she really is. I
think that real happiness is too startled that it is to mention what
it is, or say its name. It knows that within the Now, the successive is packed together with the simultaneous, and who knows
what the next Now will contain? But there is something else
about the Now, which is, I think, even more pertinent to your

situation, and this has to do with your age. You are of an age when it is possible to determine the kind of world you would like to be happy in, and I think this judgment should be more important to you than being happy for the moment, for there are worlds in which one should not want to be happy, in which it would not be normal to seek happiness. And it is in this sense that happiness, which has final value for certain philosophers, ought I think to be relativized. Socrates took this up long ago when he rejected the "happiness" of the oyster as unworthy of a man.

Perhaps you'll say that you have already chosen the kind of world you like to live in, and that you are in fact now living in it in Santa Monica. If you say this, then of course I have no further argument. I merely want to make the point here that finding one's way into the world one wants to be happy in may be a very unhappy experience. In fact, is not this the subject not only of some of our best and most famous novels, but also of the not yet published, not yet famous novel you told me you yourself were writing? So you seem to me a novelist devoted to his problems as a person, rather than a person thinking about what he should do to become a novelist.

Of course New York City is not today the city I knew when I came to it from a small town. It is not the city of the thirties, the forties, the fifties, or the sixties (when its disintegration began in earnest). It is not only the dirt, the crime, and the pornography that have changed it so substantially. There are two other negative facts about New York: One, the high rents, which make it almost impossible for anyone to live decently in the city on a low income or a low salary, and two, the fact that the city as such does not provide ways of bringing people together that do not pander to special purposes, as do the singles bars, which, to my mind, are like the special interest groups which have become so important in politics: the Right-to-Life, the pro-abortion, and the Equal Rights Amendment groups. Single-issue groups have also replaced a general public as the readership for reviews. Generally speaking, the magazines which succeed today, unless they are subsidized, try to stress single issues. And the old places of meeting, where all sorts of people met for all kinds of reasons, are no more. It has been said that the university campuses have replaced the cities, in the social function of bringing people together. I think this is probably true, and explains what I would call the intellectual bankruptcy of New York, which I have stressed in other communications with you.

Then why do I think you should come back here and leave Santa Monica where you are so comfortable, where you say things are so prosperous? Where there are jobs and where you are at least near some publishers' offices and the offices of film producers? Why give all that up, together with the physical beauty of California and its climate too, for New York City today? Come back, then, not for the beauty of this city, which is not nearly as beautiful as San Francisco, and certainly cannot compare with Paris, or Rome, or London, though it has at certain moments in the hard light that hits it even in the summer, a quality special to it that has beauty of a certain sort, too. No, not for beauty, but for something else the city has to offer still, which can be associated with beauty, its vitality, which seems today to be unconquerable, even beyond that of the great cities of Europe, which lack its extraordinary dynamism. I haven't seen Paris since 1962, but friends who have been there say that compared to New York City it is today quite dead. Also, that you have to walk further to find good croissants in Paris than you do in New York, at least uptown. Imagine that! And I have heard that in Paris people remain isolated from each other, and do not meet, as they used to, in the cafés. Also, that whatever it is that ails Paris also afflicts London, Rome, and Berlin. So New York City is still the most living of all the great dying cities of the world. That is one reason for coming back to it.

If the great cities are dying, you may ask, why is it still important to live in even the most living of them? I say it *is* important, for in a great city you are less caught in the web of everydayness than you are in average-sized cities or in small towns. There the pressure of the humdrum is constant. Of course it can be escaped, but it takes more energy to escape, and you have less energy to spend on the unusual, the bizarre, the complicated, and the breathtaking (if anything like that comes up) than you have even in as defective a metropolis as New York is today. So these are the reasons why you must come back to it.

The ease of life in California and the happiness you have found there have not, in any case, so far spoiled your epistolary style, and I'm grateful for the comments—even some of the criticism you have made of the earlier chapters of my book, of which I mean to make this letter to you the final chapter. For noting your complaint that I have so far not treated the late sixties or the seventies—the complaint is legitimate—I'm obliged to say something about what happened during these years. I've decided to make my comments on the whole period in this letter to you.

Of course I can't cover everything, nor is there any reason for me to do this. I taught at SUNY in Buffalo during the late sixties and through the seventies. In '67 I participated in a writers' conference at the Fredonia campus of the State University of New York. The day those invited gave their lectures was one during which a vast demonstration took place in New York City, and some say that this demonstration was the turning point of the Vietnam War, for after that demonstration the antiwar mood in the country crystallized. In any case some three hundred thousand people marched, one group carrying a banner which said, "Even Princeton."

I and several of the other speakers at Fredonia would have liked to participate in the demonstration in New York, but we had committed ourselves in advance to go to Fredonia. One of the group, though, felt obliged to make a public statement of apology for being in Fredonia before the reading of the text she had prepared for the occasion. This famous beat poetess managed to uplift her own spirits by apologizing for not having gone to New York to demonstrate, and to depress the rest of us, who also would have liked to join the demonstration, but thought it lachrymose to apologize for something no one had forced us to do, and which we were well paid for doing. I mention these details, for they tell something of the moralistic hypocrisies we saw beginning in the sixties.

The whole decade of the sixties was dominated by images

of catastrophe. Leon Trotsky, in writing on the Russian poet Essenin, had said that his muse, tender, lyric, and intimate, could not really make itself heard in a century that was public, epic, and catastrophic. Certainly, in the sixties, the public and the catastrophic dominated not only the television screens but also our imaginations. But nothing epical was realized, as far as I can see, in the action or thought of that time.

It seems to me even today that the public and the catastrophic find their best representation on the television screen. I recall that after I had seen on TV the fighting between the leftist youth who had come to Chicago to impose their will on the Democratic Convention, and the Chicago police who beat them mercilessly, I found I could not read Norman Mailer's description of these events in the book he devoted to them. It seems to me the Chicago riots were meant for the media, even as the Nazis were meant for the media. No one could possibly write of Hitler at Nuremberg in a manner to equal what the camera did in "The Triumph of the Will."

The thought strikes me here that however it be with the public and catastrophic, what is generally epic in quality can *never* be realized on the television screen. We have seen a real epic presented on television, Tolstoy's *War and Peace*; it was marvelously done on Masterpiece Theatre, marvelous, yes, but without the dimension conveyed in Tostoy's prose. One wonders why this should be so. But one should not wonder for very long; clearly it is the sublimity, what Herbert Read called "the sense of glory" present in all true epics, including Tolstoy's novel, which cannot but be lost to the television screen. Probably it's right that this should be so, and that we should not be able to turn on the sense of glory when in the position to just as easily turn it off. The epic has to envelop us, as do the words and rhythms of Homer's *Iliad*, which in a certain sense we do not actually hear, as of course we do not see. They simply enter into our consciousness, which is no longer directed toward them, but to what took place in Troy.

THE seventies I spent teaching at SUNY Buffalo. I watched the development, the rise and fall, of student leftism, and I suppose the cultural event which most absorbed my colleagues was the appearance on the scene of a new French intellectual movement, structuralism, which took hold of the French and English departments at SUNY Buffalo and elsewhere. I believe that interest in this development is now less than it was a few years ago, and I predict that it will be still less as time goes on. There is not enough in structuralism for it to become any wider than a university trend. It will not, as existentialism, and even abstract expressionism did, affect people's lives as lived outside the university. Of course, I hasten to qualify this remark, for, in fact, the universities have absorbed a good deal of the life which used to lie outside them, and this, I believe, to the disadvantage of life and of learning too. Perhaps I have some bias here. My image of life requires me to think of it as open to the charge Ben Johnson made against Shakespeare, whom he said knew little Latin and less Greek.

But should I not here make an effort to connect the last ten years and what happened during them with the other forty years I have covered in my account? After a point in a narrative of events not directly connected with each other, and brought together only by the will of the narrator, one is bound to ask these questions: Toward what consummation are these postures, happenings, ideas heading? What point have we reached in fifty years of travel through our culture and its changes? Surely something was learned as well as remembered. Surely there is a moral to be pointed here, if only one could find it. Let me limit the expression of whatever I had learned to answering one question, the one I raised at the beginning of this communication, the answer to the question Why come from California to New York City?

And in this connection I must reply to your question about something I wrote a couple of years ago in memory of the late Harold Rosenberg. Yes, I remember what I wrote about the "homelessness of the spirit" which I said Georg Lukàcs made fundamental to all our cognitions and recognitions, and to which he gave credit for radicalism in politics and novelty in art. And now you want to know if I still think the homelessness of the spirit is important and valuable, and if it is, why talk affirmatively about where one lives, in New York City or elsewhere?

Won't the spirit continue to be homeless whether housed in a small Western town, or in a New York City flat? Now there is a good question. I commend you for it.

I think I *can* make a clear reply. I do believe in the creative afflatus of the homeless spirit, I still think all that can be valid in art will come from it. What was Breton's phrase? "Beauty will be convulsive or it will not be." I think his point holds, as it has held ever since Breton made it. Look again at Pollock's paintings and you will understand why I say this. Are there homes for the politically minded? I have friends who have tried to find homes on the Left, in little magazines that go over for *nth* times the phrases of Adorno, Benjamin, Lukàcs, and Sartre. And I have friends who have tried to domicile their spirit in quarters to the Right. In a way they, I think, are the more logical. It makes more sense to try to have a family and a home if you are opposed to pornography and easy abortions, and if you are in favor of religious education for the young. I do not, for my part, have a family today, and I have opted for the very same homeless spirit which presides over so many creations in this century.

When I was at Buffalo I met Stanley Rosen after he gave a talk for the philosophy department, and I was rather taken by him. Recently I read his book, *The Limits of Analysis,* an excellent and serious attack on the leading figures in the philosophical world today: Wittgenstein, Quine, Kripke, and others. While much that Professor Rosen says is valid, there is one thing he cannot explain: why the creative work done in philosophy in this century, in any case in the last two decades, was presided over by the spirit of analysis, the very spirit he is attacking. He would have the same difficulty in explaining this, that the old humanists like Irving Babbitt and Paul Elmer More had in explaining why the inventive genius in the literature of their time was modernist, and neither humanist nor neoclassical.

But now the homelessness of spirit quite naturally situates itself in big cities, rather than in small towns. In a city like New York there is little pretense of deep rootedness, and one is not likely to experience very strongly here what Nikolai Hartmann (in a different connection of course), has called the "depth of succession." For we do not in a modern metropolis (at least in

America) remember well or powerfully feel the deeds of those who came before us. On the other hand, there is something equally great to be experienced in New York, what Hartmann (once again in a different connection) called the "breadth of simultaneity," and this may be an alternative to the "depth of succession," though it is not an ersatz for it. In our city, breadth can be felt almost constantly in the panoramic vista of countless different yet interlacing lives, sprouting all around us.

I grant every one of New York's faults, in fact, I insist on them. I do not like those New Yorkers who insist that the subways are safe, simply because they think that if they admit the underground is dangerous, which it is, they are lining up with conservatives against the liberals. The safety of the subways to them falls under the rubric of ideology. The subways *are* dangerous; I avoid the train whenever possible. A few years ago we read in the newspapers of a young girl being pushed off a subway platform onto the tracks, and of her right hand being severed by an oncoming train. Just the other day, a teenager was murdered in the subway, for—this is the way an editorial in the Daily News put it—"clinging too hard to a radio a gunman wanted." And no passenger in the car tried to help the teenager, or even took the trouble to report the incident. So I am not going to say things favorable about our underground system. And I am not happy on the buses, or with the cost of cabs. Happily, though, one can still walk in New York City, and even at night on a very few streets, for instance, on Third Avenue, uptown, and with a fair chance of getting home safely, that is, without being slashed, beaten, broken, humiliated, stepped on, or spat upon. One thing I do not see on the streets of New York which in the past I often saw, and that is a beautiful woman being stared at as she walks by. There are beautiful women in New York, there always were; men used to watch them as they passed. Nowadays one does not notice their being noticed. I myself try not to indulge my bent for staring at girls I do not know who seem appealing, an impulse to which I used to give free reign. On the other hand there is this to be seen on the streets which I find positive: I have noticed not a few women who come on down the streets with a kind of swagger, making a show of powerful physiques. This is something quite new to the city, and I don't suggest that these women are lesbian; happy Heddas, I call them, and they do give an unexpected glow of physicality to the streets as they go by.

New York is dirty, yes, dirtier than it used to be. The roaches are everywhere; there are more of them, they are hardier, more intrepid, more resistant to poison, and I believe, bigger than they were. And for the water bugs, they are gigantic. Every week I'm reminded of Kafka's story, *The Metamorphosis*, because I'm faced with one of these great big bugs, and, thanks to Kafka's tale, who knows who the bug might be, though so far I have not yet recognized anyone in the guise of these urban creatures. Do they have rights, too? Only the mystics would say yes, I suppose. And maybe few of them would have the hardihood not to say it. Anyway, I am not asking you to come back to this whole mess of dirt, danger, and insect-life. Happily no one has yet advocated insect rights, because if there were such groups here, I think I myself would leave New York. To what am I asking you to come back? To the city where it is still possible to talk to somebody about something that is not purely practical; to the city where the things that mean most to you are already expressed, at least in part, in the skyline, in the beauty of the bridges, and in the general intelligence of at least a very large number of people in Manhattan, in the wit and cunning of the taxi drivers, in the number of places still available for the pursuit of nonpractical activities or purely social contacts. And come back also for the handful of people still in New York who cannot be duplicated in any other of the nation's cities. They are not in Los Angeles, not in San Francisco, not in Chicago, they are not in New Orleans or Atlanta, and they have no intention of moving to Boston.

Of course a great many of the intellectuals have left New York City already, some to go to the cities I've already mentioned, and these people are not coming back. And then some of the best New Yorkers have left, not for other cities, but for that undiscovered country Hamlet speaks of with fear. They are gone, I miss them, what shall we do without them? But I shall have to go too, myself, and whoever is left in New York will have to get along without me. With this sobering thought, may I suggest to you that you may really be needed in this city, where you first have to prove something about yourself to know that you are needed. (For while "the depth of succession" may not be expressed in terms of this city's total life, it may be felt within some limited groups contributing to that life.) Come back here, then, prove yourself, and prove likewise that you are worthy to replace some one or other of the interesting and illustrious persons who made this city what it was at its best, and, such is my hope, may again be.

INDEX

Abetz, Heinrich Otto, 198
Absalom (Abel), 218
abstract expressionism, 206, 210, 285
  surrealist movement and, 104–5
  theatre and, 220, 227, 229
abstract painting, 231–32
Adorno, T. W., 44, 122, 188
Adventures of Augie Marsh, The
    (Bellow), 183
Aeschylus, 156, 237
"Age of Hemorrh" (Matta), 109
Age of Reason, The (Sartre), 122
Alexander, Brooks, 235
Alquié, Ferdinand, 95
Althusser, Louis, 147
Alzburg, Henry, 52
Ambrosino, Georges, 162, 184
American Stuff, 53
Amiel, H. F., 194
Andler, Pierre, 162
And the Crooked Shall Be Straight
    (Robinson), 277
Ansermet, Ernst, 195
Anti-Semite and Jew (Sartre), 268
anti-Semitism, 278, 279
  Sartre on, 73–74, 77, 86, 268
Apoèmes (Nonpoems) (Pichette), 170
Arendt, Hannah, 118, 122, 187, 265
  on desegregation, 277
  on Eichmann, 272–77
  on evil, 77–78, 274
  Heidegger and, 274, 278

Pasternak affair and, 243, 246–47,
    249
  on totalitarianism, 275
Aretino (Buechner), 224–25
Aristophanes, 236–37, 239
Aristotle, 124, 167, 264
Arnold, Matthew, 194n
Aron, Raymond, 189
Arshile Gorky (Schwabacher), 110
artistic movements, life and death
    of, 229
Art News, 214
Ashbery, John, 218
Athens, ancient, 236–37
Atkinson, Brooks, 234
atom bomb, 72, 74, 145–58
  Communists and, 149, 154
  intellectuals' response to, 147–58
  Sartre on, 154
  Soviet Union and, 149–50
  Wahl on, 150
Austin, John, 117, 126, 175

Babbitt, Irving, 286
Baldwin, James, 248
Bandler, Bernard, 263
Barnes, Djuna, 58
Barrett, William, 50, 187
Barthes, Roland, 210
Bataille, Georges, 174
Baudelaire, Charles, 73n, 171, 173,
    186

Baziotes, William, 206
Beauvoir, Simone de, 132–33, 146, 148, 161, 162, 173
Beckett, Samuel, 122, 219, 227, 231, 239, 252
Beethoven, Ludwig von, 181
Being and Nothingness (Sartre), 117, 118, 124, 125, 127, 128, 130, 139–41, 145
Being and Time (Heidegger), 124, 146
Belloc, Hilaire, 73
Bellow, George, 213
Bellow, Saul, 40, 183
Benjamin, Walter, 85, 100, 107, 185
Bentley, Eric, 230, 239, 243, 249
Bergson, Henri, 117
Bernanos, Georges, 83, 146
Between the Past and the Future (Arendt), 274
Birds of America, The (McCarthy), 201
Birth of Tragedy, The (Nietzsche), 203
Blacks, The (Genet), 235–36
Blues (Abel), 41
Bodenheim, Maxwell, 13, 35
Breton, André, 89–90, 93–102, 105–7, 145, 147n, 161, 170
  games as interest of, 107–8
  Gorky and, 110, 114
  poetry of, 94–95
  surrealist theory of, 95, 97, 98, 101–2, 114
  Trotsky and, 98–100
"Bride Stripped by Ferocious Bachelors, The" (Duchamp), 107
Bridge of San Luis Rey, The (Wilder), 51
Broch, Hermann, 31–33
Brody, Gandy, 205
Brown, Roscoe, 233, 235
Buchenwald, concentration camp at, 271
Buechner, Georg, 224–25
Bukharin, N. I., 62
Burden of Our Time, The (Arendt), 120, 275, 276
Burke, Kenneth, 46–47
Buttinger, Joseph, 243–44, 247, 249

Cachin, Marcel, 136
Caffi, Andrea, 161–62, 166, 175–92
  as conversationalist, 182–83
  fundamental values of, 182
  on history, 179–82
  intellectual background of, 179
  on Joyce, 182
  moral position of, 176–79
  on myth, 180
  on politics, 177–78, 186, 189–91
  Wahl on, 176
  women and, 183–84, 190–91
Caillois, Roger, 147n, 173–74
Camus, Albert, 146, 161, 175, 184, 222
  Sartre and, 119, 137, 142, 148–49
capitalism, reasons for continued success of, 43–44
Capone, Al, 15
Carmichael, Joel, 183
Castro, Fidel, 121
catastrophism, 150–52, 283–84
Catholicism:
  in Geneva, 194–95, 198
  Jews and, 263, 265
Céline, Louis-Ferdinand, 98
Chairs, The (Ionesco), 227
Chambers, Whittaker, 45–46
Chaplin, Charlie, 245, 250
Char, René, 114
Chasse spirituelle, La (Rimbaud), 170–71
Chekhov, Anton, 33
Chenon, René, 162, 167–68
Chesterton, G . K., 73
Chiaromonte, Miriam, 161, 190
Chiaromonte, Nicola, 92, 132, 161, 166, 175–76, 184, 185, 189–92, 213–14
  on atom bomb, 146, 147–48
  on Caffi, 186
  in Spanish Civil War, 135–36
  on socialism, 186–88
China, People's Republic of, 49, 255–56
Chinese Revolution (1949), 44
Chisholm, Shirley, 204
Christian existentialism, 194–95
Christianity:
  extraterrestrial life and, 197–98

Hinduism and, 198
Romains on, 197–98
Churchill, Winston, 150
Cioran, E. M., 179
civil rights movement, 233, 235, 248
Clark, Eleanor, 47–48
Clurman, Harold, 121, 218
Cocktail Party (Eliot), 222
Cocteau, Jean, 265–66
Collier's Encyclopedia, 203*n*
Combat, 114, 170
Commentary, 74, 79, 127, 202
Committee for Cultural Freedom, 243
Committee for the Defense of Leon Trotsky, 65
Common Market, 174–75
Communicating Vases, 98
Communist Manifesto, 35
Communist party, British, 39–40
Communist party, French, 132, 136, 137–38
Communist party, German, 46
Communist party, Soviet, 41, 138, 149
Communist party, Spanish, 136
Communist party, U.S., 30–32, 37, 39–41, 42, 65, 113
    appeal of, 36–37, 138
    harassment of intellectuals by, 62–63
    idealized view of rural worker and, 42, 45
    intellectuals' disillusionment with, 45–58
    Jews in, 31–32, 261
    Partisan Review and, 46–47, 50–51
    Trotskyists' criticism of, 37, 40
Communists, communism:
    European Catholics and, 194–95
    failure of, 42–44
    McCarthy and, 74–77
    quixoticism and, 138
    Sartre on, 121, 128, 137, 139
"Communists and Peace, The" (Sartre), 137
Comte, Auguste, 147
Congo, The (Lindsay), 35
Connolly, Patricia, 106, 108–9, 114

Conrad, Joseph, 60
Cournot, Antoine Augustin, 203–4
Cowley, Malcolm, 13
Crevel, René, 113
Critique of Dialectical Reason, The (Sartre), 127, 128, 139–42
Critique of Violence, A (Caffi), 177
Cuban missile crisis, 149
cultural movements, death of, 200–203
cummings, e. e., 14, 16
Czechoslovakia, 74

dadaism, 214
Danto, Arthur, 125
Davidson, Donald, 251
Davis, Stuart, 34
Death of a Salesman (Miller), 237
Death of Odysseus, The (Abel), 218, 223
Death of Tragedy, The (Steiner), 203
Deats, Lucy, 13–16
de Gaulle, Charles, 138, 174–75, 186
de Gourmont, Remy, 19–20
de Kooning, Elaine, 215
de Kooning, Willem, 39, 104, 205, 206, 207, 208, 212–16, 217
Delaney, Joe, 103–4
Democratic National Convention, Chicago (1968), 284
Democritus, 240
demonstrations, political, 29, 37–38, 283
Depression, Great, 26, 28, 29–30, 35, 39
    unemployment in, 29, 36, 37, 38
Descartes, René, 57, 119
Dewey, John, 57, 62
Dial, 13
Diderot, Denis, 182, 192
Dieu caché, Le (The Hidden God) (Goldmann), 165
Dirty Hands (Sartre), 122–23
Dissent, 55, 189, 243, 246
Dostoevsky, Feodor M., 31–33, 60, 73, 141, 162
drip-painting, 104
"Drunken Boat, The" (Rimbaud), 112

Dr. Zhivago (Pasternak), 242, 245, 249, 253
DuCamp, Maxime, 143
Duchamp, Marcel, 106–7, 109, 116, 142
Duhem, Pierre, 155–56
Durant, Will, 34
Duranty, Walter, 62, 63

"Earth Is a Man, The" (Matta), 101–2
Eichmann, Adolf, 77
    trial of, 272–74
Eichmann in Jerusalem (Arendt), 77, 272–79
eighteenth century, 179–82
Eighth Street art club, New York, 205–9, 210
Einstein, Albert, 199
Eliot, T. S., 222, 263
Elizabeth I, Queen of England, 225
Éluard, Paul, 107
Encounter, 195
Ernst, Max, 96–97
Esslin, Martin, 239
Ethiopia, 52–53
Étiemble, René, 106
Evergood, Philip, 39
evil, Arendt views on, 77–78, 274
Executioner Waits, The (Herbst), 41–42
"Exile" (Perse), 238
existentialism, 128–30, 148, 174, 285
    atom bomb and, 149, 153–54
    Christian, 194
    Heidegger and, 146, 149, 153, 154
    in New York, 145–46
    Wahl and, 145
extraterrestrial life, 197–98
Ezorsky, Gertrude, 277

Fadiman, Clifton, 98
Farrell, James T., 47, 187
fascism:
    demonstrations against, 37–38
    Ezra Pound's support of, 58–59
    Rightist intellectuals and, 253

Faulkner, William, 144, 203–4, 222–23
Fearing, Kenneth, 14–16, 18
Fernandez, Ramon, 198–99
Fieldites, 37
fifties:
    New York painters in, 205–16
    theatre in, 218–23, 226, 233
Finkelstein, Louis, 263
Finnegans Wake (Joyce), 144, 182
Fischer, Louis, 50
Fitzgerald, F. Scott, 172
Flaubert, Gustave, 179, 180, 231
    Sartre on, 137, 138–39, 142–44
force, use of:
    intellectuals' debate about, 72
    natural vs. positive law and, 85–86
    philosophy of history and, 85–87
    Pierce on, 71
    surrealists on, 111–12, 114
Ford, Charles Henry, 222
Ford, Ford Madox, 58–60
Ford, Gordon Onslow, 90
Ford, Ruth, 222, 223
For Love of the World (Young-Bruehl), 277, 278
France:
    attitude toward money in, 166–68
    classical theatre of, 203
    New York theatre influenced by, 219–20
    in World War II, 67, 68, 265
Franco, Francisco, 38, 48
Frank, Joseph, 162
Frank, Marguerite, 162
Frankel, Gene, 235–36
Frankfurter, Felix, 270
Frankfurt school of radicals, 44–45, 117, 187, 189
Frechtman, Bernard, 141
French Revolution, 43, 130
French structuralism, 97, 117, 231, 285
Freud, Sigmund, 97
    on *Hamlet*, 266–67
Friedman, Emanuel, 203*n*
Friedrich, Otto, 183
Fuchs, Klaus, 74

gangsters, 15, 20–21, 36
Garbo, Greta, 171–72
Gautier, Théophile, 171
Gellner, Ernest, 278
Genet, Jean, 119, 133, 141, 176, 235–36
Geneva, Switzerland, 193–201
    Catholics in, 194–95, 198
    politics in, 194
    Recontres conference in (1951), 193–201
Germany, Nazi, *see* Holocaust; Nazis
Giacometti, Alberto, 96, 163, 175, 182–83
Gide, André, 124
Gildea, John Rose, 35
Giraudoux, Jean, 160, 265
Glazer, Nathan, 248
Godamer, Hans-Georg, 156–57
Goedel's Theorem, 200–201
Goering, Hermann, 80
Goethe, Johann Wolfgang von, 179, 181
Gold, Mike, 51
Goldmann, Lucien, 165–66, 168, 188
Goldwater, Walter, 187
Goodenough, Robert, 209
Goodman, Paul, 42, 148
    Pasternak affair and, 243, 244–50, 253, 256–57
Gorky, Arshile, 34, 39, 102, 104, 106, 109–14
    artistic influences on, 110
    Breton and, 109–10, 114
    Matta and, 103, 110–15
    suicide of, 94–95, 111, 112–14
Gould, Joe, 14
GPU (Soviet Secret Police), 62, 66, 98–99
Grands Cimetières sous la lune, Les (Bernanos), 83
Great Britain, 72, 174–75
    theatre in, 219–20, 228
Great Gatsby, The (Fitzgerald), 172
Greek philosophers, 176
Greek theatre, 236–37
    tragedy in, 203–4
Green, William, 158

Greenberg, Clement, 50, 71, 202, 212
Greenwich Village, New York, 11–17, 20, 25–26, 35, 52, 205–9, 210
    Cedar Bar in, 209–15
    theatre in, 218–22
Griaulle, M., 194, 197
Gruen, Will, 38
Guggenheim, Peggy, 103
Guide to the Perplexed (Maimonides), 263
Gulag Archipelago (Solzhenitsyn), 138
Guston, Philip, 39, 205–6, 213–15, 241
Guterman, Norbert, 147*n*
Guys, Constantine, 173

Habermas, Jürgen, 117
Hamlet (Shakespeare), 122, 143, 224
    psychoanalytic interpretation of, 266–67
"Hamlet and Don Quixote" (Turgenev), 134
Harris, Jed, 233
Hart, Sheldon, 67
Hartigan, Grace, 209
Hartmann, Nikolai, 286
Hegel, G. W. F., 130, 167, 174, 180
Heidegger, Martin, 124, 130, 141, 145, 157, 215
    Arendt and, 274, 278
    existentialism and, 146, 149, 153, 154
    on intellectuals, 134
    on violence, 111
Heisenberg, Werner, 201
Hélion, Jean, 161, 217, 232
Hemingway, Ernest, 172
Henry VIII, King of England, 225
Heraclitus, 183
Herbst, Josephine, 41–42
Hermann, John, 42, 45
Herodotus, 182
Herrington, C. J., 156
Hess, Tom, 206–7
Hinduism, Christianity and, 198
Hippodrome meeting (1936), 55–58
Hiroshima bombing (1945), 145–48

Hiss, Alger, 66
history, philosophy of, *see*
   philosophy of history
History of the Russian Revolution
   (Trotsky), 254
Hitler, Adolf, 31, 48, 63, 68, 81, 273
   Stalin and, 46–47, 60
Holocaust, 266–77
   initial information about, 270–71
   Jewish Councils and, 273, 275–77
Homer, 104, 184, 284
Hook, Sidney, 62, 121, 248, 277
Hopkins, Gerard Manley, 39–40
Horkheimer, Max, 44, 188
"Hot Afternoons Have Been in
   Montana" (Siegel), 14
Hound and Horn, 263
"How Comrade the Present
   Addressed Our Party" (Abel),
   54–55
Howe, Irving, 189, 243, 249
Hubert's Cafeteria, Greenwich
   Village, 25–26
Hugo, Victor, 171
Humanité, 138
Husserl, Edmund, 123–24, 127, 265
Huysmans, Joris Karl, 99

Ibsen, Henrik, 221
Iceman Cometh, The (O'Neill), 220–21
Iliad (Homer), 104, 184, 284
In Defense of Terrorism (Trotsky),
   86–87
Instead, 108, 109, 185, 209, 217
intellectuals:
   atom bomb and, 147–58
   "catastrophism" and, 150–52
   dramatic models for, 134–35
   feuds between, 242–49, 256–57
   Jewish, 261–68
   leftism and, 250–57, 261
   protests against Soviet Union by,
      242–49, 252–56
   rightism and, 251, 253, 254
   totalitarianism's attraction to, 261
   Trotsky-Stalin debate and, 55,
      62–63
intoxicants:
   October Revolution and, 100–101
   surrealism and, 100

Introduction to the Reading of Hegel
   (Kojève), 174
Ionesco, Eugène, 219, 227, 239, 252
Iran, 256
Israel, 255–56
   Holocaust and, 271–72
"I Stake My Life" (Trotsky), 57

Jackson, Robert, 80
Jacob, Max, 265
James, Henry, 51, 60, 178
James, William, 100
Jewish Councils, 273, 275–77
Jews, 252, 258–79
   anti-Semitism and, 73–74, 77, 86,
      268, 278, 279
   Catholicism and, 263, 265
   in Communist party, 31–32, 261
   Freud's interpretation of *Hamlet*
      and, 266–67
   Holocaust and, 266–77
   as intellectuals, 261–68
   national identities of, 268–69
   October Revolution and, 255
   politics and, 260–62
Jews and Judaism, The, 268
Jones, James Earl, 233, 235
Journey to the End of the Night
   (Céline), 98
Joyce, James, 144, 205, 245, 250
   Caffi on, 182

Kafka, Franz, 142, 288
Kaplan, Harold J., 40, 166, 183
Karlin, Jules, 262–64
Karpov, Anatoly, 252
Kazan, Elia, 257
Kazin, Alfred, 270
Keynes, John Maynard, 237
Khomeini, Ayatollah Ruhollah, 256
Khrushchev, Nikita S., 62, 149
Kierkegaard, Sören, 24–25, 129, 142,
   179, 180
Kipling, Rudyard, 199
Kirstein, Lincoln, 263
Kleist, Heinrich von, 226
Kline, Franz, 202, 205, 212–15
Koestler, Arthur, 254, 270
Kojève, Alexander, 173–74
Korchnoi, Victor, 252

Korean War, 76, 120, 137, 202
Kosygin, Aleksei, 122*n*
Koyré, Alexander, 173, 184
Krapp's Last Tape (Beckett), 227
Krasner, Lee, 103
Kristol, Irving, 275
Krutch, Joseph Wood, 41

Labor Action, 89
Laforgue, Jules, 172
LaGuardia, Fiorello H., 67–68
language, philosophy of, 123–26
Laqueur, Walter, 270
Lasswell, Harold, 69
law, positive vs. natural, 85–86
Lawrence, D. H., 179–80
Lawrence, T. E., 138
leftism:
    Christians and, 261
    intellectuals' ambiguous support
        for, 250–57
    Jews and, 261–62
    Mascolo's notion of, 252–53
    student, 284
Léger, Fernand, 186, 217
Leites, Nathan, 69
Lenin, V. I., 254–55, 262
Lenin in Zurich (Solzhenitsyn), 253
Levinas, Emanual, 175
Levinger, Armand, 155–57
Lévi-Strauss, Claude, 117, 210
Levy, Julien, 91
Lewis, C. Day, 39–40
Lewis, John L., 158
Lewis, Wyndham, 40
Liberty, 68
Lichtheim, George, 127–28
Liebowitz, René, 161
Lindsay, Vachel, 35
Lippmann, Walter, 266–68
    on his Jewishness, 267–68
literary criticism:
    Marxism and, 120
    in *Partisan Review*, 220, 239
    by Rosenberg, 74, 221
    by Sartre, 119, 120, 121, 137,
        138–39, 142–44
    by Trotsky, 98–99, 120
Long Day's Journey into Night
    (O'Neill), 220, 221

Long, Huey, 29
Lovestone, Jay, 37–38
Lowell, Robert, 209
Lukàcs, Georg, 120, 166, 208, 285
Lunacharsky, Anatoli, 120
Luxemburg, Rosa, 184
Lysistrata (Aristophanes), 236–37

Macbeth (Shakespeare), 224
McCarthy, Joseph R., 74–77
    pros and cons of, 75–76
    Trotskyists on, 76
McCarthy, Mary, 48, 184, 187–88,
    220, 276, 277
    Pasternak affair and, 242, 245,
        246
    works by, 201, 202
Macdonald, Dwight, 50, 88, 153,
    158, 187, 276, 277
    on atom bomb, 147–48
    Pasternak affair and, 242, 246,
        247, 249
    Politics and, 74, 110, 126, 161, 186,
        189, 268
McGraw, Jimmie, 52, 53
Machiz, Herbert, 218, 223, 233
Madame Bovary (Flaubert), 142, 231,
    239
Magny, Claude-Edmonde, 117
Magruder, Agnes, 109, 112–15
Mailer, Norman, 284
Maimonides, 263
Mallarmé, Stéphane, 19, 231
Malraux, André, 41, 138, 145, 147*n*,
    169
    on art, 39, 214, 219
    on Faulkner, 203–4
    in Spanish civil war, 135–36
Manhattan Project, 149, 157
Manheim, Ralph, 53, 147*n*
Man's Fate (Malraux), 41
Mao Tse-tung, 149
Marcantonio, Vito, 22
Marcel, Gabriel, 145
Maritain, Jacques, 106, 263
Marowitz, Charles, 224
Marx, Karl, 33, 35, 152, 179
Marxism, 97, 117
    Chiaromonte on, 187
    death of, 229–30

Marxism *(continued)*
    failure in theory of, 42–44, 118,
        229–30
    Frankfurt school on, 188
    Hook on, 121
    intellectuals' break with, 188
    literary criticism and, 120
    Merleau-Ponty on, 126–27
    Schapiro on, 187–88, 189
    Wolfe on, 229
Masaryk, Jan, 74
Mascolo, M., 252–53
Masterpiece Theatre, 284
Matisse, Henri, 186
Matisse, Pierre, 101, 108–9, 114
Matisse, Teeny, 108
Matta, 88, 90–93, 97, 101–3, 106, 161,
        200, 206, 217
    Gorky and, 110–15
    humor of, 91–92
    Mrs. Gorky and, 109, 112–15
    Schapiro on, 102, 110
    surrealist theory of, 102
Matta, Ann, 91, 92–93, 106, 132
Matter, Mercedes, 213, 215
May Day, 1931, 29
Meir, Golda, 271
Memoir of an Art Gallery (Levy),
        91
Memory of Justice, 78–84
    criticisms of, 79–80, 84
Men of Good Will (Romains), 98–99
Merleau-Ponty, Maurice, 122, 137,
        167, 194, 199–200
    in Paris, 173, 174
    rhetorical style of, 126
    Sartre and, 117, 126, 174, 189
Merrill, James, 218
Metamorphosis, The (Kafka), 288
Metaphysical Journal (Marcel), 145
Meyers, John, 209, 217, 218, 219,
        223, 233–34
Midstream, 183
Militant, 71
Miller, Arthur, 237–38
Miller, Henry, 17, 172
Milton, John, 224–26
Miró, Joan, 110
Miss Lonelyhearts (West), 31

Molière, 239
More, Paul Elmer, 286
More, Sir Thomas, 225–26
Morrow, Felix, 38
Moscow Trials, 40
    confessions in, 98
    intellectuals' response to, 49,
        62–63
    Trotsky and, 62–63, 98–99, 136
Motherwell, Robert, 88–90, 93, 101,
        165, 206–8
Muni, Paul, 36
Mussolini, Benito, 52–53, 58, 183
My Heart Laid Bare (Baudelaire), 73n
My Life (Trotsky), 100–101
Myrdal, Gunnar, 248

Nader, Ralph, 45
Nadja (Breton), 107
Nagasaki bombing (1945), 145–46
Nagel, Ernest, 57
Napoleon III, Emperor of France,
        139, 142
Nation, 14, 41, 63, 218
National Review, 251
natural law, 85–86
Nausea (Sartre), 121
Nazis, 97, 145, 265
    Arendt on, 272–77
    atrocities by, 77–78, 150
    in films, 36
    Holocaust and, 266–77
    Nuremberg trials of, 79–84
    World War II and, 67–68, 146
New Leader, 246
Newman, Barnett, 212
New Masses, 46
New Politics, 274–75
New Republic, 13, 51, 63, 270
New Russian Right, The (Yanov), 33
Newton, Isaac, 184
New York, N.Y.:
    contemporary conditions in,
        281–82, 287–88
    contemporary intellectuals and,
        288–89
    crime and grime in, 281, 287, 288
    in the fifties, 205–16, 218–23, 226,
        233

gangsters in, 15, 20–21, 36
"homelessness of the spirit" and,
    286–87
movie houses in, 34
painters in, 205–16
Soviet Union and, 55–58
surrealist movement in, 88–98,
    101–15
in the thirties, 29–60
WPA's effect on, 38–39
New York Artists Theatre, 218
New York Daily News, 14, 287
New Yorker, 98, 249, 272
New York Review of Books, 79, 81
New York Times, 62, 63, 65, 234, 270
Nietzsche, Friedrich, 18, 176, 180,
    203, 221
Nin, Andreas, 136
nineteenth century, irrationalism
    in, 179–81
No Exit (Sartre), 128
Nouvelle Revue française, La, 198
Nozières, Violette, 95
nuclear energy, protests against,
    44–45
Nuremberg trials, 79–84

O'Brien, Conor Cruise, 80–81
October Revolution, 100–101, 138,
    254–55
"Ode to Charles Fourier" (Breton),
    96
Odets, Clifford, 121
off-Broadway theatre, 217–41
    abstract expressionism and, 220,
        227, 229
    antitheatrical mood of, 220
    European influences on, 219–20
    in the fifties, 218–23
    Sartre on, 218
    in the thirties, 220–21
    see also theatre
O'Hara, Frank, 210, 218
Old Times (Pinter), 227
O'Neill, Eugene, 16, 220–22, 230,
    246
"On the Kind of Socialism Called
    Scientific" (Chiaromonte), 187
Ophuls, Marcel, 78–84

Ortega y Gasset, José, 194, 199–202,
    243
Orwell, Sonia, 126, 209

painting:
    abstract, 231–32
    "action," 103–5, 206, 210
    audience for, 231–32
    contemporary, 241
    French vs. U.S., 202
    New York school of, 205–16
Paris, 159–92
    contemporary conditions in, 282
    New York artists' influence on,
        185–86
    parties in, 162–65
    Saint-Germaine-des-Prés in, 162,
        169, 173–75, 182, 186
Partisan Review, 70, 88n, 98, 118,
    187, 233, 243, 274, 276
    Communist party and, 46–47,
        50–51
    literary criticism in, 220, 239
    on World War II, 71
Pasternak, Boris, intellectuals'
    fractured support for, 242–57
Paulhan, Jean, 104
Paz, Octavio, 194, 199
Perjury (Weinstein), 66
Perry, Frank, 233
Perse, Saint-John, 238
Persians, The (Aeschylus), 237
Petremont, Simone, 83–84
Phillips, William, 52, 118–19, 187
    with Communist party, 46, 48
    on *Partisan Review*, 46, 48, 50
    Pasternak affair and, 243, 247–51
philosophy, contemporary, 33
    analysis and, 286
    evolution of, 123–26
    Russell's contribution to, 123–24,
        125
    Sartre's contribution to, 117, 124,
        127–31, 139–42, 153
    Wittgenstein's contribution to,
        125
philosophy of history, 85–87
    Trotskyists and, 86–87
    and use of force, 85–87

philosophy of language, 123–26
Philosophy of Money, The (Simmel), 167
Philosophy of Surrealism, The (Alquié), 95
Pia, Pascal, 170
Picasso, Pablo, 110, 186
Pichette, Henri, 170
Pierce, Charles Saunders, 71
Pinter, Harold, 227, 231, 239
Piri and I (Vail), 172
Plastrik, Stanley, 243
Plato, 129, 180
plays, *see* theatre
playwrights:
    audience attitude and, 220–23, 230–32
    urban environment necessary for, 222–23
Podhoretz, Norman, 243
Poetry, 41
poetry recitals, 35
poets, audience attitude and, 231
Poets' New York Theater, The, 218
Politics, 176, 186–87
    Hiroshima bombing discussed in, 147–48
    Macdonald and, 74, 110, 126, 147–48, 161, 186, 189, 268
Pollock, Jackson, 103–4, 206–7, 211–12, 214, 286
    action painting and, 103–4
    New York painters and, 206–7, 211–12, 214
    theatre influenced by, 220
Portrait of the Anti-Semite (Sartre), 73–74, 77, 86
positive law, 85–86
Possessed, The (Dostoevsky), 60
Possibilities, 89
POUM, 37–38, 136
Pound, Ezra, 14, 19, 182
    Ford Madox Ford's defense of, 58–60
poverty, in the thirties, 29–30, 36, 38
Powys, John Cowper, 34
Prall, David, 88
Pretender, The (Abel), 233–35

"Prolegomena to a Third Manifesto of Surrealism or Else" (Breton), 99–100, 105
Prometheus Bound (Aeschylus), 156
propaganda:
    art and, 228–29
    Soviet vs. American, 174
Provincetown Theatre, 12–13, 16
psychoanalysis, 89, 221–22, 266–67

"Question of Death, The" (Godamer), 156
Quintero, José, 221
quixoticism, 135, 138

Rabinowitz, Dorothy, 79
Rahv, Philip, 46–52, 70, 118, 153, 187, 212, 243
rationalism, in history, 180–81
Rauschenberg, Robert, 205
Read, Herbert, 284
Reinhardt, Ad, 102, 212, 232
Recontres Internationales, 193
Republic of Letters, 243, 248–49
Requiem for a Nun (Faulkner), 222–23
Resnick, Milton, 215
Revenge for Love (Lewis), 40
rightism, intellectuals and, 251–54
Rilke, Rainer Maria, 29–30
Rimbaud, Arthur, 17, 27, 91, 112, 170, 280
Rivera, Diego, 98, 99
Rivers, Larry, 209
Robinson, Edward G., 36
Robinson, Jacob, 276, 277
Romains, Jules, 98–99, 194, 197–99
Roosevelt, Franklin D., 31, 37, 48, 273
Rosen, Stanley, 174, 286
Rosenberg, Harold, 46, 52, 89, 100, 105, 148, 187, 202, 243, 262, 285
    "action" painting and, 103, 206, 210
    film criticism of, 79
    on *Hamlet,* 122–23
    literary criticism of, 74, 221
    Pasternak affair and, 246, 249

on Soviet Union, 50–51
on Trotskyists, 37
Rosenberg, Julius and Ethel, 120
Rosenfeld, Isaac, 40
Rosmer, Alfrd, 94
Rousseau, Jean Jacques, 179
Rousset, David, 137, 175
Roux, Gaston Louis, 162, 163
Roux, Pauline Chenon, 162, 163
Ruhle, Otto, 195
Russell, Bertrand, 34, 72, 237
  on atom bomb, 150
  philosophical contributions of,
    123–24, 125
Rykoff, A. I., 62

Sabatelli, Antonio, 190–91
Sachs, Maurice, 265–66
Sade, Marquis de, 97, 114
Saint Genet, Actor and Martyr
  (Sartre), 133, 141
Saint-Germain-des-Prés, Paris, 162,
  169, 182, 186
  intellectuals of, 173–75
Salemmi, Antonio, 207
Salemmi, Attilio, 207–8
Salmon, André, 255
Sanctuary (Faulkner), 203–4
Sartre, Jean-Paul, 116–49, 161, 173,
  174, 186, 189, 218
  on anti-Semitism, 73–74, 77, 86,
    268
  atheism of, 127–28
  on atom bomb, 154
  Camus and, 119, 137, 142, 148–49
  on communism, 121, 128, 137, 139
  on Flaubert, 137–44
  literary criticism of, 119, 120, 121,
    137, 138–39, 142–44
  philosophical contributions of,
    117, 124, 127–31, 139–42, 153
  philosophical evolution of,
    116–17, 121
  physical appearance of, 118–19
  politics of, 76, 120–22, 137,
    138–39, 141
  on Soviet Union, 122, 132, 137,
    138–39, 252, 255–56
Sayers, Michael, 227

Schapiro, Meyer, 88–90, 145, 256,
  277
  on Marxism, 187–88, 189
  on Matta, 102, 110
  Pasternak affair and, 242, 247
Scholem, Gershom, 256, 268–69,
  277, 279
Schopenhauer, Arthur, 180
Schuman, Robert, 174
Schwabacher, Ethel, 110
Schwartz, Delmore, 48, 50, 63,
  88–89, 187
"scientific" socialism, 187
Scott, George, 238
Scott, Zachary, 222
Scribner's Magazine, 42
Scully, James, 156
"Season in Hell, A" (Rimbaud),
  112
Second Manifesto of Surrealism, The
  (Breton), 95
Second Sex, The (Beauvoir), 133, 173
Sentimental Education (Flaubert),
  139–40, 142
seventies, theatre in, 226–27
sexual relations, surrealists' views
  on, 106–7, 108–9
Shachtman, Max, 56–58, 86, 183
Shakespeare, William, 143, 224–25,
  239, 266, 279, 285
Shaw, George Bernard, 120, 141,
  235
Shcharansky, A., 247
Shepard, Sam, 220
Shils, Edward, 69
Show Business, 218
Siegel, Eli, 14, 35
Simmel, Georg, 167, 179
Simone Weil, a Life (Petremont),
  83–84
single-issue groups, 281
Siqueiros, 67
Six Day War, 272
sixties:
  catastrophism in, 283–84
  theatre in, 226–27, 228, 231, 233
  youth cult in, 42
Sleepwalkers, The (Broch), 31–32
social fascism, 46, 48

socialism:
  Caffi on, 177
  "scientific" vs. "utopian," 187
Socialist party, 39, 41, 52
Socialist Workers' Party, 65, 151
Socrates, 281
Sodom and Gomorrah (Giraudoux),
  265
Solzhenitsyn, Alexander, 138,
  253–55
Sontag, Susan, 79
Sophocles, 219
Soviet Union, 33, 41, 82, 113
  atom bomb and, 149–50
  intellectuals' protest against,
    242–49, 252–56
  McCarthyism and, 75
  Mussolini and, 52–53
  propaganda of, 174
  Rosenberg on, 50–51
  Sartre and, 122, 132, 137, 138–39,
    252, 255–56
  Trotskyists' criticism of, 43
  after World War II, 43–44, 72–73,
    149
  Zionist sentiment in, 271
Spanish civil war, 137
  Communist party machinations
    during, 48, 136
  intellectuals' support for
    Republic in, 37–38, 50, 135–36
  Stalinists in, 136
  Weil on, 83–84
Spengler, Oswald, 202–3
Spitz, David, 277
SS Glencairn (O'Neill), 13
Stalin, Joseph, 72, 82, 113, 149, 183,
  271
  Hitler and, 46–47, 60
  Trotsky vs., 41, 43, 55, 57, 195
Stalinists, 62, 84, 120, 151
  at Hippodrome meeting, 55–58
  in Spanish civil war, 136
Stamos, Theodoros, 241
Stander, Lionel, 11–16, 18, 27
Stecchini, Livio, 159
Steel, Ronald, 266
Stein, Edith, 265
Steinberg, Saul, 183

Steiner, George, 203
Stendhal, 226
Stevens, Wallace, 93
Stille, Mike, 187
stock market crash (1929), 11, 33
Stoppard, Tom, 228
Stranger, The (Camus), 119
Strawson, Peter, 163, 175
structuralism, French, 97, 117, 231,
  285
Studies of Classic American Literature
  (Lawrence), 179–80
Studs Lonigan (Farrell), 47
suicide:
  of Gorky, 94, 111, 112–14
  surrealists' attitude towards,
    113–14
Sun Also Rises, The (Hemingway),
  172
surrealist movement, 88–115
  abstract expressionist school and,
    104–5
  ambiguity in, 96–97
  cynicism about relationships in,
    106–7, 108–9
  intoxicants and, 100
  in New York, 88–98, 101–15
  sadism and, 97, 114–15
  suicide as seen by, 113–14
  theories within, 95, 97, 98, 101–2,
    114
  on use of force, 95, 111–12, 114
Swift, Jonathan, 179, 181
Swinburne, Algernon Charles, 114

Tallmer, Jerry, 235
Tate, Allen, 251
Taylor, Telford, 80
technology:
  existentialism and, 149, 153–54
  and failure of socialism, 44
television, 284
Temps modernes, Les, 120, 121, 122,
  126, 154, 173, 189, 252
theatre:
  antitheatre and, 220
  audience and, 220–22, 235–36, 240
  contemporary, 232, 240–41
  Elizabethan, 203

in the fifties, 218–23, 226, 233
French classical, 203
Greek, 203–4, 236–37
lost plays and, 223–26
in the seventies, 226–27
in the sixties, 226–27, 228, 231, 233
society's interaction with, 226–27, 228–29, 230–33, 236–40
in the thirties, 220–21
see also off-Broadway theatre
theatre of the absurd, 219–20, 226–29, 239–40
influence of, 228
mood of, 240
success of, 227–28
values of, 229
Theatre of the Absurd (Esslin), 239
"Theory of Descriptions, The" (Russell), 123
thirties, 29–60
political parties in, 31–32, 39–41, 45–50
social awareness in, 31–33, 36–38
theatre in, 220–21
Thomas, Norman, 38
Thomas, Saint, 180, 263
Tibor de Nagy Gallery, New York, 209, 217
Time, 183
Times Literary Supplement, 278
Tito (Josip Broz), 49
Toby, Mark, 34
Tolstoy, Leo, 33, 179, 180, 194, 200, 284
"Toward a Critique of Violence" (Benjamin), 85
Toynbee, Arnold, 198
Trachtenberg, Alexander, 46, 51
tragedy, phenomenon of, 203–4
Tragedy of Macbeth, The (Milton), 224–26
Traube, Jacques, 233
Tropic of Cancer (Miller), 17
Trotsky, Leon, 65, 67, 262
Breton and, 98–100
Hippodrome meeting and, 55–57
Jewishness as issue for, 262
literary criticism of, 98–99, 120

Moscow trials and, 62–63, 98–99, 136
on October Revolution, 100–101, 254
Stalin vs., 41, 43, 55, 57, 195
on weaponry, 150
on World War II, 46–47, 49, 68, 69–70, 71–72, 118
Trotskyists, 52, 62–64, 76
appeal of, 37, 41
Cannonite faction of, 69, 70–71
as critics of Communist party, 40
disillusionment among, 151–52
at Hippodrome meeting, 55–58
Holocaust and, 270
Jews and, 262
on McCarthy, 76
Shachtmanite faction of, 69, 89
on World War II, 69–71, 86
Truman, Harry S, 92, 146
"Truth or Consequences," 107–8
Tucci, Niccolo, 187
Tukashevsky, M. N., 183
Turgenev, Ivan, 134

Ulysses (Joyce), 245, 250
United Automobile Workers (UAW), 37–38
United Nations, 154
universities, social function of, 282
"USSR and the War, The" (Trotsky), 49
"utopian" socialism, 187

Vaché, Jacques, 113
Vail, Lawrence, 172
Valéry, Paul, 51, 99, 105–6, 116, 159
Velikovsky, Immanuel, 150–51, 152, 157
Verlaine, Paul, 170
Vicente, Esteban, 205–6, 221, 241
Vietnam War, 117, 122*n*, 123, 245, 254, 283
View, 147, 209, 217, 222
Villager, 234
Village Voice, 218, 235
Volochova, Sonia (V), 65–67
Voltaire, 73, 141, 179, 181
VVV, 105–6, 145–46, 147

Wagner, Charles, 14
Wahl, Jean:
  on atom bomb, 150
  on Caffi, 176
  existentialism and, 145
  in Geneva, 193–94, 195, 197,
    199–200
  in Paris, 165–66, 169, 175, 184, 185
  on poetry, 96
Waiting for Godot (Beckett), 227
Walberg, Patrick, 97
Walkley, A. J., 141
War and Peace (Tolstoy), 200, 284
Warren, Robert Penn, 251
Warsaw ghetto uprising, 270
Washington Square Park, New
    York, 11–12
Wattenberg, Ben, 229
Weil, Simone, 80, 83–84, 184
Weinstein, Allen, 66
Weisenthal, Simon, 272
Weiss, Peter, 97
Wescott, Glenway, 34
West, Nathanael, 31
What Is Literature? (Sartre), 120, 121,
    141
"What is Metaphysics" (Heidegger),
    274
Whelan, Grover, 29
White, Morton, 37
"White Man, The" (Romains), 199
Whitman, Walt, 226
Whoopee Club, Greenwich Village,
    20
"Why Poets" (Heidegger), 111
Wild Duck, The (Ibsen), 221
Wilder, Thornton, 51

Wilson, Edmund, 73, 141, 249
Wilson, Robert, 240–41
Witness (Chambers), 46
Wittgenstein, Ludwig, 117, 130, 141,
    174, 286
  philosophical contributions of,
    125
Wohlstetter, Albert, 37
Wolfe, Tom, 229–30
Wolfson, Harry, 263–64
Wols, 213–14
women:
  Caffi and, 183–84, 190–91
  in Geneva, 172–73
  in New York, 287–88
  in Paris, 173
  surrealists' attitudes toward,
    106–7
Works Progress Administration
    (WPA), 37, 38–39, 52, 53
"World Consciousness," 195–97
Worlds in Collision (Velikovsky), 151,
    152
World War II, 30, 42, 43, 137, 146,
    199
  intellectuals' indecision about, 61,
    67, 71, 270
  Trotsky on, 68, 69–70, 71–72
Writers Project, New York, 47, 52,
    58, 147
Writers Union, 52, 58–60, 151

Young-Bruehl, Elisabeth, 277, 278
Yugoslavia, 49

Zionism, 271–72
Zola, Émile, 98, 99